Archie's Rivals in Teen Comics, 1940s–1970s

Also by Michelle Nolan and from McFarland

Baseball and Football Pulp Fiction: Six Publishers, with a Directory of Stories, 1935–1957 (2020)

Love on the Racks: A History of American Romance Comics (2008; paperback 2018)

Ball Tales: A Study of Baseball, Basketball and Football Fiction of the 1930s through 1960s (2010)

Archie's Rivals in Teen Comics, 1940s–1970s

An Illustrated History

MICHELLE NOLAN

McFarland & Company, Inc., Publishers
Jefferson, North Carolina

Library of Congress Cataloguing-in-Publication Data

Names: Nolan, Michelle, 1948– author.
Title: Archie's rivals in teen comics, 1940s–1970s : an illustrated history / Michelle Nolan.
Description: Jefferson, North Carolina : McFarland & Company, Inc., Publishers, 2020 | Includes bibliographical references and index.
Identifiers: LCCN 2020018952 | ISBN 9781476677583 (paperback : acid free paper) ∞
ISBN 9781476639765 (ebook)
Subjects: LCSH: Comic books, strips, etc.—United States—History and criticism. | Teenagers in literature. | Characters and characteristics in literature.
Classification: LCC PN6725 .N64 2020 | DDC 741.5/973—dc23
LC record available at https://lccn.loc.gov/2020018952

British Library cataloguing data are available

ISBN (print) 978-1-4766-7758-3
ISBN (ebook) 978-1-4766-3976-5

Printed in the United States of America

McFarland & Company, Inc., Publishers
Box 611, Jefferson, North Carolina 28640
www.mcfarlandpub.com

To my son Ray, his wife Nikol and
their daughters Logan and Myka.
Always keep the spirit of teens!

Table of Contents

Preface 1

Introduction: The Rivals of Riverdale 3

Section I: Overview: The 1940s 7

1. Here She Comes in *Miss America* Comics: Patsy Walker 10
2. Patsy Walker's Groundbreaking Title 16
3. Marvel Teens in the 1940s 23
4. Judy's Date with Success 37
5. Buzzy, Binky and Scribbly in the 1940s 40
6. Candy's Antics 48
7. Hap Hazard and the Ace Gang 54
8. Wilbur, the Forgotten Success Story 60
9. Topsy-Turvy, Cookie and The Kilroys 65
10. Why *My Date* Didn't Go So Well 70
11. Comics Advertised "For Teen Girls" 76
12. Ozzie and Babs—Fawcett's Only Teen Stars 80
13. Junior, Sunny and Corliss 85
14. Slick Chick Comics and the Dearfield Duo 89
15. Other Short Run Pre-Code Girls 96
16. Teena and the Strip Reprints 102
17. Hi-Jinx—Teen-Age Animal Funnies 106

Section II: The 1950s 111

18. Patsy Walker, Something of a Supergirl 113

19. DC's Teen Humor: A Favorite in the '50s 121
20. The Unique Wendy Parker 127
21. My Girl Pearl: Dumb and Dumber 134
22. The Joy of Meeting Miss Bliss 139
23. Henry Aldrich and the Dell Teens 143
24. Jetta, Teen-Age Sweetheart of 2052 146

Between pages 148 and 149 are 8 color plates containing 15 photographs

25. The Mystery of *Candy* in the 1950s 149
26. The Amazing Mazie and Her Boyfriends 153
27. Why Ginger Deserved a Better Fate 160
28. The First Kathy and Company 165
29. Lucy, the (All Too Soon) Real Gone Gal 171
30. Oh, What a Brother! 175
31. The Most Obscure Teen Humor Comic Book 180
32. Junior Hopp and the Hopp Rod 183
33. The Short-Run Guys in the Not-So-Nifty '50s 187

Section III: Introduction: The 1960s and 1970s 197

34. John Stanley's Masterpiece: *Thirteen* 199
35. *Patsy and Hedy*: A Novel Approach in the 1960s 204
36. An Early '60s Bright Spot: Marvel's Teen-Age Tornado! 210
37. Judy, Dobie, Freddy and the Early '60s 217
38. Tippy Teen's Surprise Appearance 222
39. Josie, Pussycats and All 228
40. A Word on the Working Girls 234

Appendix: Teen Humor Comics Outside the Archie Universe, 1940s to 1970s 237

Bibliography 245

Index 247

Preface

Why a comprehensive book on teen humor comic books outside the Archie Universe? Because there has never *been* such a book.

Teen humor (and its big sister, career girl humor) were important genres in the 1940s and 1950s. They faded in the 1960s outside of Archie's circle, although they still have a presence.

The Archie titles unquestionably dominated the teen humor field after a slow start in the 1940s during the transition from MLJ Comics (which began in 1939) to the Archie Series as the firm's superheroes began to fade in the mid–1940s. More than a dozen books, both historical accounts and Golden and Silver Age reprints, reflect the relative importance of the iconic Archie characters. In 2021 and 2022, the key characters will have been with us for 80 years!

Otherwise, though, there has been precious little written about the likes of Marvel's *Patsy Walker*, DC's *A Date with Judy*, Dell's *Henry Aldrich* and nearly 150 other titles across three decades.

This is surely understandable, since dozens of major superheroes and genres like horror, fantasy and adventure comics (especially those done by the most talented artists and writers), have been far more collectible and valuable than most teen humor titles.

In recent years, however, teen humor has begun to come into its own, in connection with the increasingly collectible nature of the once almost totally ignored romance comics. Some comic book dealers, in fact, lump teen, career girl and romance titles in the same FOR SALE boxes at major comic conventions!

After my book *Love on the Racks* (2008, McFarland) helped to popularize romance comics—which had never had a definitive book on the entire genre—I thought teen humor might also be fitting fodder. Just as part of the fun of romance comics is collecting the obscure as well as the mainstream, so too are the little-known teens part of the joy of their genre.

Teen humor has been a small part of radio, television and films, but nowhere has it been more popular than in comic books (as compared to comic strips). Part of the reason is that slapstick feats and other such wild antics, so much a part of many teen humor stories, are a lot easier to portray in comic books, just as superheroics have always had a natural home in the comic books. (Or at least they did until the coming of computer generated graphics.)

Teen humor is also the most relatable genre for many readers, not many of whom have had or ever will get the chance to be detectives, war heroes, gunfighters, space explorers and the like, much less costumed heroes.

Who hasn't read a teen humor story and laughed with the memory of a similar embarrassment? Or an argument or amusing moment with boyfriend, girlfriend, mom, dad, brother, sister, teacher, principal or boss?

Reading teen humor comics, a comic collector may be amazed at the variety of people and plots that actually existed. The Archie characters would not have lasted as long as they have if they were not the best examples of teen humor, but there are many dozens of good examples of funny and touching teens from other publishers. They deserve the recognition this book affords them.

Teen humor is also all about Americana. It's no coincidence that teen humor really got going with the advent of teens dating in cars, the increasing popularity of high school sports, the All-American chocolate malt shops and, of course, the rock 'n' roll of the 1950s to go with the great balladeers of the 1940s.

American culture, surely more than any other in the world, has made the teen years a distinct subset of the nation's ethos, whether talking about the good of the nation's lovestruck younger set, or the bad of juvenile delinquency and drug use.

Where else but in America could you actually use a title like "I Was a Teen-Age Teen-Ager" and have people understand what that means? Sort of, anyway? There are a lot more of those than Teenage Werewolves, Frankensteins and Zombies!

Introduction: The Rivals of Riverdale

What really is a teen humor comic book?

One thing it may not always be is a comic book designed to interest teenagers, such as *Calling All Girls* was in the 1940s.

Nor is it a comic book with teen action heroes, such as *Boy Commandos* was at the same time in the 1940s, or *Star Spangled Comics* with the teenage heroes The Newsboy Legion.

Neither is it a comic book with one teen humor story, even an issue as historic as the debut of Archie in the largely superhero anthology *Pep Comics* #22 (December 1941).

Rather, a teen humor title—most of which were titled with the name of the star—is first of all filled with funny situations and secondly packed with tales starring amusing and entertaining teenagers.

Humorous original stories of teens—not just newspaper strip reprints such as those that filled most modern-style comics during their birth and growing pains in the 1930s—did not make up a real teen humor comic until the first issue of *Archie* (Winter 1942–1943). That was more than four years after Superman debuted in *Action Comics* #1 (June 1938).

Just as a character as revolutionary as Superman had to wait until 1939 for any genuine superhero and/or costumed competition, so the teen humor field didn't really begin to take off until the equally revolutionary Archie and his group had had the field to themselves for more than a year. By the end of the 1960s, nearly 150 teen humor titles had appeared, featuring more than 300 different humorous teens including the backup strips.

Teen humor, though, became pretty much entirely the domain of the Archie Series in the 1970s and beyond.

But even though the three primary decades of non–Archie teen humor comics were a long time ago, that makes it even more important and intriguing to read and study the titles.

These comics were, after all, fun. True, they were often surreal and silly, but they were mostly amusing and even intriguing. When you read a vintage teen humor title, you literally never know what will happen next.

The whole concept behind teen humor comics was a constant stream of rivalries between and among teens of both sexes. The idea was that teens would hatch plans that wouldn't or couldn't work. Sometimes a teen would try to fool his or her rival for a boy's or girl's attention, or that of a teacher, or a parent or sibling. It was pretty much taken for granted that teens didn't always think logically.

There were endless plot points, either at school, in part-time jobs, around the town, at the circus or movie or park, in the great outdoors … pretty much anywhere teenagers might be.

In this book, the Archie characters' titles are used primarily for context, because they have been covered by so many books already. I'm focused on the other teen humor characters and titles from more than two dozen publishers.

I mention periods when characters served as backups, such as how Quality's long-running Candy got her start as a backup in the superhero title *Police Comics*. But I do not consider *Police Comics*, or any other such title with a teen backup, to be a teen humor comic. I list in the appendix virtually all the titles that do qualify as teen humor comics.

Nor do I designate as teen humor the serious titles such as Lev Gleason's long-running *Boy Comics*, even though teen hero Chuck Chandler (a.k.a. Crimebuster) occasionally enjoyed humorous moments.

I divide the book into three sections (the 1940s, 1950s and 1960s), with a short overview to begin each. I include commentary on any given character or title in the section in which there was the greatest impact. If a title begins in 1949 but is primarily a 1950s title, it's covered in the 1950s section.

The vast majority of comic books in the 1934–1944 period were not named after individual characters, but were anthologies, either of newspaper strip reprints or original material. Some comics, such as Harvey's *Green Hornet* and DC's *Flash Comics*, were actually very much anthologies even though they were named after their stars.

I also briefly mention the career girl–working girl comics such as *Millie the Model* and *Nellie the Nurse*, so that readers can see how they are categorized. Since teens and career girls are often collected by the same enthusiasts, and since they are usually sold in the same category by dealers, I felt it was important to mention the twenty-something women—or girls, as they were always called "back in the day."

I'm indebted to more people than I can possibly name here—literally hundreds of collectors, historians, comic book retailers and convention impresarios, artists, writers and editors. The total is probably in the thousands, not just the hundreds. And there are other categories, too. But I would be remiss for not specifically mentioning the inspiration and information provided by collectors and historians Bud Plant, Dan Stevenson, Stan Molson, Bob Carter and Gary Watson, without whose help and advice this book would not be nearly as complete. But how, then, do I also not mention the admirable and well-known likes of Maggie Thompson, Bill Schelly, Shelton Drum, Jim Vadeboncoeur and so many others who have made it possible for me to grow in knowledge and wisdom?

I could fill several pages with more names, but you know who you are. I am grateful to thousands of you!

Section I

Overview: The 1940s

Almost all of the long-running teen humor comics began in the 1940s, but that's no surprise, in retrospect. At the time, so many teen comics seemed fresh and original, although doubtlessly reminding many readers of the Andy Hardy film series of the 1930s and 1940s and the exceptionally popular *Aldrich Family* radio program, which began in 1939.

The entire concept of American teenage life as being a unique period was a 20th century innovation, in response to modernized labor practices, vastly improved communications and transportation technology, and a significant increase in the number of high school and college graduates compared to the 19th century.

Teens today fancy themselves as being far more sophisticated than their parents and grandparents were in the pre–Internet, pre–cell phone world. That's understandable but deceiving. Since the founding of the United States, the real cultural and technological differences have been not from 1776 to 1876, but rather from 1876 to 1976. The teens of 1976—when significant teen humor comics had vanished except for the Archie Series—have far more in common with today's teens than the teens of 1876 had in common with their 1976 versions.

In other words, the beginnings of teen humor were a response to social and technological developments. By the 1940s, notwithstanding the hardships of the World War II era, most teens had access to telephones, radios, daily newspapers, cars, expanded educational opportunities and much more than their grandparents had. By the end of the 1950s, the vast majority of teens had television in their homes and many had flown on passenger and/or military planes.

I can recall, from my childhood memories in the 1950s, how I heard people the ages of my parents and grandparents often say they had missed out—as children and teens—on so much of the fun of the modern world for young people. Grandparents in the 1940s, if they ever picked up a teen humor comic book, likely would have found it the most confusing genre of all to follow.

But many of the parents of the 1940s—and certainly many comic book artists, writers and editors—picked up pretty well on teen humor. And not too many years later, the same adults picked up on teen horrors, as well. Even though there were a handful of early talkies dealing with the troubles of teens in the movies, such as *Girls on Probation* (1938), films about juvenile delinquents absolutely boomed in the 1950s and early 1960s. And even though there were a number of classic horror movies in the 1930s, most notably *Dracula* and *Frankenstein* from Universal, can you imagine anyone in Hollywood in the 1930s agreeing to a title like *I Was a Teenage Werewolf* (1957) or *I Was a Teenage Frankenstein* (1957)? Now, those drive-in gems from American International almost seem like a form, however strange, of teen culture.

More than 40 different companies, using many dozens of imprints for tax purposes, published corporate-level comic books in the 1940s. Not many, however, were willing to take a chance with teen humor in any significant way. That was not true of Marvel Comics, then known as Timely Comics and published by Martin Goodman for more than three decades beginning in 1939. Goodman, with a huge post–World War II editing boost from the remarkable Stan Lee, took advantage of every trend he could, capped by the historic 1960s Marvel plunge into the universe of unorthodox superheroes.

Goodman must have noticed the success and originality of Archie and his Archie Series brother Wilbur after they gained their own titles in unrelated scenarios. Two years after *Archie* #1 hit the stands late in 1942 with a Winter 1942–1943 date, Goodman was willing to convert the budding superheroine title *Miss America* #1 to a comic for girls with the debut of Patsy Walker and several teen-centric features in *Miss America* #2 (November 1944). At the same time, the one-shot *Junior Miss* (dated Winter 1944 but actually Winter 1944–1945) appeared. *Junior Miss* may have been the victim of paper rationing, but *Miss America* soon became a huge commercial success and attracted an immense advertising base. In 1945, Marvel gave Patsy Walker and Georgie (a boy not that much different from Archie) their own titles along with the beginning of career girl comics with the debut of *Millie the Model* in 1945.

By 1948, Marvel had 13 teen humor titles on the stands, far more than anyone else. National Comics (DC), in its typically stable manner, made good financially and artistically in the later 1940s with *Buzzy, A Date with Judy* and *Leave It to Binky*. By the end of 1949, no fewer than 56 teen titles had appeared outside the Archie Universe, in addition to several more from the Archie folks in the wake of *Archie* #1 and his appearances in *Pep Comics* and *Jackpot Comics*. They're all covered in this section.

Not everyone succeeded. Ace Comics, from the same company that had a huge paperback book success with the Ace Double Novels beginning in 1952, was a teen bomb. *Hap Hazard* ran 24 issues from 1944 to 1949, but six other Ace teen titles had disappeared after running a combined 24 issues from 1947 to 1949.

In the 1940s, few publishers outside Archie attempted teen anthologies and absolutely nobody but Archie succeeded, with titles like *Laugh Comics* and *Pep Comics*. All the comics that really succeeded were named for their lead characters.

1

Here She Comes in *Miss America Comics*: Patsy Walker

Like Archie Andrews had nearly three years earlier, Patsy Walker emerged from the pages of a comic book devoted to a patriotic superhero, in her case *Miss America Magazine*. And, like Archie, Patsy got her own title within a year and went on to become the second-most commercially successful teen character series ever, behind the Archie Series.

Miss America #1 was an undated 1944 production from Timely Comics, the predecessor of Marvel. *Patsy Walker* did not yet exist; there were four stories of the red-white-and-blue Miss America, who first appeared as a supporting character in *Marvel Mystery Comics* (#49, November 1943), Timely's flagship title.

Readers must have been surprised to see *Miss America* #2 (November 1944), which was expanded to 68 pages, an unusual move during a period of wartime paper rationing. Timely had come up with the first legitimate and ultimately highly successful competitor for *Calling All Girls* from *Parents Magazine*, which began as a 68-page combination magazine–comic book in 1941.

Miss America #2 featured what would become the only Golden Age issue with a teen girl, identified on the inside front cover as Dolores Conlon, 15, dressed as a superhero—Miss America, of course—in the earliest example of costume play in comics. The publication, which also took the unusual step of early monthly production, featured a 16-page Miss America story along with page after page of text fiction and non-fiction, all directed at girls. There were fashion stories, advice columns, film stories, love-interest fiction and the beginning of what would soon become scads of advertisements.

There was also, for the first time, Patsy Walker, with a sophisticated emphasis on the redheaded teen girl's interactions with her father, drugstore owner Stanley; her mother, PTA member Mary; her kid brother Mickey; her boyfriend Buzz Baxter, and her raven-haired rival, Hedy Wolfe. Patsy's best friend, Nancy Brown, debuted in *Miss America* #3 (December 1944).

All the Patsy Walker stories in *Miss America* Volume 1 #2–6 were seven pages long and all were lettered by a machine—uncommon in comics of the time. The stories were logically plotted and illustrated, without the slapstick antics so prevalent at the time.

What the Patsy Walker stories were *not* was recognized or publicized. *Miss America* Volume 1 #2–5—all with photo covers following the superheroine-dominated first issue—did not so much as mention Patsy's name on the covers! Apparently, Timely's first series starring a high school girl, five years into the company's history of publishing primarily action-adventure comics, was not considered important enough to recognize except in the table of contents on the interior front covers.

Publisher Martin Goodman's wife Jean was listed as supervising editor and wrote letters to girls about the contents of the magazine. She did not mention *Patsy Walker*.

In Patsy's first story, she learns that glamorous rival Hedy will date heartthrob actor Swoon Strong at the class prom when he visits Centertown (soon Centerville). Patsy is so disappointed that she turns down Buzz's invitation, with Patsy coming across in this debut story as somewhat self-centered—and thus lacking a certain degree of respect from her mother and Buzz.

Patsy tells her mother, "...Don't discuss my tragedy so calmly. I'm shamed—I'm undone—I've been defeated by that brazen—that, that Hedy Wolf [spelled incorrectly]!" Her mother responds sarcastically, "Oh, I thought it might be serious!" The next day after school, Patsy tells Buzz, "Buzz, you're a nice boy—but—I want a man—strong and—and—deep!" Buzz responds, "You don't want a man—you want a well!"

Mickey has learned a secret about Swoon Strong from a gossip magazine and shares it with Patsy. She races to Buzz's house and tells him, "You don't think I really meant it when I said I wouldn't go to the dance with you, did you?" When Patsy encounters Swoon with Hedy and her retinue, Patsy slaps Swoon on the back and knocks his wig off, thus mortifying Hedy. Mickey tells the reader in the final panel, "—And that's how I got Patsy to give me enough money to see a movie each day for a week!"

What *Miss America* #2 did plug on the cover was a contest for teenagers. First prize was $500 (more than $5000 in today's dollars!) for a 250-word essay on "Tomorrow's World." In the explanation on the full page announcing the contest, the editor makes this observation:

> It has often been said that TEEN-AGERS are the FORGOTTEN PEOPLE! That's bad thinking because, truly, TEEN-AGERS are the most important people in the world; the reasons are too numerous and obvious to list here. MISS AMERICA wants to remedy this deplorable situation, but she cannot do it without your help! And because MISS AMERICA needs your cooperation to make TOMORROW'S WORLD a better place to live and develop—physically, morally, spiritually and mentally—she is offering the following in cash prizes ...

Patsy did not become the leading comic feature until Volume 1 #6 (March 1945), which was the first issue without Miss America. The patriotic young costumed heroine was in two stories in #3 and one in #4 and #5, although she continued to appear in *Marvel Mystery Comics* through #85 (February 1948).

In #6, Nancy Brown names Patsy a "woman of destiny" in history class, with the junior class election in mind. When Buzz, president of the senior class, takes nominations at a meeting, Nancy nominates Patsy following someone else's nomination for Hedy. Patsy's father, a community stalwart, calls on friends to help publicize her while Nancy and Patsy campaign against Hedy. The result: Patsy, 378 votes; Hedy, 61.

In #3, a lackluster story takes place in nearby Farmdale: Patsy tries to get a job to keep up with Hedy, but she forgets about Buzz and he gets a job instead. In a much better story in #4, Patsy greets her seldom-seen cousin Percy at the train, only to find that Hedy wants to date the handsome fellow. But Percy is caught trying to rob the Walker family and confesses that he is the wrong Percy. Hedy goes on a date with the right Percy, a scholarly looking bookworm, much to Patsy's satisfaction. In an amusing story in #5, Mickey causes all sorts of Valentine's Day card confusion until his guilty conscience causes him to confess and leads Stan to tell his family, "Remind me to tell you about the time I sent a frog—"

Miss America would remain a monthly—a span of 66 issues except for no issue dated January 1946—until a company financial slump struck early in 1950. Patsy Walker never left the *Miss America* title, but she would not be billed on the cover until Volume 7 #4 (November 1947), which promised "3 Big Patsy Walker stories" in a format change. The cover of Volume 7 #5 (December 1947) also promised "4 Romantic True-to-Life Tales!" but all four were illustrated text stories, in contrast to Patsy's comic tales.

A Puzzling Publishing History

Miss America Comics lasted 126 issues from 1944 through 1958, one of the most successful runs of any comic started during World War II. (Most of the successful long-running comics of that period began in the late 1930s and early 1940s.) By the end of 1958, when *Miss America* officially ended with #93 (November), that number was absolutely deceiving, as the ensuing chart will show.

It took comic historians, including the author, many years to figure out the publishing history of *Miss America* and to confirm that Patsy Walker did indeed appear in every issue except the superhero-dominated first issue. Her 125 consecutive appearances were more than any teen character at the end of the 1950s, including Archie, in large part because *Miss America* sold so well that it was published monthly in two sequences. In all, Patsy appeared in 337 stories in *Miss America*, including backups with the logos of Hedy Wolfe, Nancy Brown and Buzz Baxter.

Miss America **Vol. 7 #13, August 1948, copyright 1948 Miss America Publishing Corp. Patsy Walker was the primary comic attraction in *Miss America*, but the generic covers often did not make that obvious.**

Here is the publishing history of *Miss America Comics*, covering the odd numbering system, dates and publication frequency:

Volume 1 #1, 1944 (undated). Volume 1 #2–6, November 1944 through March 1945.
Volume 2 #1–6, April 1945 through September 1945.
Volume 3 #1–6, October 1945, November 1945, December–January 1946, February through April 1946.
Volume 4 #1–6, May 1946 through October 1946.
Volume 5 #1–6, November 1946 through April 1947.
Volume 6 #1–3, May 1947 through July 1947 (last magazine-size format).
Volume 7 #1–33, August 1947 through April 1950 (last monthly issue).
Volume 7 #34, July 1950, through Volume 7 #44, March 1952 (last issue with proper numbering until #55).
Volume 7 listing only, with no numbers in indicia or covers: May 1952 (actual #45).
Volume 1 listing only, July 1952, September 1952 (actual #46 and 47).
Volume 7, November 1952 (actual #48).
Volume 1 listing only, January 1953 (actual #49).
Volume 7 #50, Spring 1953. Volume 1 #51, April 1953. Volume 7 #52, May 1953.Volume 1 #53, June 1953. Volume 7 #54, July 1953.

The rest of the run is listed as Volume 1 in the indicia with the correct number and also by number and date on the covers:

#55 (August 1953) through #63, April 1954 (end monthly run).
#64 (June 1954) through #70 (June 1955) (end bi-monthly run).
#71 (August 1955) through #76 (January 1956) (end monthly run).
#77 (March 1956) through #86 (September 1957) (last Atlas logo issue).
#87 (November 1957), first IND logo (Independent News).
#88–93 (January 1958) through #93 (November 1958) (final six issues).

Besides *Patsy Walker*, the only comic stories in the early issues were *Danny* (a teen boy) in Volume 1 #6 and Volume 2 #1–3 (four stories) along with *Betty Blair* (teen reporter) in Volume 2 #1 and Volume 2 #3 through Volume 3 #4 (nine stories). Multiple *Patsy Walker* stories began to appear in Volume 7 #1 and lasted the entire run except for single appearances in Volume 7 #34–36, each of which had five different, well-established teen characters.

When romance stories became a comic book craze, one each appeared in Volume 7 #20-26 and two each appeared in Volume 7 #27–33, and returned with one each in #77–88. Wendy Parker was a backup character in #53–66.

Patsy's first cover appearance was the line-drawn Volume 7 #36 (November 1950), resuming with Volume 7 #42 through the end of the run. After the first issue, photo covers were featured on every issue from Volume 1 #2 though Volume 7 #41 except for Volume 7 #36.

After the first few issues, *Miss America* was loaded with advertisements aimed at girls. The title was either 68 pages or 76 pages (including covers) through Volume 6 #3, except for the 92-page Volume 4 #5–6 (September and October 1946). During this period, *Miss America* was a genuine rival for the iconic *Calling All Girls.*

In the final few issues of *Miss America,* with covers signed by Al Hartley for #82 to 93, some of the stories resembled those of Katy Keene, with reader credits given for designs of fashions and pin-ups.

Beginning with issues dated November 1957, Marvel was limited to eight bi-monthly issues each month (16 total titles) in 1958–1959 in an agreement with Independent News and National Comics (DC) following an implosion caused by Marvel's distribution dilemma. The total expanded every year in the 1960s, however. *Miss America* was discontinued late in 1958 in favor of a new science fiction title, since the Patsy Walker and Patsy and Hedy titles were still selling well.

2

Patsy Walker's Groundbreaking Title

After appearing in increasingly popular single stories in each issue of *Miss America* for eight months or so, in 1945 Timely–Marvel Comics made Patsy Walker the first teen girl to have her own comic book. She succeeded so well, she was also among the last teen girls to have her own title, fully two decades later after 124 issues of continuous publication.

Ironically, the cover of *Patsy Walker* #1 shows the girl who became Marvel's best-selling comic flopping on a pillow strapped to her backside while she's roller skating. Artist Pauline Loth's indelible image shows Patsy with a pretty smile to go with the cute blue hair ribbon that matches her blouse.

Since the first issue was listed as a quarterly, even though the only date in the indicia states "Copyright 1945," that issue almost surely was a Summer 1945 comic book since #2 is dated Fall 1945. By that time, the only teens with their own regular titles were boys: *Archie* #1 was dated Winter 1942–1943; Ace's *Hap Hazard* #1 was Summer (officially undated) 1944; *Wilbur* #1, also from MLJ (soon to become the Archie Series), was Summer 1944; and DC's *Buzzy* #1 was Winter 1944–1945. No other girl would get her own comic for more than a year—until Marvel published *Margie* #1, dated Winter 1946–1947.

World War II paper rationing had forced many publishers to drop from 68 pages (including covers) in 1943 to lower page counts, including many with 36 pages from Marvel in 1944 and 1945. The 36-page count would become the standard for decades after comics gave up the 52-page size at various points for ten years through 1954. Thus, *Patsy Walker* #1 through 4 were all 36 pages, but the first three had four full-length stories of Patsy, drawn by Pauline Loth and Ruth Atkinson, and #4 had three stories, all longer than any so far.

Unlike many teen titles in the 1940s and even the '50s, *Patsy Walker*, while drawn with obvious humor elements, had very few crazy, slapstick elements. This makes them great period pieces dealing with every aspect of high school life in the 1940s.

Since Patsy had been formally introduced in *Miss America* #2 (November 1944), the first story in *Patsy Walker* #1 made Patsy and her family and friends seem like established characters. That tale details the arrival of Birdseye Walker, literally a country cousin of Patsy, and how he avoids the clutches of her rival Hedy Wolfe. All four stories are light-hearted romps. The best one detailed how Patsy unsuccessfully tried to stop her father Stanley from smoking. In that story, Hedy smokes in public, shocking Patsy, best friend Nancy Brown and boyfriend Buzz Baxter. "I always say that smoking lends one an air of sophisticated mysteriousness," Hedy tells them before they make her sick with a "cure" that did not work on Stanley Walker.

A Rare Women's Rights Story

One of the most memorable of the early *Patsy Walker* stories was an untitled tale in #2. It was first spotlighted by author-artist-editor Trina Robbins, for decades the preeminent historian of women in comics, in her 1999 volume *From Girls to Grrrliz: A History of Women's Comics from Teens to Zines.* On the splash page, a sign in the window of an employment agency, BOYS AND GIRLS WANTED, offers $18 per week for boys and $12 for girls. (This would have been considered good pay for teens in 1945; factoring in inflation, that's more than $250 at the high point.)

Patsy says, "Why should boys get more money than girls—that's unfair!" Nancy responds, "What about equal rights for women?" and kid brother Mickey Walker retorts, "Aw, c'mon … the deal sounds okay to me." After debating the point into the night, the two friends are still on point the next morning, with Patsy fired up enough to contend, "But we have a duty to perform. We must free women from bondage!" in response to Nancy's observation, "I say equal rights for women are fine but I'd rather have dates and be pampered."

Patsy calls a meeting of the high school girls and they all agree to her points except Hedy, who mutters what Nancy calls a "little boo." Patsy places marching orders on a blackboard: "Don't wear skirts—wear slacks! Don't let boys carry your books or package … [It] makes them think you're weak! Don't be so helpless!" The next day, every girl but Hedy is wearing slacks, leading Buzz to ask, "Why's everybody masquerading as boys, Patsy?" Patsy and Nancy insist on paying for movies and sodas, much to Buzz's bafflement. The next morning, Nancy notes, "$1.53 for movies, 45 cents for sodas … Equal rights are pretty expensive!" Patsy declares, "The cost of freedom comes high but it's worth it!"

Hedy, true to her nature, coaxes the boys to hold their own meeting and convinces Buzz to post a sign, "Woman Power Shortage! Sign up for dates with Hedy, last real girl in town."

This is all pretty stunning for a 1945 comic book! (It wasn't until the 1960s that Patsy regularly supported women's rights again.) In this epic, the girls are miserable seeing Hedy monopolize the boys, so Patsy decides that to save face, she will ask the principal to ban slacks in school. (Pants were banned on most days at most high schools in the United States until the late 1960s!) He does just that, while elsewhere Buzz tells Hedy she would look like movie star Sonja Wildfire in slacks. On the morning Hedy shows up in slacks, Nancy dons a pretty dress and says, "I feel like a girl again." Patsy agrees: "I didn't like those slacks either." The story ends with Hedy alone and Patsy telling Buzz, "You can carry my books forever, Buzz, if you want to!"

Well, it was 1945. Women's lib was more than two decades away.

In *Patsy Walker* #3 (February 1946) four separate stories involve a cake-baking contest, a radio quiz show, father Stanley Walker's desire to avoid teen music, and a swim team for the girls. Issue #4 (April 1946), the last 36-page issue until #53 (July 1954), deals with pets, Stanley's revenge against Hedy at the ice-skating rink, and a failed attempt by the girls at sophisticated upswept hair styles.

Patsy Walker #5 (June 1946) and #6 (August 1946) were the first 52-page issues as the effects of both her own runaway popularity and the end of paper rationing kicked in. The girls thus appeared in no fewer than six stories—everything in both issues.

But from #7 (October 1946)—when Georgie appeared as a backup strip one year after his own comic surprisingly appeared out of the blue—popular characters, almost always stars of his or her own comic books, also ran as backups in *Patsy Walker*. This enabled Marvel to let readers know about the bonanza of other teen comics that begin late in 1946 and early in 1947 (see separate chapter). There were numerous house ads to that effect, beginning in #8.

The Backup List

The list of backups in *Patsy Walker* from #7 through #33 has never been presented. For the benefit of collectors, here they are, after Georgie's appearance in #7:

#8 (December 1946), Georgie; #9 (February 1947), the only appearance of Daisy; #10 (April 1947), Millie the Model and Peggy; #11 (June 1947), Georgie, Mitzi; #12 (September 1947), Rusty, Willie; #13 (November 1947), Margie, Willie; #14 (January 1948), Margie, Willie; #15 (March 1948), Margie, Georgie; #16 (May 1948), Margie, Georgie; #17 (July 1948), Margie, Georgie; #18 (September 1948), Cindy, Georgie; #19 (November 1948), Margie, Georgie.

#20 (January 1949), Georgie, Cindy; #21 (March 1949), Jeanie, Cindy; #22 (May 1949), Jeanie, Cindy; #23 (July 1949), Jeanie, Cindy; #24 (September 1949), Jeanie, Cindy; #25 (November 1949), Jeanie, Cindy; #26 (January 1950), Millie, Margie; #27 (March 1950), Nellie the Nurse, Millie; #28 (May 1950), Nellie, Buzz Baxter; #29 (July 1950), Mitzi, Jeanie; #30 (September 1950), Jeanie; #31 (November 1950), Mitzi, My Friend Irma; #32 (January 1951), Mitzi; #33 (March 1951), Margie, Jeanie.

This was a classic example of a company using its most popular comic to publicize other characters. Patsy's backups in #34 (May 1951) through #47 (July 1953) were related stories of Buzz Baxter and Hedy Wolfe. In #48 (September 1953) through #52 (May 1954), Wendy Parker and Hedy were the backups, with only Wendy in #53 (July 1954) and #54 (September 1954). Regular romance backup stories followed in #55 (November 1954) through #73 (October 1957).

Claim of Five Million Readers

Unlike some other leading publishers, Marvel seldom made circulation claims. But they did appear in 1948 on the covers of *Patsy Walker* #16 ("5,000,000 Teen-Agers Love the Experiences of Patsy Walker!") and #17 ("Over 5 Million Readers!").

Comic book publishers in the 1940s often assumed a "pass-around" rate of four to six readers per comic book, especially in the era before commercial television exploded. This explains such a huge readership claim, since no comic book ever sold five million copies; a million-copy title was considered a total success. The pass-around phenomenon also is a major reason that only a tiny fraction of Golden Age comics are found in fine or better condition.

The term "collector's item" was seldom if ever used on the cover of a 1940s comic book. At the time, they were considered totally disposable entertainment—they inevitably sold for five cents (or less) or "six for a quarter" at second-hand outlets—and thus offered no collector value beyond a reader's love for the characters.

When Patsy Beat Archie

Beginning with Patsy Walker's first appearance in *Miss America* #2 (November 1944), Marvel thought so much of her commercial value that she appeared far more often than Archie from 1945 to 1949. Archie got a head start in *Pep Comics* #22 (December 1941), *Archie Comics* #1 (Winter 1942–1943) and *Jackpot Comics* #4 (Winter 1941–1942) and had appeared in 48 issues of those three titles by the end of 1944, when Patsy made her second appearance in *Miss America* #3 (December 1944).

By the end of 1949, Patsy had appeared in 107 issues across four titles and Archie had starred in 110 issues across six titles. Thus, Patsy could be found in 105 issues in the 1945–1949 period compared with 62 for Archie! Of course, in that period, Marvel had more resources than the Archie Series, which debuted as MLJ Comics in 1939. In 1949, Marvel led the industry with 272 issues and the Archie Series had only 43, according to historian Dan Stevenson's year-by-year checklist of all corporate publishers. Very few characters in any genre appeared in more than 105 issues in the last five years of the 1940s.

The 1940s Patsy list: *Miss America* 61 issues, *Patsy Walker* 25 issues, *All-Teen* and *Teen 16* issues, *Cindy Comics* 7 issues (#29, 30, 34, 35, 36, 37, 39).

The 1940s Archie list: *Pep Comics* 56 issues (#21–76), *Archie* 29 issues, *Laugh Comics* 17 issues (#20–36), *Jackpot* 6 issues (#4–9), *Archie's Pal Jughead* #1 and *Archie's Rival Reggie* #1.

Marvel experienced a serious financial implosion in 1950—in part caused by an over-production of romance comics—and dropped to 187 issues of all genres. At the same time, the Archie Series began an expansion with titles like *Archie's Girls Betty and Veronica* and *Archie's Pal Jughead*, resulting in 57 issues.

By the end of the 1950s, Marvel had suffered a disastrous implosion caused by a distribution fiasco in 1957, resulting in a contract with DC (National Comics) that limited Marvel to 96 issues in 1958 and 1959 (eight per month). The Archie Series, meanwhile, had grown steadily and by 1959 the Archie Series had hit 100 issues, with the vast majority featuring the Archie gang.

Some 1940s Patsy High Spots

The 52-page issues of *Patsy Walker* from 1946 through 1949—#5 through #25—contained a total of 88 stories about Patsy, along with all those tales featuring other Marvel teen characters not related to the unique Miss Walker and her retinue. Each of Marvel's teens in the 1940s were part of unique universes with no story crossovers at all, unlike a variety of costumed heroes from several firms in that decade.

Patsy Walker #8 (all early dates noted above in list of backups): "What a Racquet!" Patsy plays a sport for one of the few times in the series rather than watching. A drawing has matched Patsy against Hedy in the Centerville High inter-school tennis tournament, so Hedy flashes cash and steals Buzz away for instructions. (Buzz is good in several sports, as the entire series shows time and again.) Patsy tries to get Nancy to help, but she winds up tutoring Nancy more than Nancy can help her. Nancy's tall cousin Ethelbert turns out to be the Masked Meteor, tennis player extraordinaire. Patsy responds so

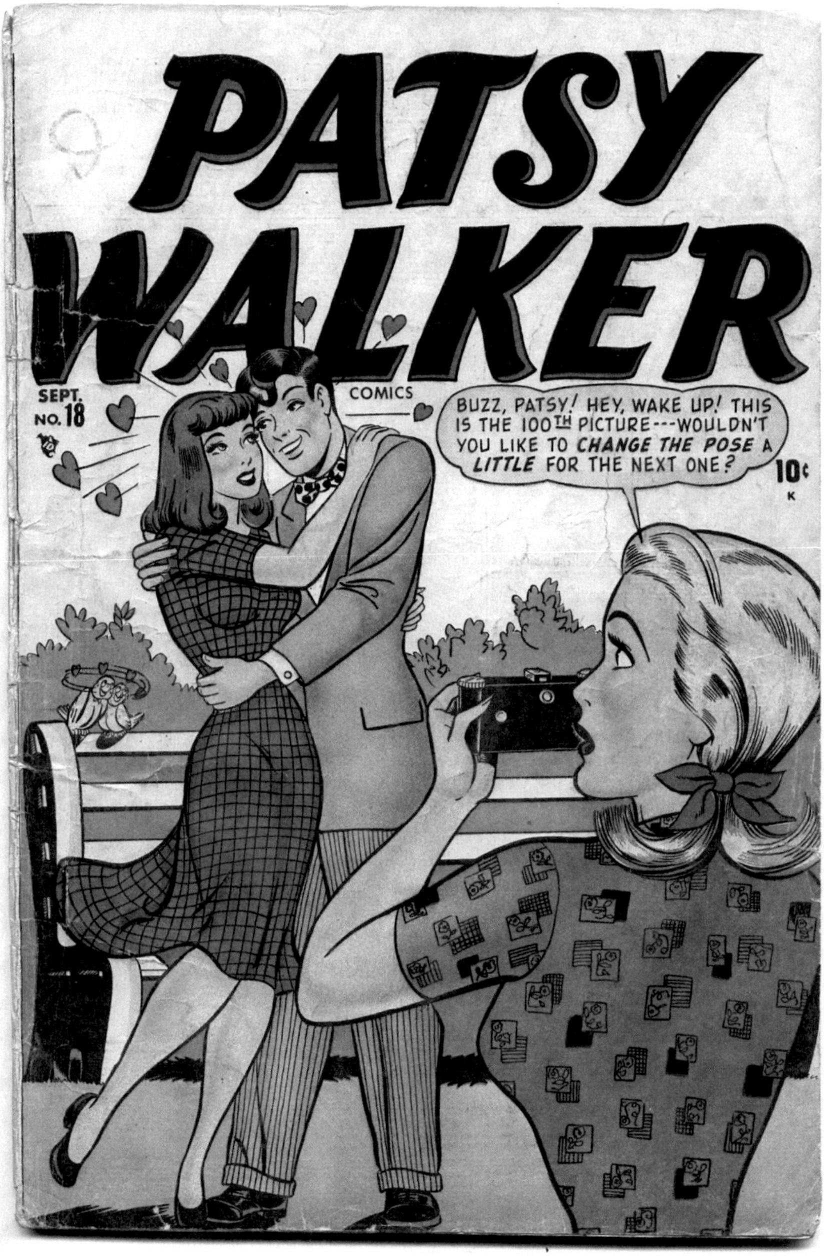

Patsy Walker #18, September 1948, copyright Bard Publishing Corp. This issue was published during a five-year period (1945–1949) when Patsy appeared in far more issues from Marvel than Archie did with the Archie Series.

well that she beats Hedy and then accepts Buzz's explanation that he needed Hedy's money to take Patsy to the dance. Patsy ends the story by talking trash to Hedy: "The next time you want tennis lessons, I can get them wholesale for you from the Masked Meteor!"

Patsy Walker #11: "Date with a Dream!" Hedy sees Patsy and Nancy enter the beauty parlor and asks them, "What are you doing here? Nothing can help you two frowsy females!" Nancy immediately calls Hedy "Dracula's Sister." Hedy swipes a pair of scissors and quickly cuts both Patsy and Nancy's hair! The sympathetic hairdresser boots Hedy out and finds a way to refashion the two girls: with sweet short bang-cuts and shimmering blue dresses with gorgeous fur coats, giving their dates an eye-opener!

Patsy Walker #14: "Cheers for the Cheer Leader!" Patsy injures her ankle while working hard in competition with Hedy for cheerleader. Hedy tries to trick a homely admirer, snack salesman Lemuel, into forcing ice cream down her back. Lemuel thinks Patsy is too pretty to deliberately hurt her chances, but he's so clumsy that the ice cream finds its target in the back of her shirt. Patsy goes physically nuts in response and wins the contest with her crazy moves, much to Hedy's disgust. This is a rare but well-done example of slapstick in the series.

Patsy Walker #18: "You Can't Stop Pop!" Stanley Walker and Dave Brown, fathers of Patsy and Nancy, both catch a prize fish simultaneously on a friendly outing. There is much recrimination between fathers and daughters until the girls make amends—they're such solid friends—and split the fish in half so they can put a trophy for each man on their walls. But in the last panel, they realize that showing the "wisdom of Solomon" won't work if either man visits the other's home! This is a truly amusing story in a long series that spotlights parents more than most in the teen humor genre.

Patsy Walker #19: "Helping Hands!" Patsy and Nancy help Joe, a veteran with amnesia, and his family avoid being evicted by Titus Skinflint. Skinflint realizes when he sees Joe that he is his long-lost son Jon, who has suffered from battle fatigue. Everyone wins in this nice piece of amusing Americana. Most teen humor stories are not overly sentimental; this one is.

Patsy Walker #21: "Patsy Goes Courting!" In an amazingly complicated story, Patsy become a judge for the day and helps solve the problems of four families in two unrelated cases. It would take an adult to understand this tale, which ends with Stanley amusingly taking in his daughter as a law partner. That was just, of course, for the last panel of the story.

Patsy Walker #25: This last issue of the 1940s begins a series of four consecutive painted covers by Louise Altson, the unknown artist who nicely painted the covers of the 1949 *Junior Miss* #35–37.

3

Marvel Teens in the 1940s

In the 1940s, no comic book company came remotely close to Marvel, then known primarily as Timely Comics, when it came to producing teen humor comics.

As successful as she was, it wasn't all Patsy Walker. Not by the long shot all the other Marvel characters turned out to be.

Unlike other major companies of the Golden Age such as Quality and Fawcett, Marvel used teen characters only in teen humor titles. For example, Quality debuted Candy in *Police Comics* #37 (December 1944) and Fawcett ran Freshman Freddy in most issues of *Mary Marvel*, among others.

In addition to Marvel's groundbreaking titles *Miss America* and *Patsy Walker* (see their chapters), which started in 1944 and 1945 respectively, publisher Martin Goodman's ambitious firm started 13 other teen titles between 1944 and 1948. This made Archie and DC seem diminished before 1950, even though in retrospect both companies got off to strong starts with characters who proved to be exceptionally durable in the teen humor genre in the chaotic decade of the 1950s.

But while Patsy Walker appeared in 124 issues of her own title through 1965 and in 125 issues of *Miss America* through the end in 1958, only one of the other 1940s Marvel teen titles lasted more than 17 issues and ran beyond 1950. That was *Georgie*, which presented at least five different artistic impressions of Georgie Foster in a 39-issue run from 1945 through 1952.

Although Marvel tried with a handful of other teens in the 1950s and 1960s, the 1940s teens are far better remembered and more avidly collected, even if by only a fraction of all Golden Age collectors. But the "working girl" titles, such as *Millie the Model, Tessie the Typist* and *Nellie the Nurse*, were more successful and today are sought by more collectors.

Goodman was famous for ordering his editors, including Stan Lee in the postwar years, to follow successful trends. Marvel put out 30 different romance titles in the 1949–1950 explosion, to see only five last into 1951 on an uninterrupted basis. Despite Marvel's financial implosions of 1950 and

1957, by the end of the decade, Marvel had produced nearly 450 romance issues. DC and Charlton didn't catch up until the 1960s, when Marvel had mostly moved on to superheroes (who were themselves created in response to DC's Silver Age successes beginning in 1956). Likewise, Marvel produced hundreds of westerns and war comics.

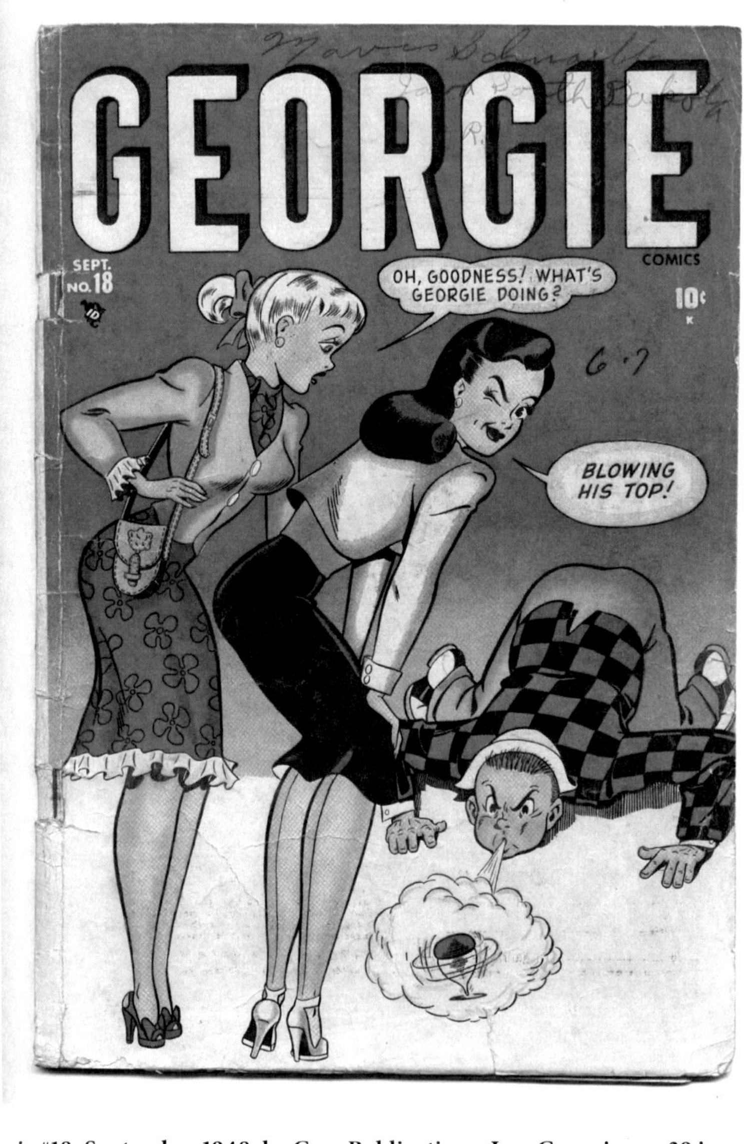

Georgie #18, September 1948, by Gem Publications, Inc. Georgie ran 39 issues as Marvel's most successful boy with his own title in the Golden Age.

Marvel's Teen Explosion

Here are the 13 Marvel teen titles that began in the wake of the success of *Patsy Walker*:

All Teen Comics #20, January 1947; *Teen Comics* #21, April 1947 to #35, May 1950; 16 issues.

Cindy #27–40, Fall 1947 to July 1950; 14 issues.

***Frankie* #10, August 1948, copyright Margood Publishing Corp. Frankie, a spunky little guy who was drawn several ways but always as a go-getter, was among Marvel's earliest teen boys.**

Frankie #4–17, Winter 1946–1947 to November 1949; 14 issues.
Georgie #1–39, Spring 1945 to October 1952; 39 issues.
Jeanie #13–27, April 1947 to October 1949; 15 issues.
Junior Miss #1 (one-shot), Winter 1944 (copyright 1944).
Junior Miss #24–36, April 1947 to September 1949; 13 issues (*Junior Miss* #37, December 1949, is all romance); *Junior Miss* #38–39, May 1950 to August 1950; two issues; actually a new and different title based on the radio program.
The Kellys #23–25, January 1950 to June 1950; three issues.
Margie #34–49, Winter 1946–1947 to October 1949; 16 issues.
Mitzi #1/*Mitzi's Boy Friend* #2–7/*Mitzi's Romance* #8–10 (actually the same comic book), Spring 1948 to December 1949; ten issues.
Oscar #24–25, #3–10, #13, Spring 1947 to October 1949 (#11–12 are kid humor titled *Awful Oscar*); 11 issues.
Rusty #12–22, April 1947 to September 1949; 11 issues.
Willie #5–19, #22–23, Fall 1946 to May 1950 (#20–21 are kid humor titled *Lil' Willie*); 17 issues.

All of these titles used some of these characters as guests for backup stories in the series. Even a star like Patsy Walker was only part of *Cindy* comics and *Teen Comics*, which was the only true teen anthology among the 13 titles.

Junior Miss

The first Marvel teen comic after the premiere of *Miss America* was the one-shot version of *Junior Miss*. This is dated Winter 1944, but it's copyright 1944 so is actually a 1944–45 issue. It's only 36 pages (including covers), showing how paper rationing was making a bigger impact.

Other than for its scarcity, the *Junior Miss* one-shot is not especially noteworthy. There are comic strip biographies of June Allyson and Frank Sinatra along with stories introducing Peggy Brooks (the cover feature) and Betty Lane. Betty Lane is still a teen but is a budding crime reporter, so there's nothing humorous about her eight-page adventure.

That leaves Peggy Brooks, who was never more than a little-known backup. This story opens with Peggy in the church choir and ends with her little sister Nema pulling an ice-skating prank on Peggy's so-called "wolfess" rival Alyce Forsyth, the junior class president. That means senior class president–heartthrob Chuck Rawlings can take Peggy to the senior prom. It's a lightweight story, with none of the impact Patsy Walker had, at least in retrospect.

Marvel's second version of *Junior Miss* began with #24 (April 1947) with the banner introduction of Cindy Smith, a glamorous redheaded rival for

***Junior Miss* #1 (first series), Winter 1944, copyright Cornell Publishing Corp. This one-shot is half teen humor, half biography and may have been the victim of paper rationing.**

Patsy Walker's circulation figures (although they were apparently seldom in the same stories). *Junior Miss* and the contemporary Marvel teen anthology *Teen Comics* both featured Cindy, who was featured in bravura, over-the-top stories of fun, frolic and fashion. Cindy also had her own contemporary title for 14 issues (often featuring Patsy Walker as a backup) and appeared in several other Marvel teen titles, such as *Georgie*.

Cindy was cover-featured on every issue of *Junior Miss* through #34 (May 1949), but she was never ballyhooed with her full name or logo-style publicity in that title. The first 11 issues were a mix of teen humor comics and teen-oriented text stories of romance, along with various features of one and two pages.

Cindy's first story provided one and a half pages of everyone important in her life at Oakdale High, including best girlfriend Goldie Adams, boyfriend Chuck Rivers, raven-haired, sultry rival Sandra Lake and soda fountain buddies Pud, Jigger and Peanuts. Most teen humor stories did not have such an introductory page, not to mention panels on the second page of Cindy's father Oliver, kid brother Oliver Junior and "Mrs. Smith," as the red-headed homemaker is identified.

"That girl is too much for me!" Dad says, while Mom responds, "Nonsense! She's just a normal, healthy girl!" Brother says, "Aw, that sister of mine thinks she's s-o-o-o grown up!"

Cindy's debut story starts at the local hangout, Pop's, where an Atomic Sundae is 25 cents. Pop tells the kids that a cute puppy at the pet store next door is the prize in this year's soda-drinking contest, which fat boy Peanuts, a big eater, always wins. Cindy and Goldie cook up a plot to fill all the boys with fudge, sidelining all but Peanuts for the contest, in which Cindy is the only entrant. After they have ten sodas apiece, soda jerk Jigger accidentally fills a soda with soap and Peanuts exits quickly. Cindy takes ill but wins the contest and spends the next day in bed.

That was a good example of what was to come through 1950, when Cindy disappeared along with all of Marvel's teen humor titles except for the earliest two *Patsy Walker* titles and *Georgie*, who by that time carried an Archie-style swiped logo!

In the Cindy story in *Junior Miss* #25 (July 1947), Sandra Lake seems on the verge of stealing Chuck for the senior prom. Cindy and Goldie trick Sandra into thinking Frankie Snorata is calling her, when in reality it's Peanuts playing the crooner's latest hit: "...When the Moo-oon in your hair is Su-Un in my eyes ..." Fickle Sandra dumps Chuck, who finds himself in Cindy's arms at the dance. The story closes with Chuck saying, "Gosh! You're pretty, Cindy!" as Goldie thinks, "And smart, too!"

The Cindy stories, many of which were drawn by Ken Bald, were consistently full of fun. She was an amusing knock-off of Betty Cooper (except for the hair) and Sandra likewise imitated Veronica Lodge (hair and big bucks included). The Cindy stories also showed how difficult it was for teen humor to achieve a level of originality, but then, teen humor didn't actually need to.

With *Junior Miss* #28 (January 1948), Cindy's story count increased to three instead of one and the title was an anthology only in the sense that several illustrated text stories made it so. But that format lasted only seven

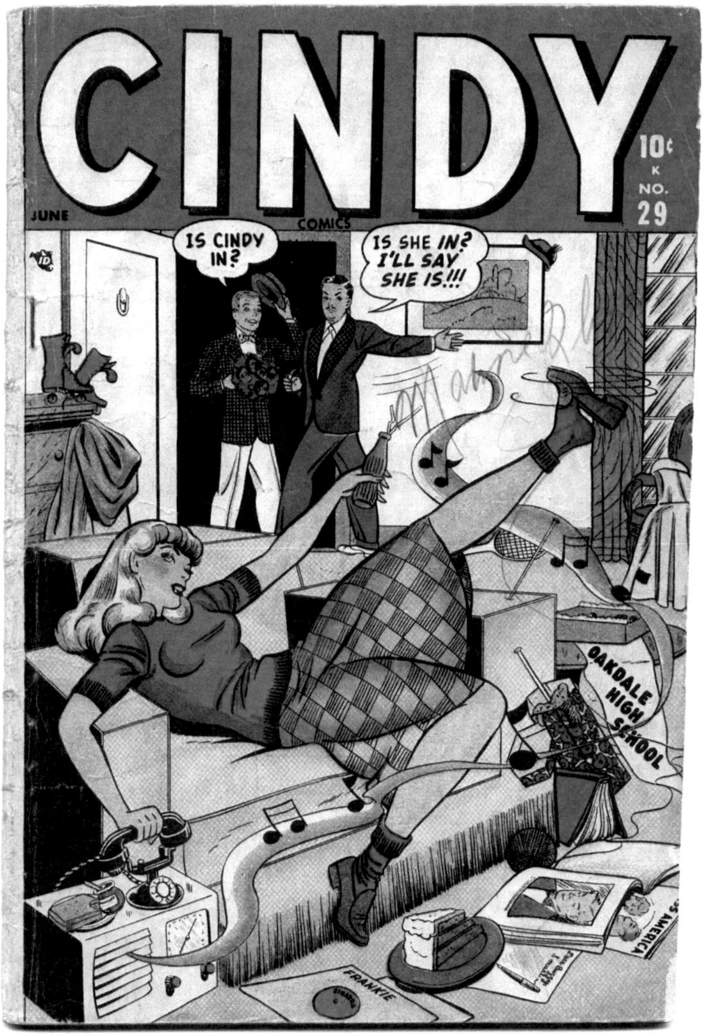

***Cindy* #29 (third issue), June 1948, copyright Timely Comics, Inc. With her big red hair, Cindy (erroneously shown on this cover as a blonde) looked a lot like Patsy Walker herself and appeared in 14 issues of her own title and numerous others as a backup.**

issues. Beginning with #35 (July 1949), the Cindy stories had to share space with the "straight" (pun fully intended!) romance stories that were proving so popular among many publishers. In fact, *Junior Miss* #37 (December 1949) was all romance—one of 30 such Marvel titles in the 1949–1950 period of what I long ago dubbed "The Love Glut." *Junior Miss* #35–37 featured painted youthful romance covers signed by Louise Altson, who otherwise was not known in comics.

Marvel soon cancelled 23 romance titles and interrupted two others in 1950. The last two issues of *Junior Miss*, #38 (May 1950) and #39 (August 1950), featured "real" *Junior Miss* stories based on the third version of the radio series, which ran from 1948 to 1954 as listed in radio historian John Dunning's huge volume *Tune In Yesterday* (1976). Based on stories by Sally Benson in *The New Yorker*, the Junior Miss of the title was Judy Graves, who had all sorts of misadventures with her BFF, the oddly named Fuffy Adams. These were not sophisticated stories, but rather short, sweet tales.

The covers were highly original: #38 has Judy stumbling over her words at a soda fountain when she tries to order the Lover's Kiss soda advertised on the wall, and #39 has Judy saying while strolling, "Fuffy, I think that boy is following us!" to which Fuffy responds, "Jeepers! Slow down before we lose him!!" The banner atop the two covers bills "Radio's Most Popular Teen-Agers!"

From the Back Seat to the Front

Mitzi Martin was the rare teen character who succeeded commercially for Marvel, yet needed more than a year to earn her own title during the firm's teen explosion in the late 1940s.

Mitzi was introduced in *All Teen Comics* #20 (January 1947), which appeared between the final two issues of the superhero title *All-Winners Comics* #19 and #21. The unsigned Mitzi strip, which made her look like a young teen, also introduced kid sister Patty and kid brother Squibby on the splash page. Mitzi and the other teen characters—Georgie (two stories), Patsy Walker and Willie—are all portrayed on a cute dancing cover, which was the only Marvel teen humor cover with four teenagers from different strips. These four did not cross over into each other's strips, so the cover was unusual.

The first Mitzi story had the clever title pun "The Inferior Decorators." In it, the three Martin children wound up with furniture chaos when their parents were away but avoided punishment because the parents were convinced the repaired furniture had become too old and fragile.

Of the 1940s Marvel teen humor comics, *Mitzi Comics* #1 (Spring 1948) was the final first issue to appear, but none of the other teen titles was cancelled to make room for it. For unexplained reasons, the title was changed to *Mitzi's Boy Friend* for #2 (June 1948) and for the last three issues to *Mitzi's Romances* with #8 (June 1949). The stories, however, were simply titled Mitzi. This was during the postwar period when most Marvel titles had shrunk from 52 pages (including covers) to 36.

For the Mitzi series, she was portrayed as a full-figured older teenager, in contrast to her stories when she did not have her own title. In #2, there were two Cindy stories and one Mitzi story in which she confuses the new vice-principal with the new janitor. The last story features Mitzi's boyfriend,

***All-Teen Comics* #20 (first issue), January 1947, copyright Western Fiction Publishing Co. This issue, Marvel's first teen anthology, appeared between the last two issues of the super hero title *All Winners* #19 and #21, then continued as *Teen Comics* with its own #21.**

***Mitzi's Boy Friend* #2 (first issue titled *Mitzi*), June 1948, copyright Timely Comics, Inc. This title ran 10 issues under three names in 1948–1949 with no change in the wacky characters.**

Chip Chambers. It's an amusing tale of bowling, in which Mitzi, BFF Daisy and Chip prevail over snooty Lydia, who shows her bowling expertise to the extent that she wears herself out for dancing later in the evening.

The "Romances" tag may have been added to Mitzi because of all the romance comics Marvel was producing at the time. Artist Ken Bald and writer Stan Lee both signed the only Mitzi story which was done in the boring, blocky eight-panel style Marvel used in most of its 1949–1950 teen humor comics. This style looked like some of the Sunday comics and it was awful. Oddly, the backup Oscar story was done in the older, more creative manner but it was a silly slapstick story.

Mitzi's Boy Friend #4 (October 1948) had one of the all-time great teen covers: Mitzi and Chip are at a cat show in front of a cat dancing on its hind legs. When Mitzi asks what kind of cat it is, Chip answers, "Why, a hepcat, of course!"

In *Mitzi* #7 (March 1949), "Disguise the Limit!" (an outrageous title pun) nicely tells the tale of Chip overcoming Mitzi's father's resistance to having him in the house. Chip disguises himself in drag and flirts with Mitzi's dad. The result is success—Mitzi and Chip get to leave the house—but Mitzi's mom ends the story with a roller pin and a battered husband. Domestic violence in those days, given the right humorous context, worked in ways that would never fly today, even for laughs.

Jeanie's Prototype Garage Sale

Raven-haired Jeanie Johnson was bannered as "Queen of the Teens" and for good reason. In fact, it will forever be a puzzle why Georgie survived Marvel's 1950 purge, if only for a couple of years, while Jeanie did not.

"Scrap-Happy" in *Jeanie* #19 (May 1948) was a good example of Jeanie's excellence. She needs $5.98 for a dress and her father gives her permission to have an "auction sale"—a 1948 version of a garage sale, not many of which were held in postwar America outside of farms. Jeanie sells so many of her father's items that he finds himself missing his things. When she tells him she needs $4 more because the dress has gone up, her father gives her the money and says it's cheaper than selling their stuff.

Interestingly, Marvel seldom spotlighted the boys, especially considering that in the 1950s, the Archieverse featured more boys with their own titles than girls—Archie, Jughead and Reggie—and ran far more logos of boys in stories than those of Betty and Veronica. In fact, the only other Archie Series titles in the 1940s and 1950s featuring females were not part of the Archie stories.

Marvel had the opposite philosophy. But then, if you included more than a dozen Marvel "working girl" titles in the 1940s and 1950s, Marvel obviously thought the "girls"—as women of all ages were often called—had a lot more commercial viability with readers of both genders.

The only boys with their own titles were Georgie, Willie and Oscar, in that order of importance. In the 1950s, the only teen boy with his own title in the Marvel stable was Homer Hooper, who lasted only four issues and was seldom used even as a backup. Georgie Lawson, who was drawn in sev-

Jeanie #14 (second issue), July 1947, copyright 1947 Chipiden Publishing Corp. Jeanie appeared in 15 issues of her own title and often as a backup in other Marvel comics.

eral different styles and seemed like several different characters, ran 39 issues from 1945 to 1952 but was seldom as funny as most of the Marvel femmes. Willie Watson and Oscar Hill were almost entirely slapstick characters, funny but not memorable.

Among the girls, Margie Foster ran only 16 issues (from 1947 to 1949) in her own title but she was featured in *many* backup tales in other titles. Rusty Rumble, oddly drawn as both a redhead and an off-color brunette, lasted only 11 issues in her own title but also was a well-used backup. Like

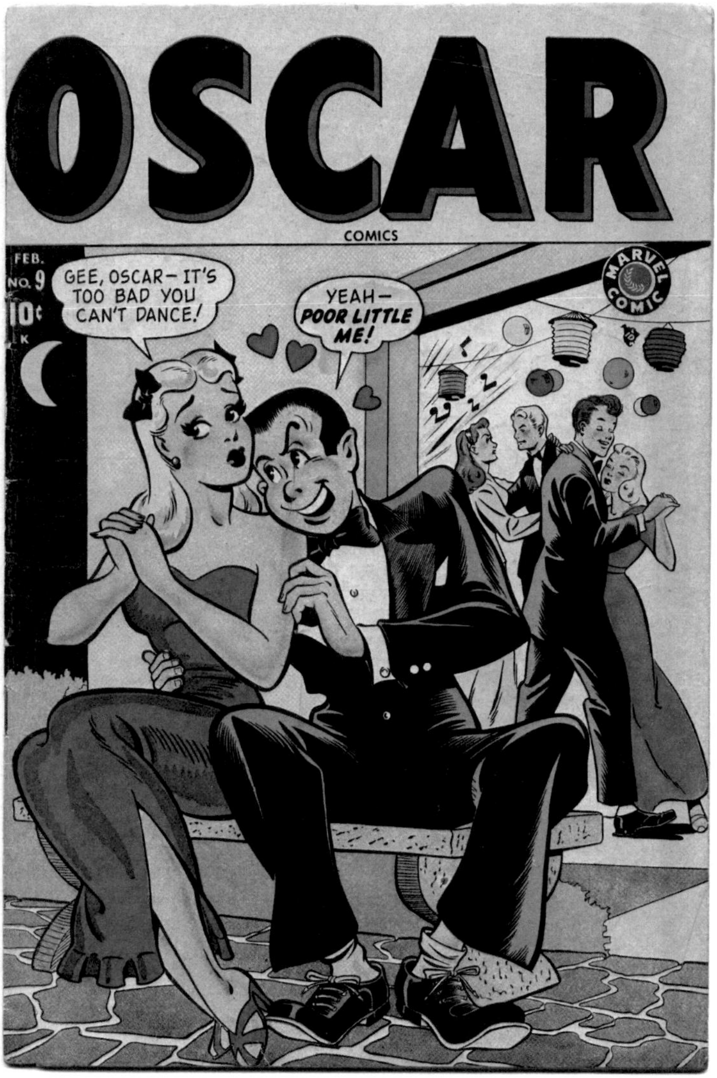

***Oscar* #9, February 1949, copyright U.S.A. Magazine Corp. Oscar was a wild wise-cracking character but ran only 11 issues in his own title. For a short time Marvel turned him into a child title named Awful Oscar.**

***Willie* #10 (sixth issue), October 1947, copyright Margood Publishing Corp. First appearing in his own title with the Fall 1946 issue, handsome heart-throb Willie was the second Marvel teen boy to get his own series after Georgie.**

Margie, Jeanie Johnson had a short run of 15 issues but was a frequently used backup. Both Margie and Jeanie had black hair, similar to Mitzi, meaning that Marvel did not have a teen title in the 1940s named for a blond, either a male or female!

4

Judy's Date with Success

A Date with Judy is noteworthy in several ways as one of the earliest teen humor comic books starring a girl. Outside the Archie Universe, the most important distinction is that her title ran longer than any comic named for a teen girl except for Marvel's *Patsy Walker.*

When National Comics (DC) launched *A Date with Judy* with #1 (November–December 1947), few fans would have been shocked if they had been told that the title, based on the highly popular radio show, would run through #79 (December 1960) on a consistent bi-monthly basis. It was DC's first radio adaptation, soon to be followed by *Gangbusters* and *Mr. District Attorney.*

Radio historian John Dunning described Judy Foster as "hyper-active, intense and unpredictable" in *Tune in Yesterday* (1976). That also makes for a precise description of her in the comics.

A Date with Judy was a summer replacement for three years before gaining full-time status on NBC from autumn 1943 to 1949 and on ABC in 1949 and 1950 for its last season. ABC's half-hour *Date with Judy* TV show ran full-time from July to October 1952 and from January to September 1953. Archie Andrews is unique in his way, of course, but otherwise only Henry Aldrich had more combined media success than Judy Foster.

DC may have been contracted to plug NBC's radio show, because her early comic book logo included an image of Judy broadcasting as "Radio's Famous Coast-to-Coast Favorite." She matched that and more in the comics. Among girls, her 79-issue run trailed only Patsy Walker's record 124 from 1945 to 1965. The only teen girl title that even came at all close in the 1940s through the 1970s was Quality's *Candy*, with 64 issues. In fact, among nearly two dozen female comic book headliners with their own titles in the 1940s, only Patsy, Judy and Candy made it beyond 1950.

Judy entered the comic book universe with an appropriate cover for #1 by George Storm, already established as the artist for Buzzy. Judy, in bobby sox, short skirt (for the time) and bright red sweater, blessed with quite the figure and holding a book with her right arm and her flowing, blonde hair with her left arm, is smiling widely and being ogled by four boys while crossing the street, apparently on the way to school. That is exactly how Judy Foster liked it; most of her hundreds of stories for DC dealt with one situation involving boys after another. This was teen humor at its height.

DC opened the issue, drawn by Storm, with "A Letter from Judy," explaining her family and friends. *Date with Judy* was unlike many other teen humor comics in the 1940s in that DC made no attempt to make puns in the early story titles, or even to title the stories at all.

Judy's First Story

Judy's first story, a hilarious ten-pager, finds the girls purposely being sent to detention in order to spend time with newcomer Greg Billings and Judy, who collided in the school hallway on the splash page and were late enough to class to be given detention. Oogie Pringle, Judy's heartthrob, also forces his way into detention, colliding with Greg, causing Greg to apologize profusely and puzzling the faculty monitor, Mr. Kibble. He thinks the kids are having too much fun, so he boots the lot out and Judy asks Oogie to walk her home. When Greg asks what's going on, Judy shows her fickle side and tells him, "You? Tootsie can have you! I like a MAN! But she isn't particular!" (Judy calls Tootsie "my bosom enemy" in her introductory letter.) In the last panel, Mr. Kibble tells his principal, "I'm a man totally in the dark!" and the principal responds, "Kibble—I'll tell you a secret. I've been that way for 20 years!"

Stan Kaye, one of DC's many good artists in the late 1940s, drew the backup strip Woody in the first six issues.

The third story, in which Oogie buys a Jeep and takes the girls for a ride in more ways than one, is also amusing, as is the fourth story, in which a beauty potion turns Judy's face blue until kid brother Randolph comes to the rescue. In the last panel, a relieved Oogie asks, "Judy, how could anything make you more beautiful than you are?" and Judy beams while answering, "Why, Oogie. How nice. You know, I never thought of that!"

In the opening story in #2 (December 1947–January 1948), Judy has noticed how well Oogie runs when he's chased by a bulldog and how well he can kick a football backward. Judy pulls Oogie out of the stands in Northeast High's big game against Greenchester—practice and eligibility rules be darned!—and convinces the coach that Oogie can win the game with unorthodox kicking. He does just that and as he and Judy are carried off the field, Judy tells him, "It only proves what men can do when they have a smart woman to inspire them!"

Judy #3 (February–March 1948), hitting the stands in December 1947, offered a wild Christmas story in which Judy convinces Oogie to serve as a replacement Santa Claus. Much craziness ensues at Lacey's Department Store, but its owner realizes that the publicity was worth millions. He gives Oogie and Judy bonuses of $200 (more than $2000 in today's dollars) and Judy tells a confused Oogie, "It's very simple, Oogie—there must be a Santa Claus!" In the same issue, Judy's red-headed friend Mitzi is introduced to the series with an utterly wacky story on the ski slopes.

Judy finds and nurtures the school principal's lost dog Socrates (!) in #5 (June–July 1948), but Judy is just as happy to see Mr. Kibble get the credit. In the same issue, Judy and Oogie have hilarious trouble from the little kids they're taking care of at the park but the kids are the heroes in the end when they rescue the teens from parental mis-accusations.

The Cutest Early Cover

The cutest of the early covers after the first issue is #6 (August–September 1948), which portrays Judy and Oogie separated on a park bench by a smug skunk! Willy-Nilly, who had a comical backup career in *Sensation Comics* #64–93, also began to appear in Judy's title in #7 (October–November 1948). But Willy-Nilly, as funny as his strip was for several years, never got his own title, a situation shared by well over 100 backup teen characters in the 1940s alone.

In one of the funniest endings to a story in the early series, Judy first gets help from her father, Melvin, and her mother, Dora, about worrying in #10 (April–May 1949). They think they've taught her about worries when she finds a book titled *How to Worry Correctly*. The result can't help but give a smile to the reader in the last panels, when Judy tells her father, "Oh, Father! I've got the biggest worry I've ever had! Now I'm worrying about whether I'm worrying correctly or not!"

There's an amusing story of confusion in #12 (August–September 1949), when Oogie buys a $3.98 blouse Judy wants but Judy's father Melvin wants the credit because Judy thinks he bought it after an argument they had over money. So Melvin gives Oogie $10 and tells the young man to buy a skirt to go with the blouse for Judy. Oogie spends the entire $10, leading Melvin to tell Judy, "Whenever you see a bargain, just buy it and charge it to me! It's cheaper that way!"

In the last 1949 issues, #12 and #13 (October–November), yet another backup strip appears, this one called Liz. In #13, Liz deduces that rival Janice is going to buy a new dress for a dance. Liz goes all out with her mother's best clothes, only to arrive over-dressed while Janice wins praise for being sweet and simple. "What some girls won't do to attract attention!" she shouts at boyfriend Freddie.

5

Buzzy, Binky and Scribbly in the 1940s

Buzzy Brown began in a six-page strip (looking like it was originally printed in the 1920s) in DC's *All Funny Comics* #1 (Winter 1943–1944). But George Storm's stylized art, highly unusual for the period, made Buzzy stand out, even if the stories were slapstick nonsense, with no relation to real life.

All Funny was an odd publication for DC, whose cover symbol did not appear until #3 (Summer 1944). The initial issue. DC's first humor title, was technically DC's first humor comic although the indicia lists Tilsam Publications as the owner and does not refer to National Comics (as DC then was officially known). Though National executive Whitney Ellsworth was listed as editor, the office of publication was not DC's familiar Lexington Avenue headquarters.

All Funny bannered "12 Big Laugh Features!" and Buzzy was the only teenage strip. Buzzy was also the only character in *All Funny*'s 23-issue run through 1948 who earned his own comic, though he did not merit a cover appearance in #1–4, after which he left *All Funny* for his new title. It's likely he was chosen for his own comic because DC focused on superhero and adventure strips in the Golden Age but Buzzy happened to come along at exactly the right time—when it was obvious that Archie had become a solid seller.

All Funny appears to have been thrown together quickly. The first issue, 60 pages (counting covers), was eight pages shorter than DC comics that appeared in most of 1943, but no doubt paper restrictions were responsible. Unlike other DC publications, the entire book was comic strips (except for a two-page text story) and the familiar list of the company's publications was nowhere to be seen, nor were there any house ads. The same was true of #2 (Spring 1944), which was 52 pages—by then the typical size of DC's comics.

Buzzy's six-page stores in *All Funny* #1–4 were nothing to shout about; the most amusing aspects were the charming, highly athletic dancing style of Buzzy and Susie Gruff, the daughter of Homer Gruff. Homer pretty much

***Buzzy* #1, Winter 1944, copyright Detective Comics, Inc. This is the first issue of DC's initial teen humor title, with old-school art by George Storm.**

stole the strip because of how Storm portrayed the burly, balding, middle-age father and his total distaste for teen music and culture. Buzzy's trumpet was the bane of Homer's life.

The first four stories were all pure slapstick with no real plots. At the end of the first story, Homer avoids a party at his home by hiding in his refrigerator. "I'm glad there's a light in here," he says. "It's cold comfort, but it's soundproof." In the second story, Homer pounds Buzzy on his backside with Buzzy's trumpet. At the end of #3, Homer takes aim from the second story of his home and splashes a blueberry pie in Buzzy's face as Susie says, "Oh,

Buzzy, you look so funny! Don't move! I'll get the camera for a candid snap!" (Susie would have gone crazy with a smartphone!)

Buzzy carries an actual plot in *All Funny* #4 (Fall 1944). Everdrip Tech students have kidnapped the mascot of Cupcake College, a goat named Colossus. Homer, a Cupcake alumnus, helps recover Colossus, but the goat boots him into the punch bowl at a celebratory party. To ease his frustrations, Homer clobbers Buzzy with his own trumpet.

Buzzy First to His Own DC Title

The success of Archie is the only logical reason that DC gave the then-obscure Buzzy his own title, beginning with #1 (Winter 1944–45) proudly emblazoned in the cover in large type. (It wouldn't be too many years before DC sometimes did not even use "No. 1" on the first issue.) Buzzy was the firm's only teen title until *A Date with Judy* appeared three years later (see the chapter on the early Judy).

Even though Buzzy had appeared in only a grand total of 24 pages in four stories in *All Funny*, that didn't stop DC from boasting "The Rib-Tickling Misadventures of America's Favorite Teenster!" at the top of #1. Storm's cover was a bit unexpected: Homer Gruff is shown bouncing in a tuxedo as Buzzy blows his trumpet and Susie says, "Daddy must be a bit off the beam, Buzzy—he actually seems to LIKE your tooting!"

There's nothing introductory overall for the first story in #1, a 12-pager, but it does bring in Buzzy's nemesis, Wolfert the Wolf. Homer Gruff, having become an alderman, is having his painting done by "the great artist, Henri Boltinoff." (The real Henry Boltinoff worked for DC but not on Buzzy.) The painter asks for live music and does a fine job, but the painting is soon defaced by mischief-making kids. Homer isn't happy until he batters Buzzy with both the painting and his trumpet. Poor Buzzy never seems to come out ahead! Actually, he's beaned in the head by Homer in four of the five stories in the first issue, but in the other story, Wolfie finds himself in the park in his underwear after his prank on Buzzy backfires.

DC wasn't shy about trying to bolster Buzzy. The cover of #2 shouted, "Another Jive-Jammed Jamboree with America's Favorite Teenster!" DC was one of the few, perhaps the *only* company to use "teenster." He does wind up on Homer's good side in the last story because he unintentionally prevented Homer from making a disastrous land deal. Once again, Susie continues to shout in all-cap letters, "POPSY IS KILLING BUZZY!" or "BUZZY IS KILLING POPSY!" during their slapstick shenanigans, which are never-ending in the 1940s. But on the cover of #4, as Homer gives Wolfie a swift, high kick, Susie shouts, "POPSY IS KILLING WOLFIE!" and Buzzy asks, "Is that bad?"

Despite the repetitious antics involving music and Homer's constant frustrations, Buzzy was successful enough to merit bi-monthly publication beginning with #6 (March–April 1946). The cover of #7 (May–June 1946) was the most clever to date, showing Buzzy lying on grass with a golf tee on his nose as Homer takes a swing and Susie pleads, "Popsy! Just 'cause Buzzy lost your tees, I don't think you should make him do this!" On the cover of #10 (November–December 1946), Buzzy is tied to a chair and Homer is blowing the trumpet in his ear as Susie shouts a variation of her favorite phrase: "Popsy's Getting Even with Buzzy!"

There were lots of successful cover gags, such as Buzzy being rescued at the beach by a female lifeguard and Susie hears him say, "Hey! I'm supposed to rescue you!" For #15, Storm does a marvelous job with comical female faces, forms and fashions as six girls stare at Buzzy as he judges the Cupcake High beauty contest. Wolfie is cover-featured for only the third time on #21 (September–October 1948) as he pays dollars for 50-cent charity kisses and Susie can only shrug at Buzzy's lone coin.

Storm continued the covers and art through #27 (September–October 1949), but DC had begun running somewhat obscure teen backup strips like the two Liz stories in #27. That provided a bit less of Buzzy but more variety. By #28 (November–December 1949), Buzzy had a new, unsigned cover artist. Homer Gruff, however, was still literally kicking Buzzy out of the Gruffs' home in some stories.

Binky Busts In

Then-youthful Sheldon Mayer, born in 1917 but already an editor, writer and artist throughout the late 1930s and the 1940s, created a terrific new DC teen title as editor with *Leave It to Binky* #1 (February–March 1948). This title, often with art by the outstanding Bob Oksner (1916–2007), was much more complex and unpredictable than Buzzy in the late 1940s.

Mayer (1917–1991) introduced Binky Biggs on the inside front cover with a page that all teen humor comics would have done well to adapt. He's the classic middle child, what with older teen sister Lucy and kid brother Little Allergy on hand to provide endless story plots. The page also introduces Binky's girl Peggy Baxter, saying, "True love never runs true, so why should Binky's?" From the introduction of Mom Biggs: "Nothing bothers Mom—she knows that with three kids in the family anything can happen!" The opposite is true of Pop Biggs: "Everything bothers Pop—he knows that with three kids in the family, anything can happen—to him!"

With Lucy and Little Allergy on hand for their own stories, *Leave It to Binky* apparently became successful right from the start. Whenever a problem or challenge for our teen hero would develop, he would say, "Just leave it to Binky!" The stories are full of what might be called "organized chaos." Binky is constantly in trouble, but not to the degree he is physically abused the way Buzzy constantly was throughout the decade.

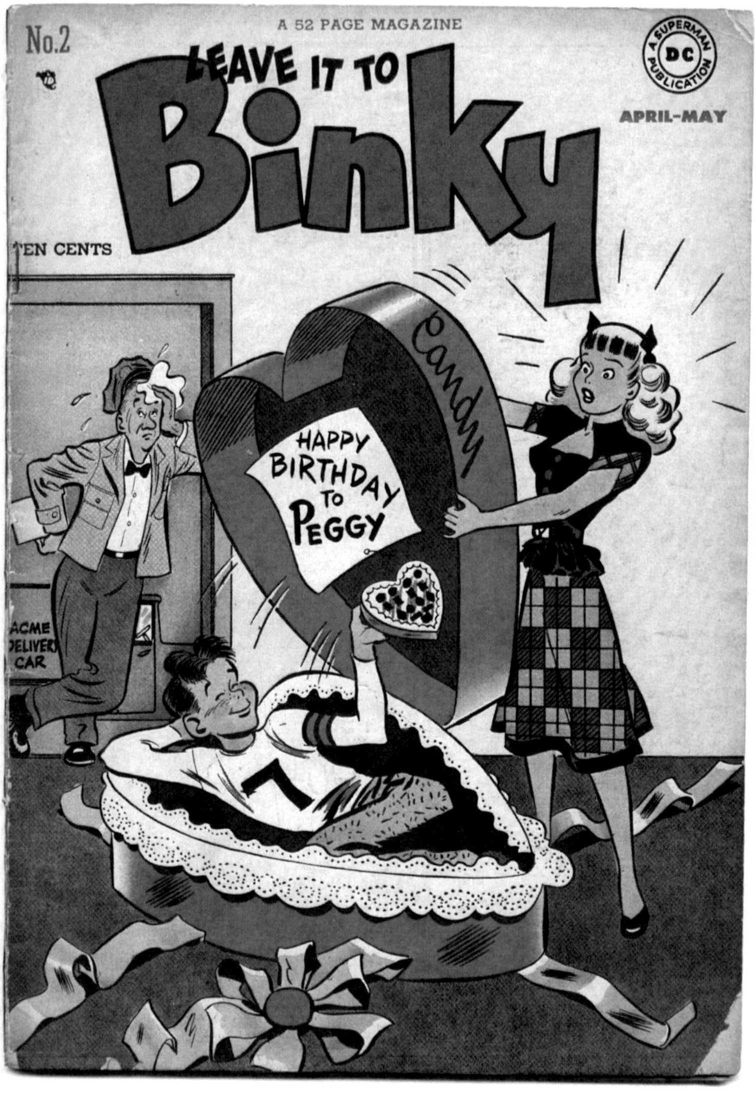

Leave It to Binky #2, April–May 1948, copyright National Comics Publications, Inc. This original title, created by Sheldon Mayer, appeared nine years before the *Leave It to Beaver* TV show.

For example, in #3 (June–July 1948), Binky gets in trouble with Principal Bigdome and admits he broke a blackboard, which the principal moans will cost $75 to repair. When Bigdome meets with Binky's father, the principal asks Mr. Biggs to sell him a larger life insurance policy than he originally expected. Binky's father is so delighted, he increases Binky's allowance 75 cents per week, but Bigdome soon tells Binky, "I promised to make things easy for you and I did! I've arranged an easy payment plan! You will pay the school $1 weekly for a year and a half—that, ahem, includes a slight six percent carrying charge!" When Peggy begs Binky to eat at lunch, Binky says, "No, thank you! I'm not opening my big mouth again for anything!"

In #4 (August–September 1948), one of the earliest television sets in teen humor history appears in the series story "A Day with Binky's Folks." Uncle Snootly has bought the Biggs family the set (commercial TV was concluding its first more-or-less–full season when this story hit the stands). But Binky breaks the antenna trying to fix it. The family fakes TV shows for Uncle Snootly, whose vision is poor, but ultimately Binky and his father are fined $10 apiece for disturbing the peace. In the end, Uncle Snootly buys the family a much bigger set because he thinks the small one he purchased wasn't good enough. It's a silly story but nonetheless fun—and the second TV set is much bigger than anything on the market in 1948!

Whitney Ellsworth took over as editor with #5 (October–November 1948) because Mayer had left his DC editor's post to focus on drawing his new Scribbly comic book along with the multitude of funny animal strips he did for DC titles.

Ellsworth immediately has Binky trying to use advice he hears on the radio in "A Date with Judy." In another story in the same issue, Superman makes a cameo appearance on the last page to move a department store to make room for a children's park, much to the astonishment of Binky and Peggy.

The cover on #8 (April–May 1949) is a classic, with a theater usher saying, "But, Boss, I couldn't find two seats together for them!" as Binky and Peggy hold hands across the aisle during the movie. In that issue, Binky accidentally knocks out Sherwood, the conceited boy who wants to date Peggy, in the locker room as they are preparing to box. Binky gets hauled off in celebration because he's so popular. Nothing like that would happen to the often luckless Buzzy in his title.

In #11 (November–December 1949), the usual chaos of his dating life ensues after an argument with Peggy because her parents are meeting with Sherwood's parents and Sherwood invites himself to join them. Frustrated by Peggy's refusal to fight off Sherwood, Binky tries to literally get "a date with Judy" but Judy Foster turns him down because she has a date with Oogie. Then Binky asks Homer Gruff if Susie is home and he says she's out with

Buzzy. So much for the crossovers: Binky eventually finds a date but ultimately winds up with Peggy talking happily on the porch as Sherwood and Binky's date Ruthie find they don't care much for each other.

Buzzy and Binky survived the 1940s (unlike DC superheroes like the Flash and Green Lantern, among many other vanished Golden Age stalwarts) and lasted into 1958. In fact, when a modernized version of the Flash returned in 1956, the original Buzzy, Binky and Judy were all still going. It's one of the most baffling developments in comics history, but such is the power of teen humor.

Scribbly Wasn't So Lucky

Mayer returned Scribbly Jibbet to the comics in *Scribbly* #1 (August–September 1948), which was only marginally teen humor in many stories through the first ten issues, but was all a fabulous parody of a boy cartoonist in his wacky world at *The Morning Bugle*. Scribbly originally appeared in a few strips for Dell Comics late in the 1930s and ran in four-page strips of urban parody in *All-American Comics* #1–59 from 1939 to 1944.

When Scribbly, weird hat, splayed tie and all, appears out of the blue in his unexpected new title, he goes ga-ga over Red Rigley when he finds out the famed cartoonist and creator of Terrificman for Rational Comics is really a fabulous looking, somewhat older redhead.

Scribbly isn't the type of comic a young reader might appreciate, but older teens and adults who love either or both comic strips and newspapers will find it fun. Unfortunately, much of the humor was too subtle or too complicated for young readers and the title was cancelled with #13 (September–October 1950), only to be brought back for the final issues #14 (October–November 1951) and #15 (December 1951-January 1952).

Scribbly found a heartthrob in Clover Cooley, with whom he shares a soda in a classic cover on #6 (June–July 1949) as kid brother Snoony Jibbet uses a long straw to cheat over the lovestruck Scribbly's shoulder. The Scribbly-Clover stories are classic tales of young life in the wacky style of a master cartoonist who mixes dreams and parody with reality and disappointment.

"Scribbly Turns to Romance" in #11 (May–June 1950) was the story in which the series truly became teen humor. In a four-chapter epic, Scribbly impressively stuns Clover by putting both feet down—and not on her toes! *Scribbly* #12 has a truly touching cover—Scribbly holds a gift for Clover as his pet Dizzy Dog accompanies him, when he sees her shadow on the window shade in an embrace with Bentley Bilgewater. Clover and Scribbly wind up happy after epic battles with Bentley.

Clover proves her love for Scribbly in three remarkably amusing stories in #13, but this temporarily was the last issue despite some of the funniest stories and art in all of comics. In many ways, Mayer was far ahead of his time as a cartoonist, his work being more subtle than what was popular in 1950.

Scribbly and Clover were back on the romance trail a year later in *Scribbly* #14, now only 36 pages. The stories weren't anything special, but the humor was back in first-rate style in #15 and Scribbly and Clover wound up feeling just fine. After numerous battles with burly Bentley Bilgewater, who also pursues Clover with many schemes, Scribbly winds up with her in the final two issues, although they are both still youngish teens. Somehow, though, you just know that Scribbly will overcome the odds and eventually marry Clover.

6

Candy's Antics

Only one comic book company outside of Archie, Marvel and DC continued into the 1950s with a girl who had become well established as a character with her own teen humor title in the 1940s. That company was Quality Comics and that character was Candy O'Connor, one of the wackiest teens in comic history.

Ironically, after appearing in 66 consecutive backup stories in *Police Comics*—still a record for a teen girl—Candy survived only in her own title after 1950. Quality changed the lineup of *Police Comics*—long a mixture of costume heroes and humorous strips—to a hard-boiled detective and crime title with #103 (December 1950), since crime comics had become bigger and bigger by that year.

Quality's move showed how hard it was for most companies to consider teen humor by 1950, although the genre was far from finished, thanks in large part to the "Big Teen Three." But that year, 20 companies published at least 36 issues of various genres—an average of at least three per month—and only four such firms had eponymous teen titles. So Candy was good company, indeed.

Candy's 1940s stories centered primarily on community events, often involving her family and friends (we'll cover her later misadventures in the 1950s section). Originally drawn by the clever humor artist Harry Sahle, the stories were out-and-out satires on life in middle America at mid-century.

Everything was outsized, from the often slapstick, wildly unlikely plots to the panels themselves. Other than on the covers, the Candy logo was different from story to story, even in the same issues. Arms and legs often spilled from one panel to another—and panels were rarely the same size. Word balloons were large and filled. The visual impressions were just as wild as the stories themselves.

Mom, It's Candy, Not Candace!

Candy's debut story in *Police* #37 (December 1944)—a seven-pager signed by Sahle—was early for a teen backup, only three years after *Pep* #21 and *Jackpot* #4 fatefully introduced the country to Archie (who himself first appeared three months after Wilbur debuted in *Zip* #18, one of Pep's sister titles). Quality had more than half a dozen other teen backups in anthologies such as *Police Comics*, but none of them succeeded like Candy.

There was an intriguing angle right from the start about Candy: She may have been the first teen humor character to make it clear that she hated being called by her real name. On the splash page of her first story, Candy's unusually stout mother, Agnes O'Connor, shouts from the porch, "Candace! Candace O'Connor! Answer me this minute!!" Ted Dawson, literally the boy next door, shouts over the back fence, "It's no use, Mrs. O'Connor! She hates her name so [much], she won't answer anybody, unless they call her Candy!" Meanwhile, Candy is hiding below the porch with a dismayed expression.

At the same time, Quality's editor George E. Brenner—or perhaps the writer—used the following caption to introduce Candy:

> And you'd better remember that, too—for you're going to see a lot of Candy O'Connor in the coming months and if you don't treat her right, she might not let you in on her escapades and adventures, her pals and her secret ambitions! So if you want to stay solid with a chick full of action, Jackson—just remember—Candy O'Connor!!!

The first story page in *Police* #37 is hilarious: When Mom yells, "Oh, Candace! Theodore is here!" Candy responds from upstairs, "Tell him to collapse, Mother! I'll be down as soon as I put on some dazzle-dust and pucker-paint!" Candy's mom invades her room and tells her, "Candace, such language! Collapse.... Pucker-Paint ..." Candy responds, "That's jive talk, Mother! Don't be a herkle all your life ... and pleeeeease stop calling me Candace!"

Mom continues, "I'm glad this is a civilized dance and not one of those hideous jitney-bug affairs!" Candy indignantly responds, "Jitterbug, Mother! Oh, you can come out of your tizzy! This is no squirm! This brawl is strictly off the cob, for squares and ickies!" Mom holds her head and mutters, "Brawl ... cob .... Ickies! ... Let me out of here before I go mad!"

Candy speeds to the dance with Ted, who it turns out hates Theodore too. But it turns out this dance is the citywide jitterbug contest. When Candy changes clothes at friend Trish's, she warns Candy that rival Cornelia Clyde plans to win the contest with Sam Engel. Candy becomes indignant: "That double-crossing goo-brain? That blue-woozy Susie?" When they arrive at the dance, Ted asks Candy, "What are you and Cornelia always pulling hair about? She's not a bad fad for a bright night!" Candy explains, "Ah, that sag-bag thinks because her father's a banker, she can lord it over everybody!"

As the night wears on, Candy and Ted and Cornelia and Sam are the only couples left. The dance committee decides to let the crowd vote and makes a sign for each couple. Candy notices her sign calls her Candace and has a fit, eventually failing to catch Ted on a dance move. He crashes into a drum and loses the contest while accusing Candy of sabotage. "I had to! I couldn't let that Candace O'Connor [sign] stay up in front of everybody for a whole year!" But Candy still came out ahead, telling Ted that Cornelia will be in trouble when her father sees her picture on the front page as contest winner.

Candy Scores Her Own Title

A little less than three years later, Candy became the only one of Quality's frequent teen backups to earn her own title in the 1940s, when Quality was among the best of the many publishers. *Candy* #1 (Autumn 1947) features stories involving confusion at Candy's babysitting service, how Candy and Ted inadvertently capture an arsonist, how Candy convinces Aunt Agatha that jitterbugging is fun, and how Candy copes with working in a rare book store. The book story is the funniest, involving a mix-up in rare books caused by Candy. But the store owner recovers his missing rare book and Candy explains her reward to Ted: "He bought me this dress—on condition that I wouldn't take another job in the book business—ever!"

The funniest story in *Candy* #2 (Winter 1947, actually 1947–1948) involves Candy's efforts to work in Eekin's Department Store at the perfume counter. Ted doesn't want Candy to work, so he takes a "de-skunked" skunk, Stinky, out of the Hartwick High lab and places the animal on the perfume counter, resulting in mass hysteria and plenty of publicity. But store management loves the headlines so much that it hires both Candy and Ted to work with a unique skunk display that draws huge crowds.

Candy apparently sold so well that the title needed only four issues to go bi-monthly with #4 (June 1948). The wild, slapstick stories were different than many other teen characters—they had an internal logic and logical endings, when that internal logic is considered. By the second half of 1950, when Quality cancelled or suspended all 14 of its romance titles after about a year or less of publication, *Candy* was among the company's few titles that survived uninterrupted or unchanged in genre format through all of 1950, including the likes of Blackhawk, Dollman and Marmaduke Mouse.

Two Companies Flop with Teens

Two second-tier but generally successful companies, Eastern and Orbit, directly contrasted with Quality's success with Candy in the late 1940s.

Orbit enjoyed success with comics in the crime, western and romance genres when the firm became known as Our Publishing Company. But two attempts at teen humor flopped, even though Patches and Taffy both often tied their covers and stories to celebrities in the entertainment world. Ironically, that makes them a bit more collectible than they otherwise would have been.

Orbit tried hard, allowing Patches to run from #3 (July 1946) through #11 (November 1947) after the small firm Rural Home Comics published the first two issues in 1945. Patches and his enormously rotund buddy Tubby suffered from some of the worst art in comics, especially considering that the teen humor genre generally had some of the best art. The stories, dealing with typical teen subjects, were some of the wildest slapstick in all of comics.

Patches #4 (September 1946) had centerfold spread announcing the adventures of Taffy Tucker in *Taffy Comics* #5 (November 1946). The first four issues were funny animal comics, though for unexplained reasons the title was named *Taffy* from the start. The way she was drawn, Taffy eventually resembles a 15-year-old tomboy, but she lasted only through #12 (January 1948). Chances are that neither *Patches* nor *Taffy* had strong circulation.

Taffy #11 (December 1947) involved Taffy and her oddly named BFF Putty in a school play with Mickey Rooney, of all people, because he wanted to make up for splashing storm water all over the girls while driving. He played Taffy's father and the play, which even had the line "Curses, foiled again!" when Mickey proved to be the hero, made Taffy a success, just as she always was when she met a star from the entertainment world.

In an unusual four-page story in that issue, Taffy and Putty tell the tale of the Y-Teens in the Young Women's Christian Association. It's a long plug for the association that concludes, "With its Y-Teen Program, the YWCA prepares youth for tomorrow, molding good citizens through democracy in action." This would not have been out of place in *Calling All Girls*, but it was unusual in a teen humor title. DC Comics did the same character plugs many dozens of times, but used only one page.

Famous Funnies, Inc., had the first regularly published comic book title with *Famous Funnies*, which ran 218 issues from 1934 through 1955. With comics printed by Eastern Color of Waterbury, Connecticut, the firm was also known as Eastern. Every Famous Funnies title bore a symbol stamp, "This Is a Famous Funnies Publication," including the short-lived teen titles *Sugar Bowl* and *Club 16*, both of which began in 1948. *Club 16* ran from #1 (June 1948) through #4 (December 1948) and *Sugar Bowl* was published from #1 (May 1948) through #5 (January 1949). (Eastern's contemporary teen-oriented title with profiles of stars in the entertainment world, *Juke Box*, ran six issues.)

Both *Club 16* and *Sugar Bowl* seem to have been aimed at some of the youngest readers in comics. Except for Alex Toth's work on a football-oriented strip named *Randy*, which began with an 11-pager in *Sugar Bowl* #3, all the other characters appear in stories (almost always six pages) with simple plots and simple lettering. Unlike most teen anthology comics, *Club 16* and *Sugar Bowl* did not have characters spotlighted with cover plugs. But then, none of the characters ever became well known in comics. That's a bit of an irony, since *Famous Funnies* itself succeeded with reprints of some of the best known of all Sunday comic strips.

***Club 16* #3, October 1948, copyright Famous Funnies Inc. This anthology title was loaded with original characters but it lasted only four issues.**

Club 16 featured the strips *Heavens to Betsy*, with Betsy and Bix; *Angela*; *Dreamboy*; *Clickety*, a photographer strip starring a young woman; *Ginger and Snap*; tales of a girl and her twin brother; *Bungling Ben*, and *Jug, the Hillbilly Hotshot*. *Sugar Bowl* also featured *Ginger*; *Just Girls*; *Ted the Tattler*; *Wendy*; and *Our Modern Juniors*.

In *Club 16* #3, the *Ginger and Snap* story is right out of an eight-year-old's dreams. Snap makes the football team at Wells High but gets the measles just before his first game. Ginger takes his place, stays unrecognized, and breaks a scoreless tie with a winning touchdown run. She is discovered when the goalpost knocks her helmet off while she's carried off the field. The coach just laughs at Snap being replaced by his sister and he tells her, "If Snap plays half as well as his twin he's a permanent member of this ball team." Snap thanks her in his sickbed and says, "Having a duplicate comes in mighty handy, yes sir, mighty handy!"

Cute as they are, there apparently wasn't a market for *Club 16* and *Sugar Bowl* with either younger readers or the teens who read the more mature stories about kids their own age.

7

Hap Hazard and the Ace Gang

Not one comic collector in 1000 could answer the following question—unless the collector reads this book:

It's easy to identify the first teen humor character to get his own regularly published comic book under his own name: Archie Andrews in 1942.

Who was the second?

Believe it or not, it was Hap Hazard in Ace Publications' *Hap Hazard Comics* #1, Summer 1944. Much more commercially successful characters such as Buzzy, Patsy Walker, Wilbur and Candy all followed in their own eponymous titles from other publishers within the next one to three years.

What's really amazing about Hap is that he was the only teen humor character of the Golden Age who began life in comic books as a young adult in a serious strip, as it were.

The same Hap Hazard was featured in a backup strip in the Ace superhero titles *Sure Fire Comics* and its successor, *Lightning Comics*, in 1940–1942 as a newspaper copy boy who constantly found himself fighting off trouble while trying to show he deserves to be promoted to reporter.

In *Hap Hazard* #2 (Autumn 1944), Ace reprinted a six-page Hap Hazard story from *Lightning Comics* #5 (February 1941). Since Hap was referred to a "demon copy boy" in one of the humorous stories in that issue of Hap Hazard, the logic may not have been lost on readers, while others may not have cared. (In the 1940s, the so-called copy boys were sometimes adults.)

Hap Hazard #1 carried three new stories of the teen Hap up front and relegated three reprints of young adult reporter Hap to the back of the book. Nonetheless, this issue is unique among teen titles. Ace showed how it perceived teen humor with the front-page box: "See Hap run in out of trouble! Fun and frolic galore!"

The *Hap Hazard* title quickly became devoted entirely to fun and frolic and ran through #24 (February 1949). In retrospect, this was a bit surprising, because the art was most often a combination of slapdash and slapstick.

***Hap Hazard* #19, March 1948, copyright A. A. Wyn, Inc. This title was unique, taking a character who began as an adult reporter in Ace super hero titles and turning him into a teen in the wake of Archie's popularity.**

The covers, most signed by an artist named Singer, were generally among the poorest of all teen humor comics.

Oddly, Hap appeared in *Four Favorites* (a super hero-mystery title for its first 28 issues) as an adult newspaper reporter in #23-29 before being portrayed as a teen humor character in #30-32. He was even a dynamic cover feature as a crime-fighting reporter in #28 (April 1947). Thus, for the only time in Golden or Silver Age history, the same person was concurrently a teen humor character and a heroic adult figure.

Few of the Hap Hazard stories dealt with high school hijinks; rather, the focus was on friends, family and other adults. The strip did not depend on the dynamics between continuing characters, as were so vital in Archie's success, but rather on plot ideas involving a borrowed car, a band and so on.

In most of the backups, Hap Hazard's own title did not appear in other comics, including his buddy Zippermouth, Stella the Starlet and Slug, an unorthodox girl who was also a friend of Hap. Dotty appeared in a few of the final issues. Dotty was similar to Ace versions of Katy Keene from the Archie Series.

26 Issues, More Than a Dozen Teen Characters

Before the romance comics phenomenon became huge in the second half of 1949, Ace tried hard to make teen humor work in the period from 1947 to '49. This was likely a response to the success of several DC and Marvel titles.

In the annals of pop culture, A.A. Wyn's Ace Publications was better known for pulp magazines in the 1930s and 1940s and for its highly successful line of paperback books beginning in 1952. But Ace was a significant comic book publisher from 1940 to 1956, producing a variety of genres in the 1940s before shifting almost entirely to romance and horror comics in the 1950s.

Teen and young adult humor, though, attracted the attention of Ace in the post–World War II era, when most publishers were gradually dropping superhero themes and finding other genres.

The title evolution of Four Favorites, one of Ace's primary titles along with superhero companion *Super Mystery Comics*, is one of the best possible examples of the 1946–1949 shift in emphasis. By *Four Favorites* #30, all the costumed heroes, detectives and crime-fighting magicians and reporters were gone, although the title remained the same when *Four Favorites* emerged as a "teen humor"–"working girl" title from #30 (August 1947) through #32 (December 1947) featuring Jerry the Jinx, Curly, Hazel of Hollywood and Hap Hazard, who was the only true teen humor character. Ace often conflated stories of college-age kids with those of Archie-caliber age.

Like so many publishers, Ace tried to save on a new postal permit on an entirely different comic book as *Four Favorites* became *Crime Must Pay the Penalty* with #33 (February 1948). The crime title resumed with #2 (June 1948) while the teen theme returned with a title change to *Four Teeners* #34 (April 1948). But the title immediately changed to teen humor character Dotty with #35 (June 1948) in order to feature accomplished cartoonist Al

Hartley's new character, who was easily the most attractively portrayed of all the Ace teens. She was a college-age hat-check girl at the El Kisco Club and combined humor with drama—kind of an early comic book dramedy, so to speak.

Dotty ran six issues through #40 (May 1949) and then became *Glamorous Romances* with #41 (July 1949)—one of nine romance titles begun by Ace that year! But #40 was yet another change—it was not a teen humor comic in any way shape or form. Hartley's Dotty emerged as a glamorous adult character in two dramatic romance stories in #40, which had the over-line title *Glamorous Romances* above the name Dotty. The other two stories were pure romance. In #40, the editor ran a contest for readers to rank and explain in no more than 50 words the stories they liked best. Wyn put a deadline of April 17, 1949, and urged readers to "DO IT NOW!! HURRY!!" Considering #40 hit the stands no earlier than March, Wyn obviously wanted to see if romance was as popular as he thought it might be.

Glamorous Romances #41 (July 1949) noted "formerly Dotty" on the cover—an unusual move in comics. The contest note appeared again, with a June 14 deadline. There was only one Dotty story, but for the third issue in a row, she exposed her love interest as a selfish man not worthy of marrying her! The other three stories were all romance. Dotty—either teen or adult—disappeared forever in *Glamorous Romances*, which ran through #90 in 1956.

Thus, in a span of 13 issues (#29 through #41), Ace came up with seven distinct changes in title and/or character themes. That might have been the quickest seven such shifts in comic book history.

At the same time, another Ace humor title, *Scream Comics*, went through five shifts in an 12-issue span. *Scream Comics*, which had been primarily little-kid and animal humor in its first 15 issues, went total teen with #16 (October 1947), featuring Andy and his twin sister Billie, Ernie, Orville, Adelbert and a new character, the Southern charmer Lili Belle.

Scream Comics changed its title to *Andy Comics* with #20 (June 1948) and #21 (August 1948) mostly featuring the same lineup. Then Andy's name was changed to Ernie in the oddly unnumbered 22nd (September 1948) and 23rd (November 1948) issues. Ernie had two numbered issues #24 (January 1949) and #25 (March 1949), but issue #26 was the first issue of the appropriately titled *All Love, sans* any teens.

The Andy story in *Scream* #16 features tomboy sister Billie as the football team's mascot and Andy's love interest Teddie as a fan who urges Andy to join the football team because of his natural kicking ability. Having made a poor showing in practice because of nerves, Andy finally get a chance in the final minute of a scoreless game after Billie convinces the coach that Andy has his competitive fire back. Andy wins the game with a 60-yard field goal and promptly faints after Teddie kisses him. The coach thinks Andy is just overwhelmed at becoming a hero but Billie breaks the fourth wall and tells the reader, "We know what really made him pass out, don't we?"

The original Ernie in *Scream* #16 was a burly redhead. But that wasn't the same Ernie a year later—that was Andy was who renamed for reasons lost in the mists of time. The Andy-cum-Ernie character still had sister Billie and girlfriend Teddie to motivate him.

***Ernie* #24 (third issue), January 1949, copyright Current Books, Inc. There were only four issues of *Ernie* but they featured two artistic versions of the same teen guy.**

Ace published another teen humor title with a character, the rich girl Vicky, who did not appear in other publications. Her last issue, #5 (June 1949), was the last Ace with teen characters. The first issue was dated October 1948 and was not numbered; the second issue was dated December 1948 and was mistakenly numbered 4; the third issue (February 1949) also was not numbered; and the real #4 was dated April 1949. Vicky's stories dealt with a social-climbing family, dogs of breeding, equestrian humor and so on.

Ace seemed to be unaware of what other comics were doing. Unlike anyone else, Ace would say "16 extra pages" when it went from World War II–era 36-page issues to the 52-page issues that were more common among the large publishers in the 1940s and often the early 1950s. But instead of designating them as 52-page issues (including covers), Ace would sometimes say "Full 48 pages"—but eventually changed that to 52 to match all the other publishers.

8

Wilbur, the Forgotten Success Story

Other than Marvel's Patsy Walker, no other non–Archie Universe teen humor character enjoyed a longer run than Wilbur Wilkin, the wacky star of *Wilbur Comics*. Now he's pretty much forgotten.

Wilbur was unrelated to Archie, although his stories appeared in some of the same Archie Series comic books as Archie and his gang did, such as *Pep* and *Laugh*.

Wilbur debuted in the MLJ anthology title *Zip Comics* #18 (September 1941), three months before Archie first showed up in the 21st issue of *Pep Comics*, another of the firm's anthology titles, then still filled with Golden Age superheroes. Wilbur, in fact, was the first original teen humor character to appear in comic books (a lot of bar bets near comic conventions have been won by the few fans who realize that). Wilbur also became the second teen humor character to gain his eponymous title, with #1 (Summer 1944), which likely beat Ace's *Hap Hazard* #1 (Summer 1944) to the newsstands. *Wilbur* ran continuously for 15 years, through #87 (November 1959). For reasons never explained, *Wilbur* returned with the same logo for annual one-shots #88, #89 and #90 in 1963 through 1965. The Archie Series later published a different version, *That Wilkin Boy*, with #1–52 from 1969 to 1982 starring Bingo Wilkin.

The early issues of *Wilbur* are nowhere near as valuable or as sought after as those of Archie, even though they are likely to be less common. It's not hard to pinpoint the primary reason: For the first four years of his title, Wilbur was not involved in a love triangle the way Archie was right away in his own book. In fact, *Wilbur* #1–17 featured only two friends of the protagonist: His buddy Red and his love interest Linda, a highly intelligent beauty with long, jet-black hair. Many of the stories revolved around Wilbur's parents, Frank and Eleanor Wilkin (at times, they were called Wilkins). In Wilbur's early comic book life, there was no eccentric friend (such as Jughead Jones); no scheming rival (such as Reggie Mantle) and no rival for Linda (such as Veronica Lodge).

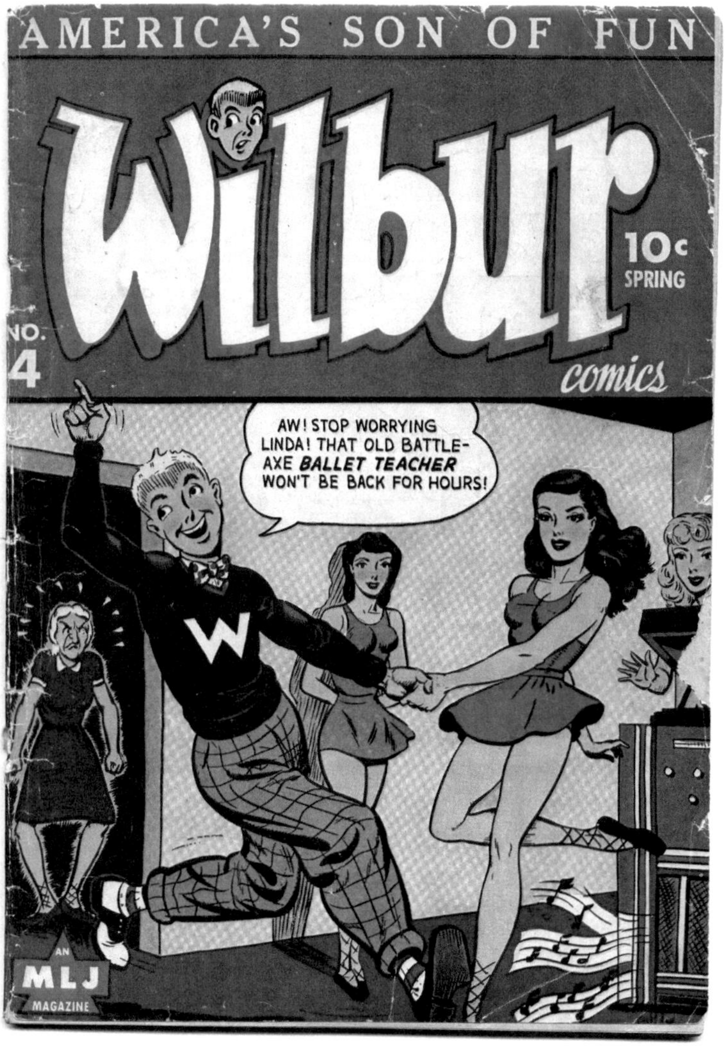

***Wilbur* #4, Spring 1945, copyright M.L.J. Magazines. Wilbur is nowhere near as well remembered as M.L.J. creation Archie, but *Wilbur* ran 87 issues without a miss, second only to Archie among boys in teen comics history.**

By and large, the early stories, penciled by Bill Vigoda and Al Fagaly, are not memorable. They are mostly pure slapstick, and many take place in Westfield but not as often at Westfield High as Archie's misadventures at Riverdale High.

That doesn't mean Wilbur's early stories aren't fun. In every story, he gets into some kind of unbelievably wacky jam involving the likes of sports, animals, cars, cops, clothing and every other aspect of high school and community life anyone could imagine.

Wilbur's Unique Comic Book Club

Wilbur #2 (Fall 1944) through #6 (Fall 1945) featured a unique comic book club for readers. There were many such organizations in the 1940s and 1950s, including the citizenship-oriented Archie Club and Supermen of America. This was "Wilbur's Trouble Club," which offered a chance to win war stamps or bonds for the best letters "telling about some trouble you got into at some time," in the editor's awkward phrasing. This letter in #6 was typical:

> Dear Wilbur, Last week I was sliding down the pig-pen door and my daddy came out to feed the pigs, but I did not see him coming. And so, when I made my last slide, I ran into him and the pigs' supper went all over us! We both had to take a hot bath and mama said we were lucky that she didn't make us stay out with the pigs!! Sincerely, Ed Cudney.

One can only imagine how much status the five winners gained at their schools!

The first four issues of *Wilbur Comics* had comical but nonsensical and thoroughly forgettable filler material without any teens. But with #5, artist-writer Bill Woggin's glamour girl Katy Keene was born, and a whole lot more letters resulted than those addressed to "Wilbur's Trouble Club"!

Katy, who existed with much younger sibling Sis outside of the universes of every other Archie Series character, became a fabulous pin-up and paper-doll hit in her own comic book in the 1950s before fading out, only to return in the 1980s in a wave of nostalgia expressed by many of the original readers. Katy was the primary, and often the only, backup story in *Wilbur* #5–69, except for #57 and #62, as listed in the Overstreet Comic Book Price Guide. The editors apparently did not realize what they had; Katy was not mentioned on a cover until #11 (Winter 1946–1947), when a blurb referred to "A New Star! Katy Keene, the Pin-Up Queen!"

Katy Keene, though, was not the most important female addition to *Wilbur Comics*. That would be the gorgeous blonde Laurie Lake, who debuted in the lead story in *Wilbur* #18 (April 1948) when she moved to Westfield with her wealthy father, Commodore Lake. Oddly, the writers and editors kept Wilbur and the two girls in separate stories until #26 (August 1949), when the girls finally began to compete with each other in the same stories.

Fittingly, their first hint of rivalry was in "Kiss Me Again," when Laurie traps Wilbur into a kiss with mistletoe. "You're just jealous because you couldn't get him to kiss you!" Laurie says when Linda calls Wilbur "a kissing fool." Linda tartly responds: "Oh, yeah, I can get Wilbur to kiss me as well as you can!" Linda tried for the rest of a funny story, but was still awaiting a kiss when it ended.

In "The Model Builder" in #27 (October 1948), Laurie convinces Wilbur to send her picture to a modeling agency, but he sends Linda's photo instead. When offered an opportunity to move to a big city, Linda realizes she would miss Wilbur and Westfield too much, Laurie or no Laurie. In the last two panels, Linda turns down the chance and then shocks Wilbur by declaring that she wants to be "a model student! And someday a model wife." That set the stage for Wilbur's wilder 1950s misadventures with the two beauties.

By the way, when a modeling agency representative meets Linda, he tells her, "We'll send you to our modeling school! A pretty girl like you doesn't need to know anything!" That tells Linda everything she needs to know about her future. This was among the few Wilbur stories of the 1940s in which there was no slapstick at all.

One of the cleverest of all Archie Series covers was that of *Wilbur* #19 (June 1948). Linda carves an update on a tree to make it read "Linda Loves Wilbur" after having scratched out Joe, Mike and Steve, then asks an appalled Wilbur, "Why Wilbur! How can you say that I'm fickle?"

Wilbur the Pitcher

In #3 (Winter 1944), Wilbur plays the unusual role of athlete in "Wilbur the Pitcher." It's the amusing story of a driver who picks up Wilbur and Linda as they head to the big baseball game. What Wilbur didn't realize while making snarky comments was that the fellow was going to call balls and strikes against Clymen. All heck breaks loose before and during the game, leading the umpire to tell Wilbur, "For the twenty years I've been an ump, I've had bottles heaved at me! Been called every name under the sun! Attacked, assaulted and divorced! But meeting YOU is the worst that's happened yet!" Wilbur, naturally, loses 13–0 and the umpire refuses to give him and Linda a ride back to Westfield.

"The Weaker Sex" in #4 (Spring 1945) finds Wilbur and Linda at a carnival, where he states unequivocally, "It takes a real man to really enjoy 'em." Right away, Linda out-shoots Wilbur on the rifle range, then illogically "needs to inform him she's captain of the girl's [*sic*] rifle team." (Why is it that editors then and now cannot catch errors in possessives?) Wilbur then loses to Linda on the strength machine and gets beaten up when a bigger guy thinks Wilbur has insulted his girlfriend. Wilbur can't even ride the roller coaster without being shown up by Linda, who on the final page pushes a car when Wilbur can't provide help. It's no wonder that in the final panel, he assaults a salesman for *Ladies' Home Journal* with "Women! Women! I hate women."

As you can see, there's nothing logical in the Wilbur of the 1940s, but it is fun to see just how much trouble he can find!

In #6, there's also an ad for NBC's new Archie radio show, which was good enough to run until 1953, minus any more radio ads in *Wilbur*. In #7 (Winter 1946–1947), a house ad proudly declares, "A New Trademark is Born: An Archie Magazine." That marked the end of MLJ Comics and the birth of what would become one of the best known of all comic companies—and still is. (Jumbo Digest format notwithstanding!)

Issue #7 also has a hysterically funny story, "The Hot Shot!," in which Wilbur and the team are forced to play basketball in ballet tutus because manager Red has picked up the wrong equipment trunk. When everyone else becomes too exhausted to play in ballet shoes, Wilbur tried to take the winning shot in the last minute and becomes so frustrated that he bounces the ball in anger—and the ball is still alive and goes into the basket to win the championship as the gun sounds. As a bonus, Wilbur accepts the trophy for having what the judges have deemed "the most colorful team in the state!" Now you can see why Wilbur is perhaps the most illogical of all early teen humor comics.

Wilbur #22 (December 1948) is even more illogical, because Our Hero wins a pole vault title with a weird move, only to be disqualified because the rule book he has submitted to the judges is more than 50 years old!

9

Topsy-Turvy, Cookie and The Kilroys

By the time an exceptionally odd one-shot comic book titled *Topsy-Turvy* appeared in 1945, teen humor was fewer than four years old and still far from established in the comics.

That's what made the first two stories of the insecure 16-year-old "Cookie" so different. About the height of a typical 10- or 12-year-old, he had never appeared in any comic, yet *Topsy-Turvy* #1 (April 1945) featured Cookie stories of 14 and 19 pages!

Cookie was always used with quote marks in the titles of his comics and splash pages, but not in the text. His surname was O'Toole and the little guy had very protective, old-looking and old-fashioned parents, but did not lack for fellow teen friends, primarily Jitterbuck Jones, the hefty Hep and The Brain, a.k.a. a boy with the odd name Murgatroyd Hibottom. Cookie has a crush on the tall, sweet blonde Angelpuss Witherspoon. Cookie's rival for the affections of Angelpuss was the tall, handsome Zoot, a football quarterback who was pretty much the antithesis of Cookie. And yes, Zoot wore a Zoot suit.

Dan Gordon drew most of the stories of Cookie, whose own title followed with #1 (April 1946) and ran through #55 (August–September 1955) as a teen humor companion but not otherwise related to *The Kilroys*, which was published from #1 (June–July 1947) through #54 (June–July 1955). Both were edited by Richard E. Hughes, as were all comics from the American Comics Group.

ACG produced Cookie under the imprint Michel Publications and The Kilroys as B.&I. Publications. Both titles enjoyed a surprisingly long run, especially considering that most teen humor titles did not have long runs. In fact, the only teens with longer runs were *Buzzy*, *Leave It to Binky* and *A Date with Judy* from DC Comics, three Patsy Walker titles from Marvel, and Candy from Quality—all major publishers of the 1940s and 1950s—along with the Archie titles.

In fact, although *Cookie* and *The Kilroys* were strictly less-than-logical teen slapstick both with featured and backup strips—in contrast to the more polished product from DC, Marvel and Quality—it's difficult to say whether they would have survived had not ACG dropped numerous titles in 1954 and 1955 including the two teen titles. By 1956, ACG was left only with the long-running *Adventures Into the Unknown* and *Forbidden Worlds* (both weird fantasy titles and formerly horror comics) and *My Romantic Adven-*

Cookie #3, October 1946, copyright Michel Publications, Inc. Comical little _Cookie_ and American Comics Group companion title _The Kilroys_ both lasted nearly a decade.

tures and *Confessions of the Lovelorn* (two of the longest-running romance titles). More titles would come later.

The indicia indicated only that *Topsy-Turvy* was published by R.B. Leffingwell, a tiny Chicago outfit that produced only three other comics in 1945. No editor was listed, although Leffingwell apparently had a connection with the Ben Sangor Shop, which provided art for ACG and other firms of the period.

Cookie appeared out of the blue in *Topsy-Turvy*—there were no explanations or origins and it was as though he had been appearing for years. On the first two pages of the opening story (the 14-pager), the gang meets up at The Sody Jerkerie and learns from Zoot that there will be a dance at Harelip High (one of the best names for a school in any teen comic). A multitude of complications ensue before Cookie finally gets his father to fork over the cost of a tuxedo for the dance and the chance to cut a rug with Angelpuss, with the deceptive help of Jitterbuck.

In the second Cookie story, he tries wolfing down box after box of Meaty-Bleaties cereal but finds they won't help him grow. Then the little guy discovers the invention "Addlepate's Escalator Boots," so he can pretend to have grown into a tall fellow, after all, with the help of Meaty-Bleaties. (Wheaties was huge at the time on the back pages of comic books.) After many more complications, including time in a hospital's maternity ward, Cookie is discovered to be the same lovable little guy he always was, only to receive credit from movie star Hortense Hoopnagle for rescuing her from kidnappers (it's so complicated, this story needed 19 pages). And as the tale ends, Cookie's mother celebrates by telling a radio audience, much to his chagrin, "He may be a hero to you, but he'll always be just our darling baby!" To which Cookie responds, "Oh, Mom—No! Anything but That!"

These two stories set the template for Cookie, who was the most slapstick teen in comics. Likewise were Cookie's friends in the backup strips in the *Cookie* comic book. For most of the nine-year run, the subtitle was "The Funniest Kid in Town."

Cookie's Long Stories

Cookie always appeared in two long stories. The logic of the 14-page Cookie football story in "Cookie" #23 (February–March 1950) was typical of most stories in the run. Zoot, the quarterback of Harelip High, and Cookie listen as Angelpuss says that Zoot has convinced her to let the player who scores the most points against Center High take her to the big Twirl and Swirl dance. "But I don't play football, Angelpuss!" Cookie complains, to which she responds, "I know! And it's a shame, Cookie.... But on an occasion like this, our alma mater comes first!" as Zoot says, "Too bad, small stuff!"

Walking away with Jitterbuck, Cookie is so angry that he kicks his math book over a fence 60 yards away and beans football Coach Clancy on the

The Kilroys #2, August–September 1947, copyright B.&I. Publishing Co., Inc. This title from the second-tier American Comics Group was far more successful than most devoted to teen boys.

head! Clancy begs Cookie to turn out for the team as the kicker … and Jitterbuck reminds him of Angelpuss' promise. Complications (there are always a whole lot of complications in every Cookie story) ensue and Cookie takes an unexpected beating (for a kicker) thanks to Zoot's skullduggery. Cookie wins the game in the final seconds 9–7 with his third long field goal but collapses with exhaustion. Doctors send Cookie to bed and he can't attend the dance, but Angelpuss brings the dance to Cookie's home and spends all her time with him.

"Kilroy was here" was a popular phrase during the 1940s and no doubt inspired "The Kilroys," a successful companion title to "Cookie." In fact, the father in the family, J. Edgar Kilroy, shouted "Kilroy Was Here!" in huge letters on the cover of #2 (August–September 1947) as teenage son Natch and daughter Katie watched from behind a tree while their dad lost it when he discovered the family car had suffered a fender-bender.

For most of its run, *The Kilroys* was subtitled "America's Funniest Family" by Hughes, who was skilled at finding ways to spotlight what differentiated his ACG titles from heavy competition on the racks.

The unsigned Kilroys stories featured father J. Edgar, mother Emma, oldest teen child Natch, his buddy Jackson, daughter Katie and Natch's girlfriend Judy Farrell in just about every slapstick situation anyone could imagine. The stories really were funny. Later in the run, Jackson—who became known as "Solid" Jackson, of course—was featured in his own stories.

"No Noise Is Good Noise" in *The Kilroys* #26 (October–November 1950) is typical of the truly funny nature of the stories, many of them 10-pagers. The mayor decides to mount an anti-noise campaign and puts in charge a judge, who in turn enlists Officer Mike Farrell—Judy's father! Natch is told to put mufflers on his noisy rattletrap but in the course of the frantic tale his dad, mom, and buddy Jackson all borrow the car and each has trouble with the increasingly frustrated Officer Farrell. The poor policeman is at his wits' end when his daughter Judy and her mother borrow the car. But they have the answer: They tell Farrell to pay for new mufflers! The story ends with Natch extending thanks to the Farrell family.

The Milt Gross creation Moronica—the politically incorrect dumb blonde working girl—was a backup feature in many issues of *The Kilroys*, but Gross did not draw most of the stories. She was always known as "Miss Nit-Wit of 1950" or whatever year was appropriate.

10

Why *My Date* Didn't Go So Well

Hillman Publications had its share of successful comics in the 1940s and early 1950s—especially for a second-tier publisher. But *My Date* was not one of them.

Hillman, best known for Airboy Comics and other action-oriented titles of several genres, decided to try teen humor for the first time with *My Date* #1 (July 1947), but the bi-monthly title ran only through #4 (January 1948), despite covers and feature stories by Joe Simon and Jack Kirby.

In contrast, shortly after beginning work on *My Date*, S&K immediately enjoyed immense success with the first genuine romance series. Crestwood's *Young Romance* #1 (September 1947), and ensuing issues were the primary reasons that within two years, love comics had exploded into a pop cultural phenomenon.

In the first edition of Simon's book *The Comic Book Makers* (1990), he didn't even mention *My Date*, despite revealing in-depth details about the bonanza of S&K successes in the 1940s, their first decade as the top team-up in Golden Age history.

In the 1970s and 1980s, well before romance comics became more-collectible artifacts of postwar America, *My Date* was sometimes incorrectly called the first romance comic. On the contrary, *My Date* really was an odd combination of teen humor, teen fantasy and teen satire. The title was also among the most overrated collectible comics thanks to the S&K art, which was their usual workmanlike job but with overly fantastic stories.

The lead feature, S&K's "My Date with Swifty Chase," involved the antics of four primary characters: Swifty Chase, Hilldale High's athletic star and budding inventor; Sunny Daye, the object of his affections; Snubby Skeemer, son of the richest man in town; and, beginning with the second issue, House-Date Harry, who refused to work and who may have been the biggest mooch in all of comics.

The first story, a 14-pager, was probably the best of the bunch because it featured the story of Hollywood star Humphrey Hogart's visit to Hilldale, where Sunny constantly pined for him but where Hogart's heartthrob, Chandra Blake, called home. Swifty and Sunny eventually help the couple get married, thanks to Swifty's Jet-Racer, and Sunny almost lands in Swifty's lap as they pass a stranded Snubby on the highway.

My Date #4, January 1948, copyright Hillman Periodicals, Inc. At one time this Simon & Kirby creation was considered a romance comic, but it's solid teen humor. S&K created the romance genre in comics in 1947 and were wildly successful, but this was the last issue _of My Date_.

House-Date Harry, looking like an underfed reject from the Boy Commandos or The Newsboy Legion, two of S&K's wartime hits for National Comics, joined the cast in #2. Readers today may not know that "house-date" was an old-time insult for a guy who wouldn't—or couldn't—take his date anywhere that cost anything. House-Date Harry wound up flying on another Swifty Chase invention, the helicopter-like Heliotrope, during a ridiculous rescue mission that otherwise resulted primarily in Sunny realizing how much she liked Swifty.

The last two stories were even sillier, with House-Date creating a "House on Wheels" in #3 and unsuccessfully trying to connive with a "Lonesome Wolf" in #4. The Lonesome Wolf of the title was the handsome but shy Howard Howard, who instead wound up with his love interest thanks to the interventions of Swifty and Sunny. The funniest aspect of that story was the final panel: Snubby and House-Date stuck with each other at a night spot.

The Complex *Ultra-Violet*

All of these stories would not have been fun for grade-school readers and thus likely helped cause the early demise of *My Date*. The same can be said of *Ultra-Violet*, a strip beautifully drawn by Dan Barry but written so as to be close to incomprehensible, especially for younger readers. All four stories involve the dreams of teenager Violet Ray and how she transforms herself into a glamorous woman. The only other character who appeared in all four issues, the freckled teen Ginny, was all-slapstick all the time.

The other feature in all four issues, *My Date*, consisted of short accounts of dating successes from the files of Jean Anne Marten, who was dubbed "My Date's famous young people's counselor." At the end of the stories in #2, 3 and 4, *My Date* presented a page of five short letters about dates from teens. There were many such "counselors" in regular romance comics, but the page of letters about dates was unique, if mostly banal.

The Even Stranger *Joe College*

Hillman had even less luck with its second and final try at teen humor, the short-lived *Joe College*, albeit older teen humor. *Joe College* #1 (Fall 1949) and #2 (Winter 1950) were actually an anthology and carried the same lineups of five long stories with different characters, all slapstick strips on the totally wild side but all drawn well.

Joe College, title character of one of the few humor strips drawn by the prolific Bob Powell in the 1940s and 1950s, was a Hardnox College freshman and found more trouble in two stories trying to romance Josie Cooley than most college students encounter in four years. Hillman brought back a different, much more comical version of Housedate Harry (even spelled differently), but that one didn't have the surrounding cast to make it interesting.

In some ways, the most interesting strip in the book was Toss-Out Terry by Dick Briefer, about a female softball player with the oddest face in the comics at the time. A gangling tomboy who just won't be discouraged, she's an unlikely heroine on the diamond in both stories, which are genuinely amusing. The other two features, Rosie Romance and Boola Boola Jones, were as slapstick as possible in comic book stories but otherwise unremarkable.

Hillman also tried its luck with a love comic supposedly based on a radio counselor, *Mr. Anthony's Love Clinic*, but it lasted only five issues from #1 (November 1949) through #5 (May 1950). The company, which produced paperback books and a small variety of slick magazines, did enjoy a 25-issue run with the orthodox love comic *Romantic Confessions* from October 1949 (Volume 1, #1) through April–May 1953 (Volume 3, #1), when the company left comics.

Dudley

The talented Gordon "Boody" Rogers was a well-established cartoonist when he decided to try his hand at teen humor with *Dudley* for Crestwood in 1949. Rogers had an outrageous sense of humor that showed to great effect when he created non-costumed super-strong boy Sparky Watts first as a comic strip and later in original comic book stories for the Columbia titles *Big Shot Comics* and *Sparky Watts*. Sparky's hilarious and satirical decade-long existence ended with the Columbia titles by the end of the 1940s, so Rogers turned to Crestwood Publishing for 11 issues of *Babe*, a working girl title that featured the phrase "Amazon of the Ozarks." He finished at Crestwood with three issues of *Dudley*, featuring small-town teen Dudley Lee, who always seemed to come out on top.

Dudley, as his amusing, slapstick-filled title was known, began with #1 (November–December 1949) and ended far too soon with #3 (March–April 1950). Rogers signed his work but had a style so distinctive that everyone in the industry could tell who drew it, and so it was with *Dudley*.

Rogers did no introductory page but he did show all of the protagonists on the splash page of #1: Spurs Lee, Dudley's younger brother who fancied himself a cowboy, lassoed Dudley; nefarious rival Milt Magee; Magee's sister Mona, who was Dudley's love interest; and Fanny Belle Smythe, who went for Miltie. Rogers, who drew amusing sports parodies, did his typical penciling and inking job on all three Dudley stories in #1, the best of which was the football yarn "Dribble Threat." In this little epic, Magee is only the water boy but creates circus-like costume diversions for the crowd to take attention away from touchdown hero Dudley, who is the athletic savior of Cherrydale High. At the end, Magee's attempt to smear olive oil all over the football backfires when he is hit by the bounding ball and finds himself with his head dunked in the bucket of olive oil while the girls mob Dudley.

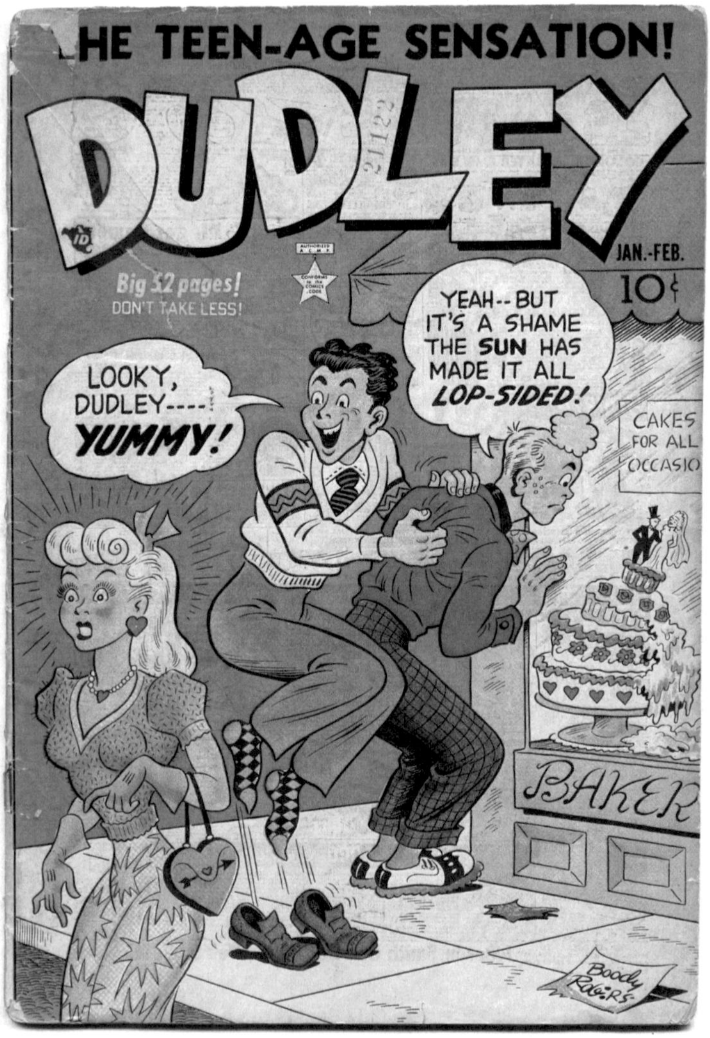

Dudley #2, January–February 1950, copyright Feature Publications, Inc. Expressive cartoonist Boody Rogers succeeded a lot more often than not, but *Dudley* lasted three issues with his last work in comics including all the covers.

In another amusing story in #1, Dudley is assigned to keep company with Dibney Dingle, Fanny Belle's homely cousin, but instead meets the train and meets Desira Drew, the "Beauty from Butte," as the Montana movie star is known. Milt tries to steal Desira away but is eventually saddled with Dibney after Desira clears up the confusion.

After several uninspired fillers in the first issue, Rogers wrote and drew the entire second issue. Dudley's story titles provide a good hint of the hilarity that ensues: "The Ski's the Limit!," "Dudley and the Dumb Belles!," "Milt Magee, Tough Guy!" and "Put on the Glad Rags!" These are all truly funny parodies of snow sports, study halls, gangster behavior and costume parties.

Equally amusing in #2 is the new backup strip *Jasper Fudd* by Rogers, who once again shows his ability to parody sports. Jasper is derided as "Mr. New Mown Hay" when he visits Northside High as a newcomer from a school of country hicks known as Looney High. Jasper bumps into the conceited Big Ben, the school's sports hero and bully rolled into one. After much mocking, Jasper attends the softball game against Southside, and when that team runs out of players, Big Ben tells them that Jasper can play for them since he has moved into that side of town. What Big Ben—who has his first no-hitter going with two outs in the ninth inning—doesn't know is that Jasper trained himself in true country style by slamming rocks with sticks. So Jasper agrees to pinch hit and wins the game while slamming the ball into Big Ben's stomach. It's typical of the "underdog wins" approach Rogers used to great effect.

Dudley was fond of saying things like "Whoa from Kokomo!," "Gee from Kankakee" and "Gosh from Oshkosh," using Midwest cities with colorful names. In the 1940s, many cartoonists made teen lingo seem like it came from another planet, not just the younger generation.

11

Comics Advertised "For Teen Girls"

In the 1940s, a decade in which many comic book historians feel girls' readership was on a par with boys, or at least nearly so, three titles were designed especially for teen girls.

Calling All Girls, published by *Parents' Magazine*, is the best-known girls' comic of the era. But it was not always targeted only to teens, especially the early issues when there were features for females both very young and perhaps in their 20s and 30s. *Calling All Girls* ran its first 51 issues from 1941 to 1946 with comic strips as well as text and photo material (and ran many more issues as a magazine and a digest into the 1960s, along with a title change or two along the way before returning to the traditional title). Likewise, post-war sister comic *Polly Pigtails* was not marketed for teens, but rather for grade-school girls.

Parents' Magazine, a significant comic book publisher from 1941 to 1949, is best remembered for *True Comics*. The firm, which produced only wholesome material in contrast to many other publishers of the period, did market the unique title *Sweet Sixteen: Comics and Stories for Girls* from #1 (August–September 1946) through #13 (January 1948).

Sweet Sixteen, slightly oversize like *True Comics* and *Calling All Girls*, did have distinct teen humor material: a unique six-page strip about a teen genius by the talented cartoonist Vic Herman titled *A Date with Dirinda*. This strip and *Dorothy Dare, Queen of Hollywood Stunt Artists* were the only storylines that appeared in every issue.

Sweet Sixteen apparently become so popular that it went from bi-monthly to monthly from #5 (May 1947) for its last nine issues, then abruptly and mysteriously disappeared. Perhaps this occurred because *Parents' Magazine* had limited comic book resources and had just acquired the license to print a comic book about one of radio's greatest favorites, "Jack Armstrong the All-American Boy." They published 13 issues of *Jack Armstrong*, from #1 (November 1947) through

#9 (September 1948) and from #10 (March 1949) through #13 (September 1949).

Parents' Magazine dropped all of its comic books midway through 1949, about the same time that Street & Smith abandoned its line of comics, so Baby Boomer collectors more often than not in the 1950s and 1960s were not aware that either large publishing company was a significant second-tier producer of comics.

Dates with Dirinda

Dirinda Jones was surely one of the most charming teen girls ever to appear in a Golden Age comic. The theme of every humor-packed story was highly unusual: Bespectacled blonde Dirinda was fascinated by boys, the way so many high school teens were, but she refused to abandon her superior academic abilities, including her penchant for spouting facts and figures in any context in which she appeared. This was not only unusual, but was downright inspirational.

Her debut story was untitled but might well have been called "Dirinda Makes Bobby Blake a Believer." The mothers of Dirinda and Bobby are close friends, so Bobby believes that's why they have set him up with a date with Dirinda. "Sure, Dirinda is a fine girl, Mother—but she's an awful drip too! All she's got is education! I admit she's the smartest girl at Central High, but ugh! What a personality … and I'll have to use up my week's allowance." On the contrary, his mother tells him: He's being gifted two radio show tickets by his dad.

Dirinda wins a raffle to appear on stage. She answers four questions, including the common name for a cypselurus hauteurus (a flying fish) and the population of Albany, New York ("Why, it's 130,577, of course"). Her reward is $240 (well over $2500 in today's dollars) and a "jiffy beauty treatment" from Madame Venus de Venus. The madame is not exactly kind: "I am only a beauty specialist, not a magician," she tells the show host. "Why did you have to pick out this one?"

Dirinda emerges from the dressing room looking like what Bobby calls "the most beautiful girl in the world." Dirinda's ecstatic response to Bobby is reflected in her diary in the last panel: "The most glorious evening in my life.… I guess it's the first time a girl became attractive (and popular, Dear Diary) because she got straight A's in history, geography, algebra and English … and, Dear Diary, did you see the way Bobby looked at me when we said good night?"

The titles of the rest of the Dirinda stories: "At the Saturday Night Dance" (#2); Untitled, about a trip to Washington, D.C. (#3); "A Blind Date"

(#4); "A Date in the Country" (#5); "Dirinda Turns Ace Reporter" (#6); "A Date on Broadway" (#7); "Dirinda Goes Pioneer" (#8); "A Date at a Dude Ranch" (#9); "A Date at the Derby" (#10); "A Date at the Goal Post" (#11); "A Date 'Neath the Mistletoe" (#12) and Untitled, about Dirinda using ham radio to save lives (#13).

Sweet Sixteen also contained "The Four O'Clock Club," about four high school girls who do good works, and another Herman strip, the charming "When Mother Was 16," set in both the present and in 1920.

Each issue not only carried comic strip and/or text biographies about the entertainment world, but large black-and-white head shots of the "Sweet Sixteener of the Month." The list of actresses (in order): Wanda Hendrix, Jane Powell with Roddy McDowall, Vanessa Brown; Elizabeth Taylor, Ann Francis, Jan Ford; Peggy Ann Garner; Shirley Johns, Ann Todd, Jean Simmons, Jane Powell with Marshall Thompson (full photo cover), Peggy Ann Garner with Lon McCallister, and Mona Freeman.

Two Much Lesser Known Titles

Two companies that were tiny in 1945, Magazine Enterprises and New Age Publishers, came up with the same formula as *Sweet Sixteen*.

Magazine Enterprises, founded and operated by Vincent Sullivan in 1943 after he began his career at DC, was known as Life's Romances Publishing Co. when the first two issues of *Keen Teens* appeared in 1944 and 1945 with no dates or numbers (their dates are obvious from interior stories about upcoming films and contests). The final four issues appeared from #3 (February–March 1947) to #6 (August–September 1947). Nineteen forty-seven was the first year in which Magazine Enterprises, then known as ME, became the solid second-tier company it would remain for a decade.

The first two issues consisted primarily of newspaper reprints of adventure strips of interest to girls, including long episodes of Claire Voyant by Jack Sparling. The first issue shows on an unsigned cover a boy and girl in a wild jitterbug dance with similar dancers in shadow as the boy reads "How to Cut a Rug [in] 6 Easy Lessons." It's a cute cover but genuinely deceiving about the contents.

Issue #2 was bannered "The Comic Magazine for American Girls." and showed two girls arguing over whether Frank Sinatra or Van Johnson was Hollywood king, while a third girl ogles the actors' images on a billboard as a boy somehow perched atop the billboard says, "What's it matter who's king? I ain't!"

Issues #3 and #4 show cartoon teen girls admiring actors Guy Madison and Glenn Ford. Issues #5 and #6 are full photo covers of Perry Como and

Bambi Lynn. These last four issues have no full-fledged teen humor strips, although Ogden Whitney's two-page Honey strip is nicely done and there are other panel and strip reprints.

New Age was among many short-lived publishers who operated in the 1940s. *Young Life* #1 (Summer 1945) and #2 (Fall 1945) became *Teen Life* #3–5 for three final quarterly issues in 1946. These comics were sometimes billed as "America's Most Exciting Teen-Age Magazine" on the covers but actually were dull in comparison to the likes of the *Parents' Magazine* publications.

The five issues were filled mostly with text and miscellaneous material of interest to teens. The comic strip art was among the worst in the industry, especially on the likes of short teen humor strips "Alvin" and "Teen Canteen" in *Teen Life* #4. The art is so poor, it makes the stories almost painful to read. What makes all 11 of these teen-oriented comics of interest to collectors is that all of them are uncommon.

There were only two more noteworthy attempts at comics boldly marketed to teenage girls: Marvel's six-issue *Girls' Life* with Patsy Walker in 1954 (see chapter on Patsy Walker in the 1950s) and Charlton's *Go-Go* #1–9 in 1966–1967.

12

Ozzie and Babs—Fawcett's Only Teen Stars

Fawcett Comics, certainly a major comic book publisher, usually made a big deal of it when Fawcett introduced characters or titles in the Golden Age, often with Captain Marvel doing the honors on the covers. But Fawcett's only teen stars, Ozzie and Babs, debuted with minimal fanfare when they replaced Captain Marvel's sister, Mary Marvel, as the lead feature and on the covers of the last 11 issues of *Wow Comics* beginning with #59 (October 1947).

There was a small plug for Ozzie (but not Babs) in the bottom left-hand corner of #59, below plugs for the three costumed heroes remaining in one of what had apparently been one of Fawcett's best-selling titles since issue #9, the first issue of *Wow* to feature Mary Marvel. Ozzie was something of an Archie knockoff and first appeared six years after the debut of Riverdale's teen sensation.

Babs was a combination of Archie's girls Betty and Veronica, since Fawcett apparently had no desire to create a love triangle in what turned out to be a highly amusing gag strip. *Ozzie and Babs* was one of the funniest and most creative of the 1940s teen humor strips, albeit a lot more slapstick than most of the primary imitators of the Archie gang.

When *Wow* #69 (August 1948) last featured Ozzie and Babs and immediately morphed into *Real Western Hero Comics* #70—one of more than a dozen western-themed titles Fawcett produced by the end of 1950—*Ozzie and Babs* had become a monthly title with #4 (September 1948) after three quarterly issues. That was highly unusual for a teen humor title, since Archie himself was still being published bi-monthly in 1948.

Alas, *Ozzie and Babs* ran for only nine monthly issues through #11 (April 1949) before returning to quarterly status for the final two issues, #12 and #13 (Summer and Fall 1949).

Ozzie and Babs may well have been an economic victim of Fawcett's deep dive into the burgeoning romance comics market in 1949, which the company did not advertise to its mostly young readers who were not

***Ozzie and Babs* #4, September 1948, copyright Fawcett Publications, Inc. Ozzie and Babs took Mary Marvel's place on the last 11 issues of *Wow Comics* and they were also stars of Fawcett's only teen humor title.**

yet supposedly into romance comics. At the top of the title page for all non-romance Fawcett titles, a circular symbol stating "Wholesome Entertainment" with "Approved Reading" in the center appeared next to a list of the company's titles, sans all the love stuff. The circular symbol did not appear on the ten romance titles Fawcett produced in 1949 and the 17 in

1950 before the romance market greatly contracted for almost all comic companies in the second half of 1950.

Ozzie and Babs Return

Ozzie and Babs seemingly had disappeared forever by the end of 1949, only to reappear as a back-of-the-book story in *Master Comics* #107 (September 1950). But that issue of *Master Comics*, which had long been the home of Captain Marvel Junior—who could sometimes be a pretty amusing teen himself—did nothing to spotlight the return of Fawcett's only teen stars. In fact, the inside front cover featured an unusual house ad with images of 13 Fawcett costumed hero and western hero titles published at various times in 1950—but not an image of Ozzie and Babs, which was still on the stands.

Even so, *Ozzie and Babs* stubbornly—and deservedly—held down a Fawcett home as a backup feature though the end of *Master Comics* with #133 (April 1953). Sometimes the strip was simply titled *Ozzie*, but the teens appeared in every issue of *Master* from #107 through #133 except #108, 112, 116 and 124. By the time Fawcett published its final comics, with January 1954 dates, Ozzie and Babs were seen in no other Fawcett titles in the 1950s.

Ozzie and Babs did make a brief comeback after low-rent Charlton Comics purchased the rights to many Fawcett characters in 1954. Charlton published *TV Teens* #14-15 and then changed the numbering to the correct #3-5 for the final three appearances of Ozzie and Babs. Ozzie and Babs were never on TV, but that didn't matter to Charlton. *TV Teens* #6 featured 1940s Fawcett hero Don Winslow (whose serials did appear on TV) and then reprinted the Mopsy working girl strip from #7–13 before the title left the comic book scene in 1956.

Ironically, the nine-page Ozzie and Babs return-to-action story in *Master* #107, "No Base Like Home," is one of the funniest of all. Ozzie is coaching the girls' powder puff baseball team (they're pitching overhand, so it's not softball). When Winkleview High's catcher is injured in pre-game warm-ups against Highview, Babs takes Ozzie into the locker room and disguises him as a female catcher. Ozzie's rivals among the guys make fun of him coming out of the locker room: One guy says, "That's the queerest looking girl I've ever seen" and the Reggie Mantle–like Slick agrees: "She's got a face like ten miles of bad road." Ozzie responds, "Fresh!" and lands a knockout punch on Slick. Ozzie takes a beating during the game—Babs is too nervous to pitch well—and Ozzie's rivals eventually realize who the catcher really is. But Ozzie is so well armored up as catcher that Slick can't land any punches and all ends well when Babs treats Ozzie to her post-game cake.

Ozzie and Babs #1 (December 1947) features "Buy-Buy Babs," in which

Babs takes her first job in the lingerie department of a Winkleville store and laugh after laugh ensues. In "It's a Dirty Deal" in the same issue, Ozzie ruins the dress Babs hopes to use to beat her rival, Glitter Gaye, in a fashion contest. But Babs wins anyway, because Dip, Ozzie's buddy, finds a dress worn by his grandmother. Dip, who is Jughead to Ozzie's Archie, has a philosophical line when it seems Ozzie is in trouble: "Women never understand anything! That's why they're women!"

It was ironic that Dip said this, because Fawcett's romance line published story after story about how the women had to learn life lessons from seemingly wiser and more aggressive men.

A Cover Slogan Appears

Ozzie and Babs receive a cover slogan in #2 (Spring 1948): "Laugh a Mile-a-Minute with the Clown Prince and Princess of the Teen-Agers." Wonder what Archie Andrews and Patsy Walker thought of that claim?

There are a lot of laughs in "Sloppy Jalopy," in which Ozzie uses a $10 bill from Babs to buy a junkyard special with ensuing hilarity, and "Bedlam at Bigibells," in which Babs unleashes mice, monkeys and birds on the customers at a women's sale but avoids trouble because the owner thinks it's great publicity.

The cover-featured story in #3 (Summer 1948), "The Secret Life of Ozzie Turner," rivals its inspiration, Danny Kaye's movie *The Secret Life of Walter Mitty*, for sheer fun. Ozzie wakes up from his last dream to find himself sharing a soda with Babs—a fitting finish.

Babs' huge, shaggy dog Mephistopheles sends Ozzie to an unfair punishment for his kindness in the hysterical "Ozzie and Babs Go to the Doghouse" in #7 (December 1948). Dogs also play a major role in "Use Your Headline" in #8 (January 1949), in which Ozzie volunteers to help Babs find a sensational "man bites dog" photo for the *Winkleville High Courier*. Instead, Babs catches a newsworthy photo of Ozzie accidentally tumbling off a bridge into the water.

The highly creative "Front and Center" in #10 (March 1949) takes place entirely in a theater as teens and adults battle for the best seats. It's one of the funniest stories in the run. A similar story in #11 (April 1949), "Social Success," goes through all the wacky steps Ozzie and Babs need for the prom—only to see Ozzie too exhausted to stay awake that night.

Ozzie and Babs #1–11 were all 52 pages, though Fawcett did not make a cover blurb for that the way the firm did for other titles. Oddly, when the title reverted to 36 pages for the final two issues, the longest Ozzie and Babs story of all appeared in #13 (Fall 1949); the cover plugged "a compete comics novelette in this issue" for the 21-page "Queen for a Day," based on the highly popular radio program (the television show was yet to come). Stories like this were telling reflections of the popular culture of the day—and even though "Queen for a Day" was not designed for kids on radio or TV, every kid who read the Ozzie and Babs version knew what was up.

Alas, there would be no more long Ozzie and Babs stories. When the teens returned a year later in *Master* #107, they were destined for short backup tales. The same applied to their five Charlton appearances, some of which were signed by Chic Stone. Apparently none of the Fawcett tales were ever signed or credited.

13

Junior, Sunny and Corliss

Other than the early issues of *Archie* and *Pep Comics*, by far the most valuable teen humor comics are the three titles Al Feldstein created for Fox Comics in the late 1940s.

Feldstein (1925–2014) is among the creators still held in highest regard by collectors, what with his historic work for EC Comics in the late 1940s and early 1950s, followed by his editorship of *Mad* from 1956 to 1984. He was that rarest of talent in the comics—a top-notch editor, artist and writer.

Before he turned 22, Feldstein already had the uncommon distinction for one so young of having written and drawn an entire comic book by himself: the first issue of *Junior Comics* (#9, September 1947) for publisher and editor Victor Fox. He went on to produce most of the content as a whole for *Junior* #9 to 16 (July 1948); Sunny #11 (December 1947) to #14 (June 1948) and *Meet Corliss Archer* #1 (March 1948), which ran only through #3 (July 1948). In very fine to near-mint condition, those 13 issues all can fetch more than $2000 apiece, and likely more at auction when professionally graded. Even in low grade, they are hard to find and a collector would be lucky to find a complete copy even in fair condition for less than $100.

Collectors thus are fortunate that IDW published *The Complete Junior and Sunny* (2014), edited by EC Comics expert Grant Geissman, who was in a position to do an outstanding job thanks to his extensive knowledge of Feldstein's work for EC. Thanks to Geissman, we have the only complete runs of Golden Age non–Archie teen humor comics ever reprinted.

Fox gave Feldstein, who began with work for S.M. "Jerry" Iger's comic art shop, the chance to produce the only teen comics the publisher ever printed other than *Zoot* #5–6 in 1947 (the title changed genres from funny animal and *Romeo Tubbs* #26 and 28 in 1950 [see separate chapter]).

Fox began publishing comics in 1939 and essentially finished following a bankruptcy in 1950, along with returning with a mysterious handful of issues dated August and September 1951. Though always a controversial figure, his line of comics did not gain genuine notoriety until after World War II, when the rapid growth of crime and romance titles offered Fox the opportunity to capitalize on some of the most violent, sleazy comics in the industry.

Most Fox comics were illustrated and written in less-than-skillful style. There is little doubt that most parents of school-age readers were appalled by what they saw produced by Fox, other than the spate of 1940s funny animal and humor titles he published while seeking alternatives for his largely defunct superhero line. Fox, indeed, did try a little of almost everything.

Feldstein's skills, however, produced some of the better teen humor issues of the era. No one ever put it better than Grant Geissman in his reprint volume:

> Junior was, of course, an intentional knock-off of Archie, which was the leading "teenage" comic book at the time. The cast of characters in Junior were essentially inspired by those appearing in Archie; Junior Hancock, Deena, Gwenny, Goofy and Tuffy all have somewhat similar counterparts in the Archie characters Archie, Betty, Veronica, Jughead, and Reggie.

Feldstein was careful, however, not to get too close with the character designs and personalities, thus avoiding lawsuits. In stark contrast to *Archie*, Feldstein's artwork is rather boldly salacious for a "teenage" book, something Victor Fox not only encouraged but insisted upon. Actually, according to Geissman, Feldstein's art for Fox's "teenage" titles, "titillating as it is, is fairly mild for a Fox comic book."

Title Changes

Junior picked up from the funny animal title *Li'l Pan* #8 but it wasn't shocking to see the title continue as *Western Outlaws* #17, one of the most violent of all western titles. Salacious *Sunny* was spun off from *Cosmo Cat* #10, of all titles! (Fox and other comic book publishers tried to save money on postal permits by continuing numbers even if the genre changed.) Ironically, the gentle teen creation Corliss Archer—created by F. Hugh Herbert in stories for *Good Housekeeping* and a longtime radio sensation—became the first Fox romance comic, *My Life* #4 (September 1948).

Romance comics boomed in late 1949 and early 1950 in the wake of Joe Simon and Jack Kirby's historic creation of *Young Romance* in 1947. But there were so many titles industry-wide at one time—about 150 by the first half of 1950—that the public wouldn't support them all. By the summer of 1950, Fox had dropped all 21 of his romance titles. He wasn't patient with them; his 21 titles represented only 101 issues (plus two continuations for one issue each late in 1951).

But then, Fox was also impatient with his teen humor books. Almost surely the primary reason the clean-cut Junior lasted as many as eight issues was the sheer talent of Feldstein, who told entertaining but far from sleazy stories in *Junior Comics*.

Sexy Sunny Sanders was bannered as "America's Sweetheart" on her first cover, but such braggadocio was far from uncommon on the increasingly crowded newsstands of the late 1940s and early 1950s. This was before the impact of commercial television began to be felt in greater measure every succeeding year of the 1950s after a record of more than 3100 newsstand comic books appeared in 1952.

By the second issue of *Sunny*, #12 (February 1948), Feldstein had her in panties and a bra for a panel after she flashed her legs in the bathtub in the previous panel of "An Ice Story"—a tale of ice skating. When she wore a sexy costume for the skating, she tried to impress the handsome instructor but proved to be dangerous on the ice. "I couldn't help noticing your skating since you came on the lake," he told her. "You did? And what did you think of it?" Sunny responded. When he replied, "Well, personally I think you need some good instruction!! You're a menace to the other skaters…," Sunny interrupted him with a slap and the story ended when she joined Teddy at the movies and told him, "And don't ask any questions." That loud ("Wham!") slap was not something you could imagine Betty Cooper doing!

That was the last issue in which Feldstein drew *Sunny*; #13 and #14 saw her stories drawn by lesser artists.

Victor Fox did not allow Feldstein to sign his work with his real name, the way EC did, so the artist used the likes of Bill Brown, Bob Brown and Jed Duncan to let friends and co-professionals know of his work.

Unlike most writers of teen humor, Feldstein almost never allowed high school sports to play a part in his stories. In the eight issues of *Junior*, the only page with a team sport was the end to "What an Eyeful!" in #10 (November 1947). Deena wants to compete in a beauty contest and Junior wants to help her, but she gets a shiner when Junior kicks a football at practice—directly into her face! Deena is understandably upset about being shut out of the contest, but Junior doesn't quite understand. "Gee, you try to be nice to a woman and look where it gets you!" he says in the final panel.

One of the funniest Junior stories is "A Junk Drive" in the first issue. Junior's mother wants to join the local women's club, but her "jury" leaves the Hancock residence in dismay after they see all the junk Junior has temporarily left in his front yard for a good cause, a camp fund for needy children. It turns out that the women's club supports the same charity and the women relent because they think Junior is an enterprising teen. "Gee! What'd I do!" Junior asks the reader in the final panel.

Another great story is "A Record Breaking Day" in #11 when two albums change hands three times, including both Deena and Gwenny, and the records in one of the albums are inadvertently smashed. Junior winds up with his copy of the album and Gwenny can't figure out why he's so grateful to receive such a present from Deena.

Meet Corliss Archer

Corliss Archer was among the sweetest things on the teen scene, so it was ironic that she would briefly be a companion to the sexy Sunny and the intriguing Junior for the notorious Fox Comics line.

F. Hugh Herbert's creation first appeared in a stage play, *Kiss and Tell*, and in *Good Housekeeping* short stories; they were later collected in the Random House book *Meet Corliss Archer* (1944). Corliss, her family and friends lasted more than a decade on radio after debuting in 1943 on CBS. Janet Waldo played Corliss on the radio most of the time. She also played Corliss in 39 live TV episodes in 1951 and 1952, and Ann Baker played Corliss in a short-lived TV series in 1954.

Feldstein drew an attractive introductory page in *Meet Corliss Archer* #1, including boyfriend Dexter Franklin, best girlfriend Mildred Ames, Mildred's brother Raymond, and parents Janet and Harry. Feldstein also included the family dog, a female cocker spaniel named Moronica. The dog plays a key role in the first story in #1, in which she has puppies in the family car instead of on the back porch. There is nothing the least bit sexy or salacious about this story except the way Feldstein drew protruding breasts on the females. But that was the same style he used in all his teen humor work, perhaps in response to Fox.

There is absolutely no slapstick in the three Corliss stories in #1; the stories are basically unusually wordy slices of teen life. School and any romantic complications had almost nothing to do with those three stories.

14

Slick Chick Comics and the Dearfield Duo

Of the more than 50 major and minor comic book publishers that released at least three dozen issues of multiple genres in the 1940s, the Dearfield Publishing Company of Chicago made one of the most intriguing gambles on teen humor with two unusual titles.

In contrast, more than four dozen other truly tiny publishers tested the market in the first 15 years of the "modern" comic book era (1934–1949), but only one other tried a teen humor title during that span. Leader Enterprises published three issues of *Slick Chick* comics, all numbered but all undated except for their 1947 copyright (and #2 was among the few comics published with no indicia).

Slick Chick listed Iger Shop owner S.M. "Jerry" Iger—who supplied stories and art for hundreds of issues in the 1940s and 1950s—as the managing editor.

Dearfield, which produced children's material, was the only small comic publisher to try teen humor in the 1940s with *Junie Prom Comics* #1–7 from 1947 to 1949 and *Dexter Comics* #1–5 in 1948–1949. Those 12 books represented more than one-third of the little-known publisher's output of 34 issues in the last three years of the 1940s! Dearfield otherwise published only humor comics and is best known for the 22-issue run of the funny animal title *Red Rabbit* from 1947 to 1951.

Junie Prom and *Dexter* were among the "purest" teen humor comics ever published. Unlike titles like Standard's *Kathy Comics*, which dealt mostly with community and family stories, *Junie Prom* and *Dexter* were all about high school friends and rivals for love and affection and school events.

Junie Prom was an outrageous pun for a comic title, of course, but the publisher played it straight and referred to Mr. and Mrs. Prom and so on. Neither Junie nor Dexter had much time for siblings, just a whole lot of fellow teens with whom they hung out. Junie and Dexter did not have cross-over stories but their little epics showed up in each other's titles, along with house ads plugging the other character's title.

The uncredited art was an odd mixture of overtly sexual and slapstick styles. It's hard to imagine the Comics Code Authority passing on a reprint of the Junie and Dexter stories. But the style actually worked: These sto-

***Dexter* #2, Fall 1948, copyright Dearfield Publishing Co. *Dexter* lasted only five issues but is popular with collectors for its period-piece art.**

ries are fun to read, in part because they are tightly focused on their plot points.

No artists, writers or editors are listed for *Junie Prom*, which ran from #1 (Winter 1947) through #7 (August 1949), and *Dexter*, which ran from #1 (Summer 1948) through #5 (July 1949). But maybe that was just as well, considering how wild these stories were.

The Sophisticated Look

Junie Prom was among the few comic book teen girls who always wore her hair in a high upsweep with adult sophistication. She was clearly a high school student, but she looked 25, in much the same way that many actors in 1950s juvenile delinquent films looked years older (in large part because many of them *were*). Junie Prom also was among the few teen humor titles with a serious advice column: "Girl to Girl," credited to Bee Sparks. These were common in romance comics, but not in the teen titles.

On the splash page of the first story in *Junie Prom* #1, best friend Lollie reads about a glamour contest being held by *Scoop Magazine* and her first words are "Oh Junie, just look at these headlines! They're just too utterly-utter!" Then she uses the word "supersonic"—1947 was the year Chuck Yaeger became the first pilot to break the sound barrier—to describe Junie's sexy afternoon dress. Junie responds, "And jeeps, I've got billions and skillions of miles to hem around this formal [dress]."

Lollie soon becomes even more enthusiastic: "Oh, you'll win! You'll be strictly date-bait in this! No male could resist your trap-line! You'll be a fluffy, soft, earth-bound cloud in this creation!"

Soon, at the malt shop, Junie and Lollie encounter their competition, red-headed glamour girl Drucilla Dare and her friend, the tomboyish "fat stooge" Double-Bubble. Drucilla calls Junie "revoltingly juvenile" and gets this response from Junie: "I'm very afraid Drucilla's going to die of old age before she turns eighteen!" Ouch!

At the contest, Junie wins the first of three divisions against the other five competitors including Drucilla. There's a knock on her dressing-room door and Junie discovers a double-chocolate strawberry sundae, only to have a firecracker explode the sundae to ruin her beautiful formal dress. Lollie loans Junie her dress, but Drucilla prevails. Then Junie's bathing suit is stolen but it's again Lollie to the rescue with an improvised and attractively pinned school flag. The winner, of course, is Junie.

The rest of the first issue is two Dexter stories and the debut of Debbie Dale, one of the many teen characters that appeared out of nowhere in the comics. In that odd story, Debbie's girlfriends tell her about a visit by the movie star Van Crawford, except when Debbie meets him in her role as a waitress, he's Peter Crawford … obviously meant to imply the popular real-life star Peter Lawford.

Junie's boyfriend Mike Cunningham soon shows up to add spice to the stories. Naturally, Drucilla wants Mike too, and that was the plot element of many stories. The stories became shorter when the title dropped from 52 pages with #1 to 36 pages. There's a funny Dexter backup story in #3 (Summer 1948), in which Dexter buys an advice book on how to be a sophisticated gentleman only before he takes girlfriend Jill to a swanky restaurant. There, Jill spots a man gobbling down his food and the waiter tells her that's Elmer E. Post, the author of the advice book on which Dexter now figures he wasted $5. Why? Because in the last panel, Jill says of Post, "Oh!! Isn't he wonderful! So uninhibited and masculine!" to which Dexter says with his typically sour look, "Grrr!! Women—bah!! Crunch! Crunch!"

In *Junie Prom* #4 (Fall 1948), little brother Buster wins the admiration of Hollywood producer David Sellswick, who admires his authenticity over Junie's hysterical efforts to gain his attention. In the second story, Junie's plot to take a course from the new science teacher falls through when a switch leads the old maid of the faculty, Miss Parrott, to teach the course. In the third story, Junie realizes she really had encountered a ghost at a haunted house. Such stories add an element of creativity, since Junie, like Dexter, doesn't always get her way.

In the clever backup story in #4, Donna Dale (maybe Debbie's sister) misses the big basketball game and its fantastic finish because she has to keep a commitment to work. But then the players offer a weary Donna a ride home; they realize they're too tired and too banged up to go to the big dance. Donna is shown eating and listening to music at her home, surrounded by five nice guys.

One of the funniest Dexter stories was in #2 (Fall 1948), "The Soft-Boiled Yegg." Dexter, who often looks like he has a chip on his shoulder, is inspired to be tougher by the latest Lank Burtcaster mystery movie, *How Tough Can You Be*. This wasn't long after Burt Lancaster's remarkable performance with Lizabeth Scott in the classic noir film *I Walk Alone*. Dexter and Jill are forced by two real bad guys to rob a bank, but Dexter becomes the hero thanks to his wild driving.

In the second story, Dexter manages to rescue Jill, save himself from an unfair charge and rescue his father from the same. The story concludes with the police chief asking the limber Dexter to teach him a certain dance step. In the third story, Dexter teaches his friends how to play hard-to-get with the girls, with decidedly negative results as he hot-foots away from his angry buddies. The Junie Prom backup story is hysterical, with Junie inadvertently setting a school record in the high jump in the big meet while fleeing from a mouse.

"Platter Panic" in *Dexter* #4 (May 1949) sees Our Hero winning Jill's favor along with a radio contest called "Can You Take It?" with rival Hector muttering "Bet It Was Fixed!" as the story ends.

The backup story, starring a new character named Bobbie, finds her avoiding boredom in a never-named new town by catching a cross-dressing criminal for the delighted cops. But in the last two Dexter stories in #4, he does not get his way as Jill wins the day.

A title from Superior Comics, *Aggie Mack Comics* #1–8 from January 1948 through August 1949, also was a short-run title, but Superior clearly was not a tiny firm. It was a second-tier publisher with 230 comics published from 1947 through 1956. Superior was based in Canada, with Canadian advertisements, but also sold comics in much of the United States as the only such company in the 1950s.

Slick Chick Comics

In one of the oddest comic books ever printed, a 15-year-old high school girl named Tiny finds herself making friends with the new kid in town—a really tiny little guy who calls himself Sox. When he first meets Tiny across a fence in #1, he's standing on a box!

Tiny is worried she might be embarrassed if she dates Sox instead of handsome Tommy Bright, but at the big dance, Tiny gets drenched by the contents of a punch bowl, thanks to Tommy's foolishness and prejudice against Sox. "I guess Pops was right when he said character is all that counts!" Tiny tells Sox on the way home. Sox responds, "What a character I am."

Sox thinks he's out of luck with Tiny, but she tells him, "I'm proud of the way YOU made a fool of Tommy Bright, Sox! It served him right!" And the story ends with Tiny lifting Sox off his feet for a goodnight kiss. This is among the most endearing moments in teen humor comics.

The cover, showing five teens in a jalopy, has nothing to do with any of the stories. That wasn't unusual for teen humor, in contrast to many other genres.

Some teen humor comics might puzzle readers who aren't familiar with 70-year-old teen slang. For example, when the family phone rings, Tiny calls it "The Ameche!" This refers to Don Ameche's performance in the 1939 film *The Story of Alexander Graham Bell* and how he invented, well, the Ameche.

The second story involves a radio contest that Tiny wins by accident and how she forgives Sox for spilling all her prizes by calling him "Dear" when she thinks he's been hurt. The story thus ends, "Course I know I'm only delirious from shock … but Tiny … call me Dear again."

The cover of #2 can only be described as one of a kind: Tiny jitterbugs with Sox as an organ grinder shrugs while his two fully dressed monkeys join in the dance!

Slick Chick Comics #1, 1947, copyright Leader Enterprises, Inc. This was a typically amusing teen title but it couldn't compete with Marvel and DC and ran only three issues.

The Tiny stories in #2 and #3 are credited to Frank Little, of all names. In #2, the stories "At the Beach!" and "Working Girl!" once again involve embarrassing problems for Sox and Tiny but they are happy together in the final panels. On the cover of #3, Tiny is a magician pulling Sox out of a hat. In the two Tiny stories, Sox appears puzzled but comes out okay for the fifth and sixth time in as many comic book appearances for the unique little guy.

It's too bad *Slick Chick Comics* became one of the first teen humor comics to fail. It was the first such teen comic to go out of business after World War II paper rationing had ended.

15

Other Short Run Pre-Code Girls

Avon was a major mass-market paperback publisher in the 1940s when the firm began publishing comic books and pulps in 1947. Among the first comics was a six-issue teen humor syndicated newspaper reprint series titled *Penny* from 1947 to 1949, which was quite an investment during a three-year period when Avon published its first 40 issues as a distinctly minor publisher in the ever-expanding comic book field.

But Avon made significant contributions to the crowded news racks of the first half of the 1950s. From 1950 to 1956, however, the only Avon teen humor comic was *Betty and Her Steady* #2 (March–April 1950), which was cover-marketed to look like one of several exotic romance titles that Avon contributed to the love comics craze in 1949 and 1950. *Going Steady with Betty*, as it was known for one issue, was totally teen humor with #1 (November–December 1949).

For a company that invested so heavily in *Penny*, it was remarkable that Avon published more than 375 issues through 1956 yet not a single one involved teen humor after *Betty and Her Steady* #2 (see more below). *Penny* was successful in newspapers but not in comic books, perhaps in part because it was the only teen humor reprint comic of its period and looked radically different from other teen humor comics.

Penny was actually two comic books in one, but you would never know it from the covers, unless you recognized the identity of the blond boy who was with Penny on all six covers. He was Our Bill, the first teen newspaper strip creation of Harry Haenigsen, in 1939—more than two years before Archie debuted in comic books. Penny Pringle came along in 1943, as detailed in a Haenigsen biography on the inside front cover of *Penny* #1. It was rare for any creator to get a bio in a comic book. This bio, however, did not begin to do justice to Haenigsen, but the noted cartoonist-historian Jerry Robinson corrected that with his magnificent survey book *The Comics: An Illustrated History of Comic Art* (1974). By the time Haenigsen created Penny in 1943, he

***Going Steady with Betty* #1, November–December 1949, copyright Avon Periodicals, Inc. This title ran only two issues, changing its title to *Betty and Her Steady* with #2 as part teen humor, part romance.**

was 43 years old and had been doing a wide variety of illustrations including compelling work for *Collier's*.

Penny and Our Bill did not inhabit the same teen universe except on the covers of *Penny*. In all six issues, a two-page Penny Sunday reprint from the original source, the *New York Herald Tribune*, would be followed by a two-page Our Bill Sunday reprint. It was, to say the least, a highly unusual format.

Robinson noted that *Penny* ran all the way to 1970, which was a healthy 27-year run for a teen strip. Robinson was impressed with Haenigsen's style, evaluating the strip with these perceptive observations:

> Although Our Bill remained his personal favorite, Penny was his most popular and widely syndicated feature. Penny … was a teen-ager of blithe spirit. The strip was frequently punctuated by warm sequences with droll dialogue between Penny and her exasperated but sympathetic father. Haenigsen captured Penny's pert manner and supple but awkward gyrations in precise lines punctuated by a few discriminating blacks. Expert use was also made of selective focus, close-ups and long shots, not usually seen in strips of this genre.

Robinson nails Haenigsen's excellence perfectly, but Avon's format was not comic book–friendly for a teen character, especially considering the long, highly entertaining concurrent original misadventures of the likes of Archie Andrews, Patsy Walker from Marvel and Candy from Quality Comics. In the biography in *Penny* #1, the uncredited writer says Haenigsen maintains that Penny is 13 to 15 years old, but she often seems a bit older, although definitely still a high school girl.

In one strip in #1, Penny waits eagerly for her new dress to arrive the day of a big dance. She then asks her mother, aunt and father if the stylish, light-blue frock suits her, showing all the insecurity of youth. But when her date Sylvester arrives, he raves about her: "Jeeps, you sure are pretty, Pigeon! That dress is pure dream dust!" To which Penny responds: "This dress, Sylvester? Why it's just a little old burlap I simply threw on in the last minute."

The only copyright listed in the indicia of *Penny* #1–6 was that of the *New York Herald Tribune*. The comic book was not dated in the indicia until #6 (September–October 1949). Considering how well-written Haenigsen's dialogue was, it's too bad that *Penny* could not have run in longer stories.

Going Steady with Betty

The cover of #1 is unusual, showing Betty Bates and boyfriend Ozzie Olan dancing in front of the Ray Anthony Band while Betty says, "Oh, Ozzie, isn't it a beautiful sight?" Ozzie, eying another girl dancer, replies, "Wow! It sure is."

Betty appears out of the comic book blue with four stories, with no introduction or explanation of who she is and where she lives. The simple stories all involve identity confusion and misadventures, with unsigned art that can charitably be described as non-compelling.

However, the second story is one of the earliest in all of comics to portray teens arguing over television. Ozzie wants to watch a hockey game (few of which were ever televised that early) and Betty talks him into watching *The Hollywood Screen Test*, which turns out to be a filmclip of their local high school play. When Betty receives recognition, she tells Ozzie, "From now on I'm dating only movie stars!" Ozzie scratches his hand and mutters to himself, "Hmff!! Television sure is changing our habits … just like it said in the newspaper ads!" The story ends with a slapstick screen test encounter between Betty and Ozzie. The director loves it but Betty says, "I'm through with televi-

Kitty* #1, October 1948, copyright St. John Publishing Corp. The only issue of the title features this cover by Lilly Renee. She was much better known for action-oriented art, but demonstrates her versatility here.

sion! I just want to be a dramatic actress!" That leaves poor Ozzie shrugging and telling the reader, "I still can't understand women! Can you?"

With the title change to *Betty and Her Steady* with #2, Avon published a comic book like no other. The top half of the page contained six panels of four very short Betty and Ozzie stories and the bottom half was two text romance stories, "There's An End to Caring" and "I Paid for My Desire." On the cover, "Teen Age Romance" (no hyphen) and "Two Complete Illustrated (barely) Confession Stories" were plugged, with a banner across the cover plugging "Two Big Books in One!" The new style of Betty and Ozzie art, showing the two looking more like college students than high school kids, was signed F. Carin.

Whether the format bombed or Avon decided it had too many romance titles can't be determined. Avon suspended or cancelled all five of its romance titles in the first half of 1950, along with cancelling *Going Steady with Betty*.

Aggie Mack and *Linda*

Aggie Mack #1–8 (January 1948 to August 1949) from Superior Comics and *Linda* #1–4 (April–May 1954 to October–November 1954) from Ajax-Farrell both had almost identical—and identically poorly printed—art from the Iger Studio, some from Jack Kamen, who was outstanding in his work for EC Comics. Ironically, publisher Robert Farrell cancelled *Linda* to begin a four-issue series of a sexed-down Phantom Lady (a costumed crime-fighter) when Farrell acquired the rights to the formerly infamous strip from defunct Fox Comics.

The *Aggie Mack* series, apparently based on a newspaper strip, and the *Linda* series, which resembles reworked *Aggie Mack* stories, both had such an odd art style that it was sometimes challenging to look at and a chore to follow. Aggie's boyfriend Bobo was printed with black holes for eyes and several characters were portrayed with equally strange eyes in *Linda*.

These two titles might be among the most over-valued of all teen humor comics. Kamen's art skills, so effectively used in other genres by EC Comics, were wasted on *Aggie Mack*.

The One-Shot *Kitty*

Lilly Renee did awe-inspiring 1940s action material for Fiction House such as Senorita Rio in *Fight Comics*, Lost World in *Planet Comics* and Werewolf Hunter in *Rangers Comics*. She tried her hand at teen humor with *Kitty* #1 (October 1948), a one-shot for St. John. Renee did an unusual two-page spread of paper dolls, although she (or the editor) headlined them as "Kitty's Cut-Outs."

This was a 32-page issue with only three stories: one-shot appearances by three unknown characters titled *Kitty* and the unsigned strips *Kenny* and *Sally*. Kitty was by far the cutest of the strips, with Renee's talent for drawing cartoony facial expressions in great evidence.

Kitty's ten-page story told of her amusing experiences in trying to find the funds to buy a new gown for the mid-summer formal dance. She capped her efforts by taking a job at the Stacey Brothers department store, and selling $300 worth of dresses—to herself! But, as she tells her puzzled father, "With my employee's ten percent discount, all you'll have to pay is two hundred seventy!" She ends the story by calling best girlfriend Wanda and telling her, "Just thought I'd let you know I've several new formals. How? Sorry—that's a trade secret!"

St. John, however, was too busy joining the romance explosion of 1949 and *Kitty* was cancelled.

16

Teena and the Strip Reprints

In the rush to capitalize on newspaper strip reprints among the financial possibilities of the late 1940s teen humor craze, one publisher in particular tried to make a go of it. It would be another two decades before we could say "a go-go of it"!

That might have been why none of the teen humor and working girl strip reprint comic titles succeeded: The strips had been around a long time and likely did not seem as fresh to readers as what became iconic original comic book characters from Archie, Marvel and DC (National) Comics.

Nonetheless, Standard Comics, with its superhero line fading, gave *Freckles and His Friends* an eight-issue run (1947–1949) and both Magazine Enterprises and Standard tried to make *Teena* work with three licensed issues apiece across 1948, '49 and '50.

Teena was created in 1941 by Hilda Terry as *It's a Girl's Life* with a unique, minimalist art style that was both charming and unmistakable. There were lots of girls and women on the newspaper comic pages when she debuted, but Teena was among the few genuinely funny teen females. Her antics must have caused many older readers to laugh out loud, especially if they brought back memories.

Teena was so well known that when Magazine Enterprises, a solid second-tier publisher, decided to publish its first teen humor comic, publisher Vin Sullivan and editor Ray Krank used Teena's name and cartoon head across the top of what really was a teen anthology title: *A-1 Comics* #11 in 1948. The cover, however, featured the first and only teen scene for a Honey story by Ogden Whitney. It's a clever but illogical cover by Whitney: Somehow, Honey has acquired lipstick and a mirror while being carried out of the water by a lifeguard at the beach as Honey's rival glowers. The cover blurb below Teena featured the other six teen strips in the issue: *Bobby Sox, Wendy, Honey Susie Q. Smith, Flipper* and *Babs.*

Honey Russell was the only original comic book character among the group and Whitney, who drew mostly action and adventure stories in his long career, did her proud in a six-page story. The plot wasn't unusual but it was well realized. Honey made the most of visits by teen movie star Tess Tingle and suave film star Walter Midgeon to fulfill a request from Honey's father and also to win election as her school president. In the final panel, Honey's father acknowledges, "Sometimes, the younger generation scares me. My dear, it's so self-sufficient." Wonder what he would say about today's youthful generation!

There were eight pages of *Teena* Sunday reprints, two of *Susie Q. Smith* by Linda and Jerry Walker and four of *Bobby Sox* by Marty Links, who went on to great success. The short stories of *Wendy, Flipper* and *Babs* were uncredited and not drawn to syndicated strip standards. All in all, this is a highly unusual teen humor comic with seven different characters.

A-1 Comics #12 was *Teena*'s second appearance and *A-1* #15 was third and final under the ME brand. *Teena* was the cover feature for both, signed by Hilda Terry and apparently drawn especially for the firm. All three of the A-1 issues were undated 1948 comics. The A-1 series featured many different titles through 1955.

A-1 #12 made one of the greatest format flips in comic book history; this occurred less than two months after *A-1* #11 hit the stands with seven different characters. The entire contents of *A-1* #12 consisted of 31 *Teena* Sunday reprints from 1944 through 1946! The mind boggles at such a quick shift, even before the sales reports of *A-1* #11 could have been received. Likewise, *A-1* #15 also contained 31 Sunday reprints, all from 1945.

Standard Takes *Teena*

The *Teena* license from King Features Syndicate shifted from Magazine Enterprises to Standard Comics in 1949. With a banner reading "The Teen-Age Girl That Millions Love!" Standard inexplicably started a three-issue run with *Teena* #20 (August 1949) with a different style and ran two more issues, #21 (November 1949) and #22 (October 1950).

Hilda Terry received the byline for the first multi-page Teena story, the eight-page "Flat Tires" that opened #20. It's an amusing tale of Teena and BFF Pipsie cycling to a dance in their honor, with all sorts of complications including torn dresses. The next story, "Date Bait," involved Teena's sophisticated cousin Kate, who is two years older but seems at least 30. The copyright dates of 1946, 1947 and 1949 are used, so this issue has a mixture of short stories (possibly connected Sunday reprint material) and single page reprints. This issue may have been rushed into print, since there are no advertisements except for a back cover ad and two house ads on the inside front and back covers. This was uncharacteristic of Standard.

Terry signed all three Standard covers, just as she signed the #12 and #15 from Magazine Enterprises. It's uncertain if these were adapted from Sunday pages or purely original art.

Teena #21 features one of the best of all teen humor covers. Teena is sprawled in an easy chair reading a magazine titled "Reducing Diets" as the detritus of snacks surrounds her on the floor and she's reaching for chocolate on a table laden with snacks. All told, more than a dozen types of snacks are portrayed—enough for Teena to have gained pound after pound!

The copyright dates on #21 are the same as #20. Oddly, the lead story is again called "Date Bait" as cousin Kate reappears, although this 14-page epic is not bylined by Terry even though it's certainly drawn in her style. Teena goes through all sorts of histrionics as she gets a job as a private eye's assistant. She and cousin Kate attend the big dance, but each has the other's date (don't ask). The second story in #21, the six-page "School Daze!" signed by Terry, displays her minimalist style with only the words "High School" on the front door as she goes to a class.

Terry also has a byline on the four-page filler "Woody," in which a teenage boy decides it's time to date and takes along a variety of self-help books with titles like *Rules for Dating, How to Drive* and *How to Dance*, much to his date Maud's consternation. But Woody saves the day on the last page when he overcomes a pair of thugs; Maud gives him an enthusiastic kiss to end the story as Woody holds the book *How to Kiss Good Night*. Obviously, these stories are a bit surreal.

Teena's last comic book appearance in #22 consisted of five multi-page short stories and only one single-page Sunday reprint, but the copyright dates of 1947, 1948, 1949 and 1950 indicate possible use of linked Sunday material. Terry's clever cover shows a frustrated date sitting in a hammock next to Teena with a softball bat in her lap and a catcher's mask on her face while wearing a distinctly un-softball like delicate dress.

Freckles and His Friends

The eight-issue Standard run of *Freckles and His Friends* started with #5 (November 1947), typical of Standard in the postwar period, and ended with #12 (August 1949). (Standard obviously titles that started with #5 or #11 to seem better established to retailers with crowded newsstands.) The unsigned covers made the title look like a typical teen humor book, but *Freckles* was really more of a series of sports, outdoor and adventure stories. They were not credited to Merrill Blosser, the cartoonist who originated Freckles in 1915 as a pre-teen youngster, but were reprints of Blosser's daily and Sunday work syndicated by the Newspaper Enterprise Association from the late 1930s through the 1940s.

When the N.E.A.'s Argo Publishing Company issued a series of newspaper reprint comic books in 1955 and 1956, one of the first was *Freckles and His Friends* #1 (November 1955) and one of the last was #4 (June 1956). These contained the same style of reprints used by Standard but Blosser was credited. They looked very dated by the 1950s, however, as did many of the Argo titles. Argo published 40 issues across more than a dozen titles.

Freckles was listed in the category "The Old Stand-Bys" in the first comprehensive book about comics, Martin Sheridan's *Comics and Their Creators* (1942). Sheridan quotes Blosser in a brief entry: "I am trying to show the clean and humorous side of an American boy's life." He accomplished that quite nicely, but his more-than-competent style was not that of the creators of the *Archie* and *Leave It to Binky* comic books, among many other titles devoted to teen boys as well as girls from the 1940s through the 1960s.

Etta Kett

Standard also tried to take advantage of the teen humor craze with reprints of *Etta Kett* from #11 (December 1948) through #14 (September 1949). Paul Robinson's *Etta Kett* was syndicated by King Features and ran five decades, from 1925 through 1974, but like *Freckles and His Friends* was much more of a social and adventure strip rather than a teen humor comic.

Comics historian Ron Goulart, in his excellent survey book *The Funnies* (1995), wrote: "Etta Kett started in 1925 as a strip aimed at giving etiquette tips to young people. It was by Paul Robinson, who'd spent several years working in animation before switching to newspaper cartooning." But, after noting a change in emphasis, Goulart added, "Etta Kett became a flapper strip, but a very mild-mannered one in which youth was tepid rather than flaming."

À la Freckles and His Friends, Standard contributed original splashes to introduce stories in *Etta Kett*. But the heroine seldom looked like a teenager, even though Standard used the blurb "Teen Age Darling of Millions of Readers" at the top of each of the four issues.

Today, both Freckles and Etta are seldom remembered, in contrast to the highly collectible original teen humor characters for comic books. But they are both worthwhile period pieces dealing with how young people lived in the first half of the 20th century.

17

Hi-Jinx—Teen-Age Animal Funnies

Teen humor didn't come any wilder than in the short but highly entertaining run of *Hi-Jinx*, subtitled *Teen-Age Animal Funnies*. The seven-issue, highly entertaining bi-monthly run in 1947–1948 is a real challenge for the collector to put together, but it's well worth it for one of the most esoteric Golden Age Comics.

Hi-Jinx carried no credits or signatures for art and writing other than the famed cartoonist Milt Gross, who wrote and drew a backup strip, *Pete the Pooch*, in #4–7. *Pete the Pooch* had nothing to do with the teenage funny animals. The editor, Richard E. Hughes, is listed in the indicia of *Hi-Jinx*, just as he was for all the American Comics Group titles from the late 1940s, when the firm began using Ben Sangor Shop art in titles listed from a number of sub-publishers. *Hi-Jinx* was produced by B.& I. Publishing Company and the title vanished before the ACG logo began appearing later in 1948.

Hi-Jinx #1 (July–August 1947) introduces the Hepcats, feline students at Lowdown High in Jive Junction, U.S.A. (There really was a minor 1944 movie titled *Jive Junction*, about musical teenagers.) The featured Hepcats are Tommy Tabby and Kitty Catt, who solve typical teen problems involving clothes and rivalries in the first story where they are shown at the Fish Fest dancing to the music of Pussy Willow and His Cat O' 9 Tails.

The second story introduces I.M. Square from Delaware, a bulldog who hates dancing, and Heppity Hare, who is always up to some clever mischief. The wild tale also features Frank Sinatra—the real one!—along with all the Hot Hepcats led by Tommy and Kitty. Mr. Square, as he is always called, learns to jitterbug while wearing Frankie's bowtie (a gift from Heppity). That leads Mr. Square to decide the Hepcats and jive dancing aren't so bad after all.

By now, you're either going to love the potential of this series or you're going to move on to human teens!

The highlight of the final four stories, all with the Hepcats, is "Hi Jinx at Lowdown High," in which Heppity Hare and Mr. Square help the Hepcats convince the faculty leaders to dance and sing, "Let's Cut a Groovy Rug to Sing—It's Called the Academic Swing!"

Professor Weirdbeard and the Cats

Hi-Jinx #2 (September–October 1947) introduces Professor Weirdbeard of the Lowdown High faculty and Jitterbug the frog in another all–Hepcats issue. One of the charms of teen humor comics of the 1940s is just how many weird names were applied to adults!

Hi-Jinx #3 (November–December 1947) features a hysterical eight-page lead story, "Let 'Em Eat Cake," in which the Hepcats overcome difficulties to open a jitterbug dance school in order to combat the rumors that jitterbugging is fading in popularity. In another side-splitting story in #3, Tommy fulfills the dream of every teen when he gets a phone in his car—and finds trouble with the police.

Hi-Jinx #4 (January–February 1948) is the least interesting of the seven issues, without memorable stories and with two non–Hepcat tales for the first time. In *Hi-Jinx* #5 (March–April 1948), Tommy is left in charge of the Kitty Kola (the Jive Junction teen hangout) with outrageous results. It's one of only three Hepcat stories in the issue.

Hi-Jinx #6 (May–June 1948) features the only tale resembling a sports story in the series, in which Mr. Square shocks himself by winning a swimming contest. In *Hi-Jinx* #7 (July–August 1948), like in a few other stories in the series, teen slang is identified and explained, as when Kitty says, "What a drag!" and "drag" is defined as "No life, no pep! A bore!"

No comic book series ever mixed totally disparate genres—see Charlton's six-issue run of *Space Western Comics* (#40–45 in 1952)—and enjoyed any real commercial success. What's intriguing about *Hi-Jinx* is that it mixed two genres that did not really begin to succeed in comic books until only a few years earlier, with funny animals making their first splash in 1940 followed by teen humor in 1941.

It's too bad that *Hi-Jinx* didn't last longer, because it truly was among the most entertaining humor comics on the stands The approach was original and made wonderful use of the term "hepcats."

A *Hi-Jinx* Index

An index to multiple-page stories in *Hi-Jinx* #1–7 (no art credits except for Milt Gross on *Pete the Pooch*). All issues are 52 pages including covers and all covers feature the Hepcats:

Hi-Jinx #1 (July–August 1947)
"That's How Jive Was Born" (Hepcats), 7
"Mr. Square from Delaware" (Hepcats), 10
"External Combustion" (Hepcats), 7
"Are Rivals Reet?" (Tommy and Kitty, Hepcats), 6
"Hi Jinx at Lowdown High" (Hepcats) 7
"After the Brawl" (Hepcats), 6
Hi-Jinx #2 (September–October 1947)
"Circus Stuff" (Hepcats), 7
"Square and Warmer" (Hepcats), 7
"A Rude Awakening" (Hepcats), 7
"The Groove Gang in The Mystery Voice of Jive Junction" (Hepcats), 6
"Mr. Square in Silence Is Golden" (Hepcats), 7
"Bubble Trouble" (Hepcats), 7
Hi-Jinx #3 (November–December 1947)
"Let 'Em Eat Cake" (Hepcats), 8
"Juke Box Jamboree" (Hepcats), 7
"Tale of a Telephone" (Hepcats), 8
"Ignorance Is Bliss" (Hepcats), 7
"Baby Bizness" (Hepcats), 8
"Hepcat Hi-Jinx" (Hepcats), 6
Hi-Jinx #4 (January–February 1948)
"King of the Carnival" (Hepcats), 7
"Making a Record" (Hepcats), 7
"Chair Up, the Worst Is Yet to Come" (Still Life Sillies, no connection with Hepcats), 7
"Sundae, Monday and Always" (Hepcats), 7
"Pete the Pooch and Elwood" (Milt Gross strip), 8
"The Genius Was a Dope" (Hepcats), 7
Hi-Jinx #5 (March–April 1948)
"Tommy Takes Over" (Hepcats), 8
"The Real Lowdown on Little Bo Peep" (humor strip), 9
"Mr. Square in Corn Off the Cob" (Hepcats), 7
"A Bird in the Clock Is Worth Two in the Bush" (Still Life Sillies), 7
"Heppity's Big Case" (Hepcats), 7
"Pete the Pooch and Elwood" (Milt Gross strip), 7
Hi-Jinx #6 (May–June 1948)
"Gettin' In the Swim" (Hepcats), 8
"The Real Lowdown on Humpty Dumpty" (Still Life Sillies), 9
"Wash Your Dog, Lady?" (Hepcats), 8
"King Midas and His Funny Money" (humor strip), 8

"Raisin' The Roof" (Hepcats), 8
"Pete the Pooch" (Milt Gross strip), 4
Hi-Jinx #7 (July–August 1948)
"All Fowled Up" (Hepcats), 7
"You May Be Down, But You're Never Out!" (Still Life Sillies), 8
"By the Sea" (Hepcats), 8
"What Really Gives with Old King Cole" (humor strip), 7
"The Egg and Why" (Hepcats), 6
"Pete the Pooch" (Milt Gross strip), 8

Section II

The 1950s

The Archie Universe overwhelmed the rest of the teen humor field in the 1950s, publishing slightly more than 400 issues with the Archie gang across 17 titles. But there were also a handful of successes elsewhere, primarily involving the ubiquitous Patsy Walker and her retinue.

The only non–Archie teen comic that began in the 1950s and ran 100-plus issues before it expired was the 110-issue run of Marvel's *Patsy and Hedy* (1952-67). That's how well done the rivalry between Patsy Walker and Hedy Wolfe was presented.

Dozens of titles in the 1950s were limited to short runs, at least in part because of the chaos of criticism that engulfed the comic book industry in the period before the Comics Code Authority's symbol began running on comics in the spring of 1955. The chaos also extended to the ever-increasing heavy-handed influence of television throughout the decade, not to mention the most crowded newsstands in American history. Much of the phenomenon was caused by a record five-year comic book publishing total from 1950 to 1954 of more than 13,600 issues. (Note: That's issues, not titles.)

All told, including the 17 Archie teen titles, no fewer than 78 teen humor titles appeared at some time in the 1950s, including all of the successful ones. And this doesn't count the flood of career girl titles such as Millie the Model and Sherry the Showgirl, both largely done by Dan De Carlo in their heydays. (The former ran 207 issues in her own title alone; the latter appeared in nine issues of her own two titles, *Sherry the Showgirl* and *Showgirls*.)

But there was lots of non–Archie fun to be found in the 1950s, not the least of which was in the DC teen titles. There were six of them: the successful *A Date with Judy*, *Buzzy* and *Leave It to Binky*, and the shorter-run but still influential *Here's Howie*, *Scribbly* and *Everything Happens to Harvey*. Why DC never created an early teen girl star of its own will forever be a mystery; Judy Foster hit DC in 1947 a fully formed figure, licensed because of her successful radio show. The five boys were all original.

DC took pride in publishing generally "clean" comics in the 1950s, with violence held to a minimum and even the stories in the few horror comics requiring a logical rather than a supernatural explanation. The exotic men and women—especially the women—from so many other publishers during the era did not appeal to National Periodical Publications, as the firm was known for so long.

One character, Mazie from the little-known Nationwide Comics/Magazine Publishers and later picked up by Harvey, spun off three titles devoted to the fellows in her life: Stevie, Flat-Top and Mortie. She wound up appearing in a total of 45 issues, all in the 1950s. She started in a smallish, nickel-size digest for seven issues and she has an intriguing story.

There were titles that were aesthetically pleasing and enormous fun to read: *Meet Miss Bliss, My Girl Pearl, Ginger and Jetta* (rocket-powered sweetheart of the future). Alas, they were among more than three dozen 1950s teen humor titles that all lasted less than a dozen issues.

Archie, of course, appeared in more different titles in the 1950s than any comic character in the first 50 years of the industry's history, which began in the mid–1930s. But not many comic collectors realize that at one point during the decade, Patsy Walker appeared in six different titles: *Miss America, Patsy Walker, Patsy and Hedy, Patsy and Her Pals, Wendy Parker* and *Girls' Life*. When Lois Lane got her own comic in 1958, Superman finally overtook Patsy. He appeared in five DC titles and his younger version Superboy starred in two.

Wendy Parker was that most unusual teen humor strip—a college girl—of the 1950s. Howie Howe, when he was drafted out of college after four issues, spent 13 issues in the Army as the only such teen boy of the 1950s. Pearl Dimly was a recent high school athlete and still qualified as a teen, but the star of *My Girl Pearl* was definitely not college material.

Only one other teen humor comic that started in the late 1950s, Marvel's *Kathy, the Teen-Age Tornado*, enjoyed moderate success. Kathy appeared in her first two issues in 1959 and 25 more from 1960 to 1964. She spun her way to a longer non-reprint career than any other non–Archie girl created in the 1950s or the 1960s, and yet Kathy is virtually unknown today.

18

Patsy Walker, Something of a Supergirl

In the first half of 1954, Patsy Walker appeared regularly in a phenomenal six Marvel Comics titles. That was the year that Superman began appearing in six titles, too, with the publication of *Superman's Pal Jimmy Olsen* #1 (September–October 1954), if you count his youthful incarnation Superboy in his own title and in *Adventure Comics*.

Not counting annuals, only Archie and his gang appeared in more titles in 1954: eight. But then, only the Archie characters appeared in more teen humor stories than Patsy Walker and her retinue, Hedy Wolfe, Buzz Baxter and Nancy Brown.

By the end of the 1950s, however, Marvel (also then known to readers and collectors in most of that decade as Atlas) was down to the Patsy Walker and Patsy and Hedy titles. *Miss America* was cancelled in 1958 and *Patsy and Her Pals* departed in 1957, a victim of the Marvel implosion.

Even more intriguing, Patsy was a backup feature in only one Marvel title in 1954—in the last four issues of *Wendy Parker* (see details in the chapter on Wendy).

Although *Girls' Life* lasted only six issues, that was the most unusual comic in which Patsy appeared in 1954. The title ran from #1 (January) through #6 (November). The banner was "Patsy Walker's Own Magazine for Girls!" running on all six covers.

Girls' Life was similar to Miss America in the 1940s, when that title rivaled *Calling All Girls* from *Parents' Magazine* as the leading comic book marketed only to girls. *Girls' Life*, however, had only 36 pages including covers in regular comic book format.

Girls' Life was supposedly edited by Patsy Walker herself! That was a first (and a last) in comic history!

The cover of the first issue stated "Edited by Miss Patsy Walker" and plugged her fashion facts, beauty tips, home advice, love letters and more. The term "home advice" was immediately replaced by "party ideas." The best of the covers—all signed by Al Hartley—was #1, showing Patsy in dungarees, flats and sweater looking into a mirror showing Patsy in an exotic blue ball dress.

A full-page house ad—unusual for Marvel Comics in the mid–1950s—displayed Patsy with the latest issues of all six titles. She's shouting, "GOOD NEWS! Now we can get together regularly in these 6 super simply sensash magazines!" "Sensational" was often "sensash" in teen lingo of the day.

Each issue led off with a typically short Patsy story. The story in #1, "Just a Quiet Evening," is a hoot. It opens with Patsy and the gang enjoying a loud party instead of a study session at the Walkers' home, what with Patsy's father Stanley having mistakenly overruled Patsy's mother Mary, because "Pops" had no idea what would happen. He invited the gang back, but for real study, and after Patsy mutters "Trapped!" Buzz tells her, "Let me handle it, Doll." And so Buzz does, coaxing Mr. Walker into saying, "I can guarantee that I know enough to answer any question in high school science." So Buzz asks him what he knows about Dr. Heinrich Himmelhock and stumps Mr. Walker, who spends the rest of the evening researching the German doctor while the teens spin their platters. Finally, at bedtime, Mary tells him that the doctor is in the phone book! She then advises him as he blows a gasket, "Please, Dear, relax.... I'm sure you'll outsmart them next time!"

In "Heart Clinic," Patsy comes across as motherly, telling a 14-year-old reader, "Personally, I believe 14 is much too young for a girl to wear cosmetics" and advising another reader, "A girl under sixteen is entirely too young to go out on a date with a boy alone."

There is a unique feature never seen in another teen humor comic. On "Patsy's Own Page," she uses two covers of real back issues of *Patsy Walker* with blank word balloons and asks readers to fill in the dialogue. The prize: "A picture of me—Patsy Walker—with my own autograph!" She announced the winners in *Girls' Life* #3 (May), complete with new dialogue, but the contest was discontinued.

Patsy's Appearances in the '50s

Here are Patsy's 1950s appearances:

Patsy Walker #26–86 (61 issues)
Patsy and Hedy #1–67 (67 issues)
Patsy and Her Pals #1–29 (29 issues)
Miss America Volume 7 #29-#93 (65 issues)
Girls' Life #1–6 (6 issues)
Wendy Parker #1–8 (8 issues)

That's a total of 236 issues over a 120-month period—an average just shy of two issues per month.

When Marvel was limited to 96 comics per year (eight per month) beginning late in 1957 and chose to go with 16 bi-monthly titles to be printed

Patsy and Hedy #1, February 1952, copyright 1951 Gem Publications Inc. *Miss America* and *Patsy Walker* sold so well that this third regular title was added. Cover by future *Mad Magazine* great Al Jaffee. All three titles ran more than 100 issues.

by the publisher of DC Comics and distributed by the related Independent News, the company made Patsy its star. Her three primary titles were chosen to continue; only *Patsy and Her Pals* was discontinued. That's an amazing statement about the popularity of the character, who by 1957 had become Marvel's only teen humor feature.

In 1950 and early 1951, Patsy still carried one or two backup strips in each issue of *Patsy Walker* from either or both the teen humor or working girls genres. Beginning with #34 (May 1951) and continuing through #47 (July 1953), it was all Patsy: The backups were Buzz Baxter and Hedy Wolfe stories. Wendy Parker became the backup in #48–54 and a "Dear Patsy" non-humorous romance story was featured in #55–73.

The only genuine crossover story in *Patsy Walker* in the 1950s was in #76 (April 1958) when Millie the Model appeared in a bittersweet story signed by Stan Lee and Hartley (as were almost all Patsy stories in the late 1950s after talented artists Chris Rule and Al Jaffe left the feature earlier in the 1950s).

Millie visits Centerville when offered a nice financial incentive to model dresses. The boys, of course, react with wild enthusiasm when Hedy breaks the news. When the girls realize they are headed for a bleak Saturday night, they decide to go see Millie, too. When Patsy says, "She's not bad looking, is she, Buzz?" he responds, "She makes other girls look like boys!" Soon, Hedy says of Millie, "I'd like to pull out her blonde hair by its black roots!" (Ouch!)

Millie lets the boys down gently while telling them she has a flight to catch back to New York City. (Pretty much all of Marvel's characters lived in New York.) But Millie has made special arrangements for Patsy, Hedy and Nancy: "My boy friend, the famous photographer Clicker Holbrook, is remaining in Centerville to shoot a series on typical teen-age girls!" Clicker, of course, immediately announces, "And I've found just the girls." The girls immediately tell the boys they won't have time for them; Patsy tells Buzz, "He makes you look like a child!" As the story ends, the boys have seen their egos severely dented and Buzz says of females, "They're all fickle!"

In the next story in #76, Patsy is right back with Buzz, as is typical of the entire series. She may be fickle, but not for long! But to earn her date, she had to outwit her father, who insists that she stay home because she's been going out too often with Buzz. Patsy immediately tunes the TV to *Lawrence Silk and His Soda Pop Music*, which her father can't tolerate. When he insists that Patsy just join a nice family conversation, she proceeds to talk about fashion: "Personally, I adore the new cloche look! Of course, it depends on a girl's figure! Now you take Nancy Brown, for example.... She has the darlingest little boufonttte outfit ..." (Note the creative spelling of bouffant!) This drives her father crazy and soon he phones Buzz: "Are you gonna let my daughter sit home alone all night? I thought you wanted to take her out!" And Buzz is back in Patsy's good graces with a typically amusing story.

Patsy Lingers at 52 Pages

Marvel provided evidence of just how important the Patsy Walker franchise was when the *Patsy Walker* title ran 52 pages, covers included, all the way through #52 (May 1954). (The first four issues were 36 pages in 1945–1946.) Several other companies continued to run 52 pages with their best-selling titles into 1954, which was the last year when any regular ten-cent comics were published with more than 36 pages.

While Wendy Parker's own title ran for eight issues in 1953–1954, Patsy's four primary titles ran Wendy backup stories (see the Wendy chapter for the list). But Wendy was the last true teen star for Marvel until another original character, Kathy the Teen-Age Tornado, was introduced in her own title late in 1959. Pearl Dimly was an older teen in the short-lived *My Girl Pearl*, but not a student.

Marvel went big with full-fledged romance titles in the mid–1950s and ran one romance story for a while at that time in Patsy's titles. They appeared in *Patsy Walker* #55–73, *Patsy and Hedy* in #33–54, *Patsy and Her Pals* in #18–29, and *Miss America* in #75–88.

Young high school teacher Miss Bliss, who lasted four issues of her own title in 1955—but deserved much better!—played an amusing role in a four-page story in *Patsy Walker* #82 (April 1959). When Miss Bliss asks Patsy to bring her mother Mary to school, Patsy spends the night worrying about what she did wrong. (In the 1950s, parents were rarely asked to come to school except for parent-teacher conferences and open house nights, and not many schools in most parts of the country asked parents to provide volunteer help.)

Mary arrives with class in session; that would never happen today, because outsiders must check in at the main office of schools. Hedy thinks, "This is too good to be true." But Miss Bliss wants to tell the class that Mary is something special: "Those cookies you baked for the last PTA affair were so delicious that the principal asked if you'd show our cooking class how to bake them?" Mary responds, "Why, I'd be delighted!" By this time, Miss Bliss has turned toward Patsy to say, "You're such a lucky girl to have a mother who's such a wonderful cook..." Patsy faints into the arms of Buzz! And Hedy ends the story in fitting Hedy fashion with this comment about Patsy: "Bah! If she ever fell in a mud hole, she's probably strike oil!"

By 1959, most issues of the titles with Patsy had evolved into comics similar to *Archie's Joke Book*: three or four four- or five-page stories and lots of one-page gag strips along with plenty of pin-ups and fashion pages with paper dolls. In *Patsy Walker* #82, there were only 23 pages of comics of any type.

The one-shots *Hedy Wolfe* (August 1957) and *A Date with Patsy* (September 1957) were routine. Part of the Patsy Walker title looked like leftover

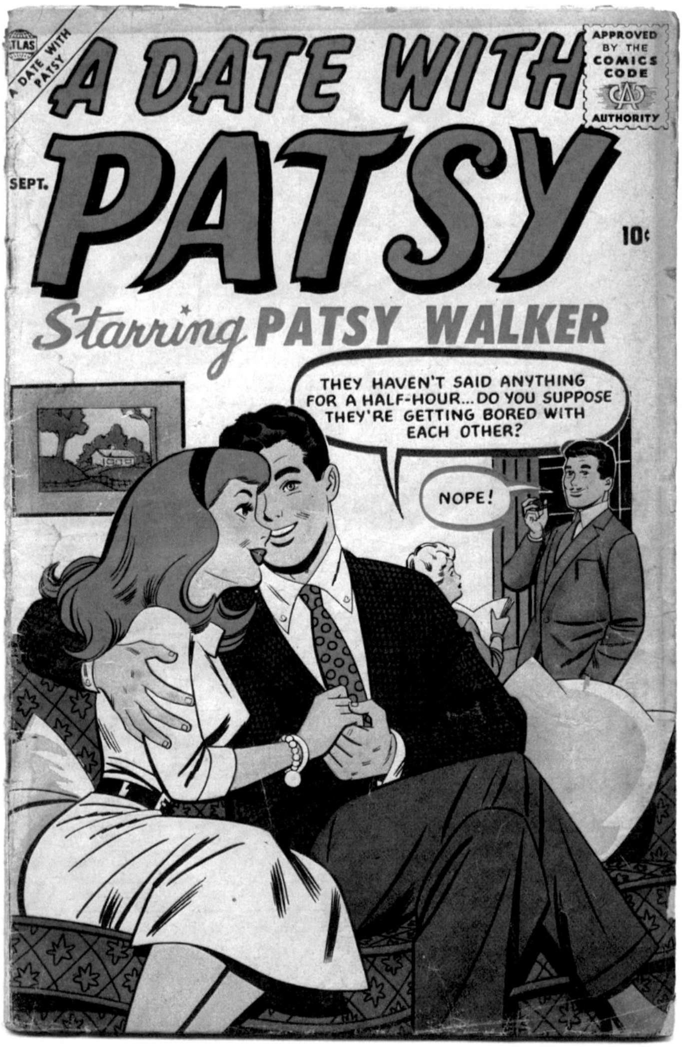

***A Date with Patsy* #1, September 1957, copyright Mutual Magazine Corp. Marvel's Atlas imprint was about to disappear; this one-shot was among the final issues with the Atlas logo. Cover by Al Hartley.**

material from *Girls' Life*. This wasn't surprising, however, and the Marvel comics always did have numerous ad pages in the late 1950s. Almost all the stories in all genres were short.

All told, Patsy and her friends appeared in at least 527 issues from 1944 to 1967 in a total of slightly more than 1350 stories—far more than any other

***Hedy Wolfe* #1, August 1957, copyright Emgee Publications, Inc. Patsy Walker's rival Hedy was in more than 1,300 stories with her, but this one-shot was the only comic with Hedy's full name on the front. Cover by Al Hartley.**

Marvel character to that point. Phrases like "at least" and "slightly more" are necessary because Marvel published so many comics, it is possible a Patsy story or two sneaked into other titles as backups or deadline fillers.

At the end of 1959, Marvel was continuing to make a stronger appeal to girls than any of the six remaining significant comic book publishers. In 1960,

Marvel began its pattern of slowly increasing the number of issues from the late 1957 agreed-upon limitation of 96 issues per year. In 1960, when Marvel had not yet begun to both introduce and revive many superheroes, there were 103 issues—and no fewer than 45 were directly aimed at female readers!

Of the 18 titles in 1960 (a few did not run the entire year), ten were named for characters—four westerns and six of what the boys called "girls' comics" (two other titles were romance comics). It wouldn't be that way for much longer. By 1969, Marvel published 249 comics—and the only non-super-female comic was Millie the Model!

19

DC's Teen Humor: A Favorite in the '50s

DC Comics was nothing if not stable when it came to teen humor in the 1950s.

Archie's domination of the genre was not to be contested; nor was Marvel's amazing Patsy Walker franchise. DC, though, was the only non–Archie company to feature three distinct characters in regular titles for seven full years in the '50s.

Up to the point when *Buzzy* and *Leave It to Binky* suspended publication after their February 1957 issues, leaving only *A Date with Judy* in their teen lineups, there were 169 teen humor issues published across a 74-month span—an average of more than two per month. This includes the runs of *Here's Howie* #1–18 from 1952 to 1954 and *Everything Happens to Harvey* #1–7 in 1953–1954, plus *Scribbly* #9–15 in 1950–1952.

In that 74-month span, the "Big Three" were always at least bi-monthly, with Buzzy Brown and Binky Biggs appearing in 47 issues apiece and Judy Foster in 43.

Total issue publication, however, dropped by more than half across the entire industry from a then-record high of slightly more than 3150 issues in 1952 to about 1500 in 1959. Comic publishers saw their issue totals and sales drop across the board from 1952 to 1956. That helps explains why *Buzzy* #75 (February 1957) and *Leave It to Binky* #58 (also February 1957) were in essence their last issues. Both added issues dated October 1957 and October 1958, however, with no advertising other than house ads.

A Date with Judy was among the most stable comics through the tumultuous end of the Golden Age through the early years of the Silver Age. Judy ran bi-monthly for 13 years, until #79 (November 1960).

Judy featured gorgeous Bob Oksner cover and interior art in most of her final few years, doubtless contributing to her popularity. DC first plugged her TV show on the cover of #26 (December 1951–January 1952) along with her radio show. DC mentioned them all through #57 (March 1957), long after the original runs of both had ended.

The last 52-page issues of the trio were *Buzzy* #39 (September–October 1951), *Binky* #22 (September–October 1951) and *Judy* #25 (October–November 1951). That meant DC had to shift their format primarily to six-page stories instead of the longer tales often used earlier.

These three titles were always highly accessible to young readers who could only imagine their teen years seemingly a long way off. Everything was as clean as could be, although the girls on the covers—and there were always both girls and boys—nonetheless showed their share of skin in casual circumstances. Beach scenes were popular, especially in Judy's title. In the last 26 issues (#54–79), Judy and often her friends appeared in bathing suits no fewer than 18 times!

The covers were often among the most clever in the industry. Clichéd circumstances, such as asking the boy of the piece if there was anything else he wanted to take out in the library—while he ogled the librarian—were generally avoided in favor of more original ideas.

The 1940s emphasis on outrageous slapstick in *Buzzy* didn't extend to the 1950s, when there were different cover artists. Among the best covers was #29 (January–February 1950), when Susie says "Would you like a kiss, Buzzy?" and he answers "Sure, Susie!" while reaching for a piece of candy as her father Homer looks stunned in the next room.

In a beach scene for the cover of *Buzzy* #44 (July–August), he kicks his foot up with a sea creature biting him as Susie tells him, "Oh, Buzzy! How sweet of you to catch a lobster for me!" *Buzzy* #57 (July–August 1954) features Susie enjoying a drive while asking, "Buzzy! Do you prefer a girl with beauty or brains?" and Buzzy says, "Personally, I like a girl with a good head on my shoulders!" Likewise, #65 (July 1955) has the couple leaving a theater as Buzzy asks, "How did you like the movie, Susie?" and she replies, "Terrible! I could hardly sit through it the third time!" The title of the film was *Tropic Romance*.

Cute Covers

Buzzy readers were likely surprised when 1950 issues #32, 33 and 34 and 1951 issue #39 each featured Sheldon Mayer's Scribbly stories involving his fascination with Clover Cooley. They were doubtless intended for *Scribbly* #14, which was delayed a year after the title was suspended with #13. In the Scribbly story in #13 (September–October 1950), Clover is reading the DC romance title *Secret Hearts*, even though the title was suspended with #6 (July–August 1950) and was not resumed until #7 (December 1951–January 1952).

Binky featured a cute cover with #22: Peggy grins on the beach as Binky says, "Oh, Peggy!" while his dog Dopey licked him with his eyes shut. *Binky* #30 (January–February 1953) has a dance-floor scene with Binky saying, "Golly, Peggy, I could waltz like this forever with you!" and she looks startled while muttering, "That's nice, Binky, but this is a rumba!" *Binky* #36 (January 1954) shows Peggy chopping down a fence with her name posted with every boy's name except Binky's. He looks amazed as she explains, "See, Binky? I'm tearing up all my old love letters!" *Binky* #55 (August 1956) shows our hero being hit by a beach ball as he ogles a girl while Peggy warns, "Next time, Binky, keep your eye on the ball, not the belle."

One of *Judy*'s best covers is #32 (December 1952–January 1953), with Judy and a friend straining to fix a flat tire while Oogie and his buddy look on and Oogie says, "You're the ones who were always yelling for equal rights for women!" For #40 (April–May 1954), Oogie tries to cope with three children while Judy reads *How to Baby Sit* and tells him, "Courage, Oogie! I've only got 300 pages to go!" For #44 (December 1954–January 1955), Oogie is surrounded by cheerleaders after a football game while Judy stands aside in her cheerleading uniform and listens to Oogie explain, "But Judy, you wanted me to be a touchdown hero!" In a beach scene for #60 (September 1957), Judy is indignant as a girl with the same bathing suit walks up and hapless Oogie asks her, "Judy, why don't you get yourself a bathing suit like that?"

Howie Drafted for Readers

Not long after DC introduced *Here's Howie* #1 (January–February 1952), the playboy college student was drafted into the Army in #5 (September–October 1952) along with his best buddy Melvin Higby. He even beat Harvey's Sad Sack back into the service.

Nothing was ever said about the Korean War and Howie Howe spent his military stint on U.S. bases, ending with the final issue, #18 (November–December 1954). The stories were consistently funny but for some reason, military humor failed a lot more often than it succeeded in 1950s comics. Atlas tried it at least six times and always struck out despite commendable efforts.

Winnie the WAC appeared in 14 consecutive issues (#5–18) as a backup. Again, she was always funny and nicely drawn, but she was quickly forgotten.

Another DC teen title was *Everything Happens to Harvey* #1–7 (September–October 1953 to September–October 1954). DC tried book-length stories in #1–3, which were rare in teen humor that isn't thinly disguised drama. But apparently they didn't work and DC went back to four short stories per issue.

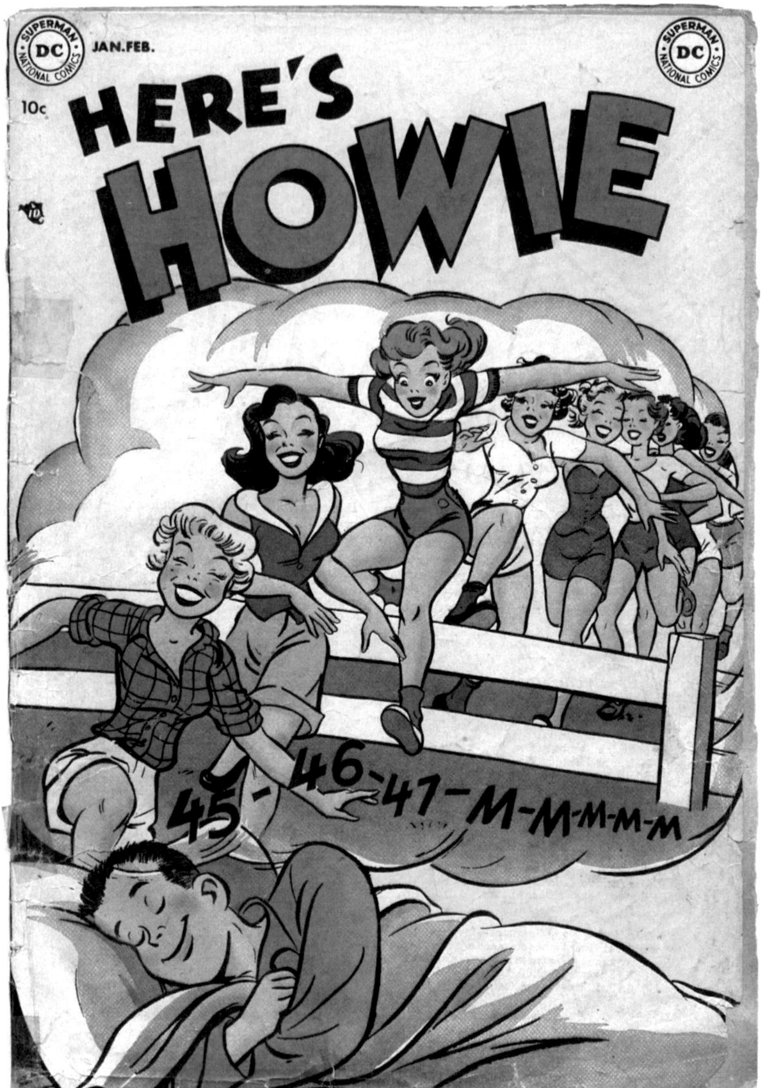

***Here's Howie* #1, January–February 1952, copyright 1951 National Comics Publications. Howie Howe joined the Army in #5, beating Sad Sack's return to the Army in his Harvey title.**

Harvey Payne's covers were always funny, as were the misadventures with his father, a real estate tycoon.

On the cover of #6 (July–August 1954), Harvey is umpiring a girls' softball game and the batter asks, "Well, Harvey, was that last pitch a ball?" The catcher asks, "Or a strike?" as both glower at poor Harvey, who looks as if softball is not his game no matter how pretty the players are.

In an untitled lead story in #6, Harvey's girlfriend Sue can't figure out why Harvey doesn't like her attractive new dress with a star pattern below

***Everything Happens to Harvey* #1, September–October 1953, copyright National Comics Publications, Inc. DC created a clever cover for the first issue, but the title ran only seven issues.**

the waist. But then she's really puzzled when Harvey says he likes her friend Millie's new dress—even though it's identical! Two more women walk by in the same dress and Sue and Millie try to return their frocks. Harvey goes with them but tells the saleswoman, "I don't know why [he doesn't like the dresses] and I don't even know what I'm doing here!" before a box beans Harvey. He tells Sue her replacement dress is "a knockout!" as the amusing story ends.

Harvey actually wasn't bad, but apparently he just had too much competition at DC.

20

The Unique Wendy Parker

Marvel's Wendy Parker was among the most unusual comic book characters of the 1950s, even though she appeared for less than two years.

Wendy was one of the few college students in the teen humor and career girl-working girl humor market of that decade. Possibly because she was different than almost all of Marvel's other humor strips (and far different than those of almost all the comics from other companies), Marvel could not have tried harder to make her a hit.

Amazingly, *Wendy Parker* began as a monthly for its first four issues (#1, July 1953, through #4, October 1953) of its eight-issue run, which finished with a bi-monthly schedule for #5 (January 1954) through #8 (July 1954).

Millie the Model was running monthly in 1953, befitting what was almost surely Marvel's best-selling title, as was *Patsy and Hedy Comics* that year along with *Miss America Comics* with Patsy and Hedy for the last eight months of 1953. Patsy Walker, who starred on the covers and in four monthly or bi-monthly titles that year, was still running bi-monthly in her eponymous comic book and basically would be throughout the title's 20-year, 124-issue run.

But for *Wendy Parker* to begin on a monthly basis was startling. Just as surprising was that along with 24 Wendy Parker stories in her eight-issue run were Patsy Walker backup stories in each issue. That would be similar to DC Comics using strips of its teen leader, *A Date with Judy*, as backups in *Everything Happens to Harvey*, a seven-issue teen humor failure in 1953–1954.

But then, all four Patsy Walker titles ran Wendy Parker backup stories in much of 1953 and '54! That was pretty much unheard of in comic book history at the time: a new character running in five comic books, including her own title, at the same time.

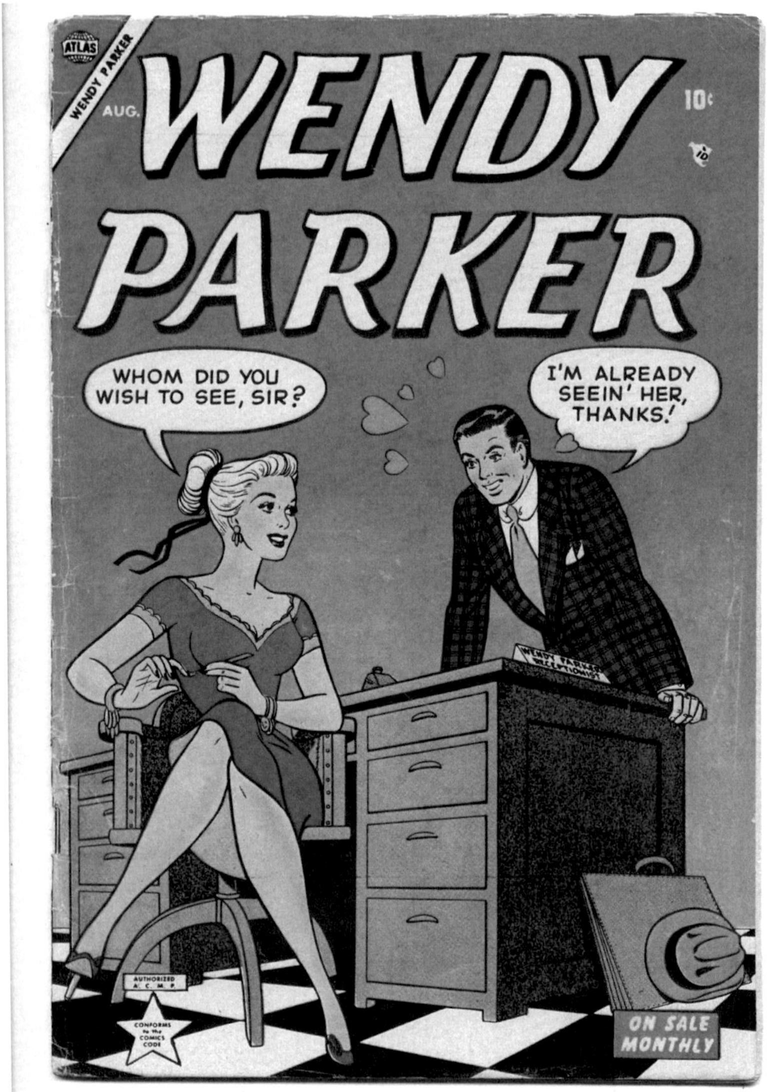

***Wendy Parker* #2, August 1953, copyright Official Magazine Corp. Marvel tried hard to make attractive college student Wendy Parker a hit, but she ran only eight issues. While her series was published, she was a backup in all four Patsy Walker titles.**

Wendy's Big Numbers

The total number of Wendy Parker backup stories was 44 in an 18-month period. The list:

Miss America #53 (June 1953) through #66 (October 1954).
Patsy and Hedy #17 (July 1953) through #32 (December 1954).
Patsy Walker #48 (September 1953) through #54 (September 1954).
Patsy and Her Pals #3 (September 1953) through #9 (November 1954).

One reason Marvel pushed *Wendy Parker* so hard was that the company likely wanted another teen humor hit, since less than a decade earlier, Marvel was unquestionably the postwar leader with no fewer than 20 teen titles alone, along with four career girl titles. By 1953, however, the only Marvel titles in those categories were Patsy Walker's four along with *Millie the Model* when *Wendy Parker* debuted.

But Wendy was destined for only a short run along with most of the firm's attempts at teen and working girl humor after 1953. By far the most successful such post–1953 comic was the three-title incarnation of *A Date with Millie* #1–7 (second series), *Life with Millie* #8–20 and *Modeling with Millie* #21–54 from 1959 to 1967.

Wendy Parker deserved better, even though her stories were almost always basic five- or six-page accounts of confusion among boyfriends, family members, rivals and bosses. It was admirable, especially in 1953 and '54, to see Wendy working her way through college as what today would be called an administrative assistant or office aide. Most colleges in those years were *far* more affordable than they are today. Of course, her work life enhanced the variety of plots she could be involved in.

Unlike most titles from Atlas Comics, as Marvel was known during part of the 1950s, the Wendy Parker stories were not signed by artists or writers. Marvel editor Stan Lee not only signed much of his own work along with the artist, but he did not automatically erase artists' signatures. (It wasn't until the 1960s that comics officially began to credit artists and writers, and Marvel was the first company in that regard.)

The first Wendy Parker story appeared with no cover fanfare in *Miss America* #53 (June 1953) and was typical of the jams she would often find herself in. Timmy Foster, whom she described as her "semi-steady" in the story, was busy studying for a psychology class test, so she wanted to go to the big dance with Ken Collins, whom she acknowledged to a friend was dating Sherry Schloggelholtz (Marvel loved having fun with names at times). When Ken greets Wendy with a smile on campus and asks if she will be home at six p.m., she agrees to meet with him, thinking he's sure to surprise her with a ticket to the dance. She turns down another prospective date request from her friend Foxie, only to learn she won't be going to the dance after all. Ken just wanted to ask her to help pick out a corsage to match Sherry's red dress! Wendy kicks him out of her house. When her father asks her why she's not at the dance, she responds, "Daddy—you should know how unimportant a dance is to me!" Wendy was always a master at trying to save face.

Unlike most comics companies of the period, Marvel ran a house ad at the end of the story, with big letters declaring "She's here to stay!" followed by "Queen of the teen-agers! Belle of the campus! Not-so-sophisticated young modern! The apple of her father's eye! That's Wendy Parker! And you'll see her every month—in every issue of Miss America Comics!"

There was no mention of the soon-to-be-published *Wendy Parker* #1. In fact, *Miss America* #54 (July 1953) plugged Wendy's addition to the lineup in *Patsy and Her Pals* but did not mention the debut of her own magazine, dated the same month! But.... *Wendy Parker* #1 received this plug (at the end of the Patsy Walker story) in *Miss America* #55 (August 1953):

> What is everything? Everything is good, clean wholesome humor ... a beautiful girl with a figure to match ... a natural charm ... tops in teens ... college romance ... written and drawn by your favorite artists! [No, the artists usually didn't write the stories.] Put them all together and they spell one thing.... Wendy Parker ... and Wendy Parker Comics.

The Wendy Parker stories were drawn with a special dignity not always afforded teen humor stories, which tended to contain an oversupply of slapstick antics.

The first issue of *Wendy Parker* made no attempt to introduce the characters, nor were there any story titles. In the opening story, Wendy's Latin instructor asks Timmy to tutor Wendy in preparation for exams at an unnamed college. Wendy coaxes Timmy to take her on dates involving anything but study. But Wendy finally cracks her books and gets a 95. Timmy, in contrast, did not and "failed miserably," as the teacher says, while asking Wendy to tutor Timmy!

Wendy soon gains a rival, Laura Lee, to add to the consistent pattern of circumstantial complications involving Wendy's relationships with everyone in her orbit. For example, in *Wendy Parker* #4 (October 1953), Laura tells Wendy that she should not want Timmy winning the college field day competition because if he does, he will become so popular that Wendy will have many rivals. Wendy thus tries to wear out Timmy but only succeeds in tiring herself so badly that she misses his winning performance. Timmy tells her that he has won and will use the $100 prize to buy her a special birthday gift. Remember, $100 in 1953 was worth more than $1000 in today's dollars. The story finishes with a clinch and Wendy thinking, "Oh.... I hope Timmy never finds out how hard I tried to stop him."

If you get the impression that Wendy was occasionally shallow and impulsive, you would be right. But her portrayal is not always so, and Wendy is basically a decent young woman, even if the sometimes misogynistic storylines sometimes betray that.

In *Wendy Parker* #8 (July 1954), the last issue, there is no indication she will not reappear. But this, of course, is typical of almost all comics of the Golden Age. In fact, at the end of one of Wendy's last stories, the publisher ran a house ad for *Girl's Life*, the sixth Patsy Walker vehicle to appear regularly in 1954. Patsy, the purported editor, writes:

> Dear Everybody: Here we are only in our fourth issue and you wonderful readers have made *Girls' Life* the most terrific success in the publishing world! And your thousands of wonderful letters have made me the happiest gal in the world! I read 'em all, every single letter! Love to you, every one of you! P.S. Be sure to look for the readers' own corner in *Girls' Life*!

Girls' Life ran only two more issues. Ironically, Atlas-Marvel did well enough in 1954 to lead the industry with 379 issues published, as noted by comics historian Dan Stevenson's year-by-issue list.

Homer Hooper Strikes Out

Other than Wendy Parker and the Patsy Walker titles, the only new teen humor comic book Marvel introduced in the 1953–1959 period—until *Kathy* debuted late in 1959—was *Homer Hooper*. His title ran from #1 (July 1953) through #4 (December 1953) and was the least successful teen humor character Marvel ever introduced in his own title, even though the comic book's banner was "The Funniest Teen in Town."

Most of the covers and stories were signed by artist Hy Rosen, never a well-known comic book artist. The majority of the material was recycled from Marvel's nine-year history (by 1953) of teen humor jokes and plots. For example, the cover of #4 has a female library worker asking Homer, "Is there anything special you'd like to take out?" to which Homer responds "Yeah.... When do you finish working?" This joke appeared often in teen humor comics.

The first story in #4 was typical: After an uncharacteristic two weeks of good behavior, Homer makes a paper airplane note to his girl and the paper strikes Miss Hacksaw in her behind. "This is probably how the Wright Brothers started!" he tells her, only to be sent to Principal Pillpot's office with the response, "The Ritz Brothers would be more like it!" The principal is in a good mood before Homer arrives in his office: "Maybe now I'll get a chance to read some of those confiscated comic books." Homer demonstrates his technique with the principal's in-box paper but a wind gust takes the plane and causes havoc until it's recovered. It is, of course a note from Miss Hacksaw commending Homer for two weeks of good behavior—an element echoing an earlier story in *Leroy* (see Chapter 28).

Homer's girlfriend Jeanie had no connection with Marvel's 1940s Jeanie.

There is a wild, if incredibly sexist by today's standards, "Life at Midville High" strip starring the girls in the Homer Hooper strip. Coach Fungo (!) forms a girls' softball team and tells the girls, "Let's get warmed up by catch-

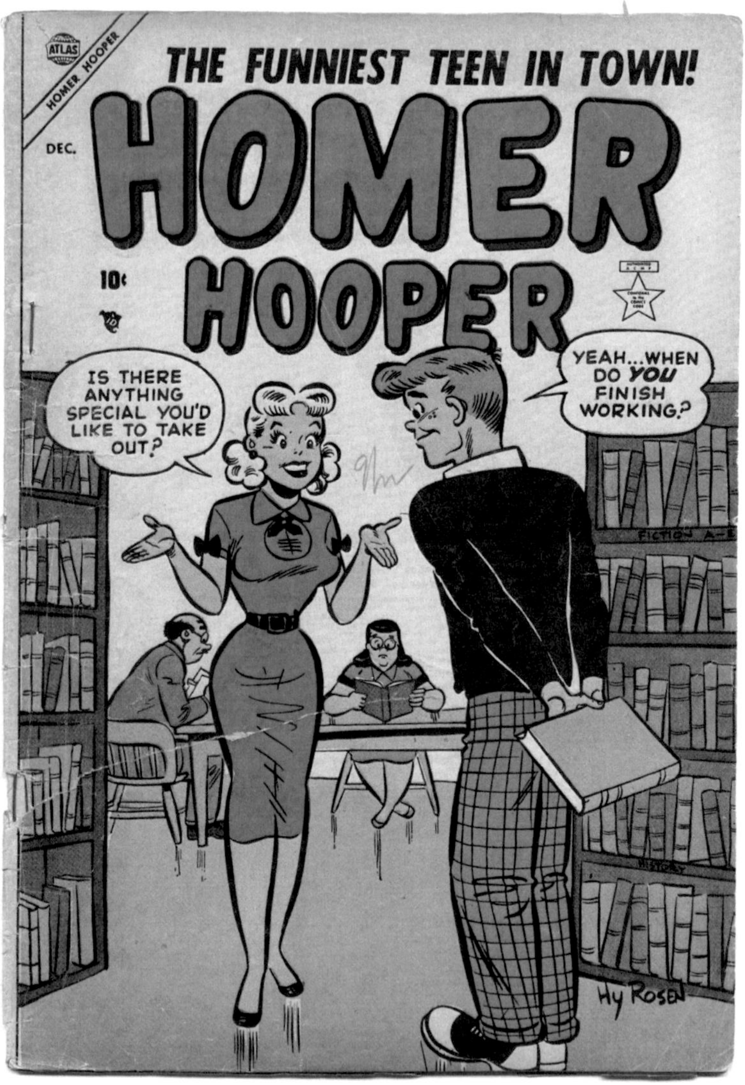

Homer Hooper #4, December 1953, copyright Animirth Comics, Inc. This is the last issue of Marvel's Homer, who like many teen humor boys in the 1950s did not last long. Cover by Hy Rosen.

ing a few infield flies." Jeanie's rival, Rita Dunn, quips, "You can use Jeanie, Coach! She attracts [flies] better than anything I know." The entire story is filled with puns like that until Jeanie provides the capper by running toward home plate and clobbering Rita with a catcher's mitt while shouting, "Touchdown! I did it! I hit a touchdown!"

And to think that two decades later, millions of girls would begin playing interscholastic high school sports in earnest with the passage of the Federal Title IX law!

21

My Girl Pearl: Dumb and Dumber

My Girl Pearl was unique among Marvel Comics, the industry's largest line of comics marketed primarily to girls during the ten-cent era.

Among more than three dozen such titles involving teenagers and career girls at Timely-Atlas-Marvel comics from 1944 through the final ten-centers in 1961, Pearl Dimly was the only character to devolve from working girl to "the teen-age doll," as the covers bannered her.

Blame it all on the creativity of longtime editor Stan Lee, who spent much of his time writing about teenagers and young working women—and signing much of it—in the decade immediately before he began to create the most unusual line of superheroes in the field's history.

In fact, Lee went from either or both writing and editing eight titles for girls—half of the Marvel line!—in the second half of 1960 to becoming the most fondly regarded creator, writer and editor in comics history, thanks to the superhero groups.

Just imagine: Only months after writing the last issue of *My Girl Pearl* in 1961, Lee penned the debut of the Fantastic Four that year. Talk about versatility!

It's no wonder Stan flashed a wide grin and said, "Oh, you remember Pearl?" when I told him I had never forgotten reading *My Girl Pearl* in the late 1950s. This was fully four decades later at one of the annual dinners that the American Association of Comic Book Collectors, of which I was a board member, gave in the 1990s to celebrate both fandom and as many highly regarded professionals as we could pack in one room during Comic-Con International in San Diego.

Lee was well aware that *My Girl Pearl* was not the type of comic book that could ever be done today. This was during the height of the "dumb blonde" craze and well before everything changed forever—and so much for the better—with *The Feminine Mystique*, *Ms.* magazine and women's liberation.

In *My Girl Pearl*'s first incarnation, she was dubbed "America's Darling Dim-Wit" atop the covers of #1 (April 1955) through #4 (October 1955). For her two-issue return with #5 (July 1957) and #6 (September 1957), the banner phrase was "She's Beautiful, But Oh So Dumb!"

My Girl Pearl #4, October 1955, copyright Margood Publishing Corp. Sometimes a backup character, Pearl Dimly had three cracks at success from 1955 to 1961 in her own series, but never made good despite Dan De Carlo's covers and interior art in the first six issues.

When Pearl and dozens of other characters disappeared with the Marvel Implosion late in 1957 in the wake of a financial disaster caused by a distribution crisis, nobody knew if she would ever return. But return she did in *My Girl Pearl* #7 (August 1960) through #11 (April 1961), but this time as "The Teen-Age Doll."

Dan De Carlo illustrated the covers and art for the first six issues and Stan Goldberg portrayed Pearl's covers and art the final five. Lee signed almost all the stories as writer.

Pearl Returns in High School

For her third incarnation, Pearl Dimly was surprisingly several years younger, although no more competent in coping with the many multiple meanings of English terms. But the words "dim-wit" and "dumb" would never again appear on any comic books referring to the female of the species.

It says a lot about both 1950s society in general and the Comics Code Authority, founded in 1954, that the organization had no trouble accepting "dim-wit" and "dumb" on a humor title about a youthful working woman but had banned words like "terror" and "horror" from the covers of fantasy titles.

My Girl Pearl's return to the newsstands gave Marvel eight titles marketed to girls among the 16 titles the firm published in the second half of 1960. The others included two romance titles, two Patsy Walker teen titles, two Millie the Model comics and Kathy, which was a teen humor comic that ran bi-monthly for 27 issues from 1959 to 1964. (See Kathy's chapter.)

Publisher Martin Goodman and editor Lee were limited to eight comics per month in 1958 and 1959—only 96 total issues compared to more than 400 they produced in 1956—in a distribution agreement with Independent News Distributors, owned by National Comics (DC). The Marvel powers decided on 16 bi-monthly titles per year and made several changes in the 1958–1960 period. In 1960, Marvel somehow managed to publish 103 issues—including eight issues that year for the science fiction–weird titles *Journey Into Mystery, Tales of Suspense* and *Tales to Astonish* and seven for *Strange Tales.*

Thus, for the second half of 1960, Marvel marketed eight titles to girls and eight to boys, including the four weird-story comics and four westerns: *Gunsmoke Western, Kid Colt, The Rawhide Kid* and *Two-Gun Kid*. Marvel expanded its numbers considerably every year for the rest of the 1960s, more than doubling from 122 issues in 1961 to 249 in 1969, as indexed by comics historian Dan Stevenson.

In the longest of all *My Girl Pearl* stories, the eight-page lead story in #1, the splash panel said it all as a cab driver asks Pearl, "Do you want a cab, lady?" to which Pearl responds, "My goodness, are you giving it away?" There followed dozens of such jokes in a comic book unique in 1955. Many involved Pearl's tendency to take questions and comments literally and her inability to understand how the same words could mean entirely different things, at least in English. Nuance was not her name. (We can only imagine Pearl responding, "No, my name is Pearl!")

"Say, are you trying to pull my leg?" the handsome young cabbie asks her. "Goodness, no! I can't even reach it from here," she replies from the back seat.

When the cabbie seeks the help of a traffic cop who knows Pearl, he tells the driver that Pearl works at 655 Madison Avenue, which just happened to be the Manhattan address of Marvel's editorial headquarters! When Pearl arrives at work, we meet her co-worker Daphne Dazzle; her boss Mr. Wortle; and Wortle's love-struck son Marvin, who offers to change her name and asks for her hand, both with predictable results. When the cabbie returns the purse Pearl has left in his cab, he gets a bowling date with her and tells her his name is Flash Grogan. Later in #1, we meet Pearl's roommate Nan Smith and their long-suffering landlady, Mrs. Lumpkin, along with Nan's boyfriend Ronald.

The cover of #2 is the funniest of all, in part because it doesn't involve an obvious synonym. Sitting on a park bench, Flash woos Pearl: "Pearl, when I'm with you I'm dizzy! I'm feverish! I can't eat or sleep! Say those three words that mean so much to me!" Pearl touches her beautifully done lips and responds: "See your doctor!"

On the regular four-panel single pages, "Pearl's Pearls of Wisdom," Wortle tells her, "Pearl Dimly! I don't pay you to sit and polish your nails!" She tells him, "That's okay! I'll do it for nothing!"

On the cover of #3 (August 1955), Pearl is about to jump into an empty pool when Flash warns her, "Pearl! The pool is empty!" She tells him, "Good! I hate crowds!" The cover of #4 is just as funny, as a motorcycle cop stops Pearl and asks her, "Where's the fire, lady?" and she answers with Dimly logic, "I don't know, but if I see one, I'll call you!"

In #4, the less-than-bright Sturdley Blump makes a guest appearance "by permission of *Meet Miss Bliss* Comics," a concurrent publication that ran only four issues (see the chapter on *Meet Miss Bliss*). Sturdley gives De Carlo one of the few guy strips he ever illustrated. The funniest Pearl story in #4 involves a burglar who goes nuts trying to rob Pearl and asks a cop for "a nice quiet cell."

With the nearly two-year gap between #4 and #5, it's understandable that Flash returns with black hair, *sans* cab, in both #5 and #6, which contain a plethora of laugh-out-loud one- and two-page jokes.

Three years later, Pearl surprised readers who remembered her by showing up on the cover of #7 in a high school classroom. Lee used younger versions of Pearl and Flash, and Mr. Wortle became the principal instead of the boss in the office. On the cover, Miss Agony, a gray-haired Miss Grundy type, tells her dunce, "Pearl!! You scored 20 percent on this test!! How do you explain that??!" Pearl throws up her arms and explains, "I've been studying real hard!!" as her classmates explode in laughter.

Pearl gets new friends, Hortense and Liz, and a twin sister, Shirl, for the five-issue run of the high school version of Miss Dimly (no Ms. then), but we don't see Pearl's parents. Lee recycles some of the gags, such as how Pearl meets Flash. All five issues are filled with high school fun with Pearl & Co.; there are no other strips. Beginning in #8 (October 1960), Pearl is given a cute bob haircut for the rest of the series.

So, what replaced *My Girl Pearl* on the Marvel docket? *Amazing Adventures* #1 (June 1961) is the answer. But *Amazing Adventures* gave way to *Amazing Adult Fantasy* with #7, which in turn became *Amazing Fantasy* #15 with the last issue. And even Pearl Dimly must know that *The Amazing Spider-Man* debuted in *Amazing Fantasy* #15 …

22

The Joy of Meeting Miss Bliss

One of the last of the many "working girl" or "career girl" characters created or adapted for Timely-Marvel-Atlas Comics from 1944 to 1955, the vast majority by Stan Lee, was also the least successful. Yet the little-known *Meet Miss Bliss* #1–4 (all 1955) deserved a much better fate than a run of only four issues, all with the ironic cover plug "Now in Her Own Magazine!"

The quips and jokes in these four issues, all written by Lee and illustrated by Al Hartley, likely went over the heads of most of the young readers the title was intended for. *Meet Miss Bliss*—what a pun!—starred vibrant 20-something blonde beauty Betty Bliss in her first job as the teacher of the few junior high school teens ever to appear in the Marvel line.

Even in the pre–Comics Code days before 1955, very few humorous comic book titles—or characters in the teen titles—presented gorgeous teachers and high school boys mixing together. Romance comics occasionally did so, since they were primarily designed to be read by older teen girls and young adults. But the 13- and 14-year-old junior high school types were safe; it was the faculty men who ogled Miss Bliss.

Comics books seldom were shy about boasting about the popularity of their characters, whether well-established like Marvel teen queen Patsy Walker or virtual unknowns like Betty Bliss.

The cover of *Meet Miss Bliss* #1 (May 1955) boasted "All-New Adventures of America's Favorite School Teacher!" The scene outside Centerville Junior High School showed a boy about 13 telling classmates, "I'm holding teacher's books" while enchanted male faculty member Don Grant stands behind the object of his obvious affections and tells her, "I'm holding teacher!" Another box in the bottom right corner boasts, "You'll love the students and faculty of Centerville Junior High!"

On the opening page of the untitled first story, Miss Bliss meets Principal Periwinkle Potter and Miss Murkle, a kindly, white-haired Miss Grundy–type teacher. They introduce Miss Bliss to gym teacher and coach Whiz Wilson and English teacher and drama coach Don Grant, both of whom instantly fall for Miss Bliss but otherwise could not be more different. Along the way, the school janitor, the bald Curley, sees Miss Bliss for the first time and tells Miss Murkle, "My my! Those gal students are getting' purtier all the time!" to

***Meet Miss Bliss* #1, May 1955, copyright Leading Magazine Corp. *Betty Bliss* ran only four issues but they were all amusing. She returned as part of the faculty at Patsy Walker's Centerville High. Cover by Al Hartley.**

which Miss Murkle responds, "She's not a girl student!" Curley mutters, "Well, if she's a boy, I'll eat my hat!" When informed Miss Bliss is a new teacher, he responds, "If she's a teacher, I'm gonna go back to school!" Miss Murkle instantly replies, "If you go back to school, I'm gonna quit teaching!" That's the flavor of a clever book filled with fun.

The students pop up in the third story, soon after school nurse Mary Meeke confesses in the second story to Miss Bliss that Whiz Wilson "doesn't seem to notice that I'm alive." The quick-witted Miss Murkle interjects, "Humph! That muscle-bound blow-hard doesn't even know that he's alive!"

The first student we meet is the Big Moose–like Sturdley, who answers this question from Miss Bliss: "Sturdley, do you know Lincoln's Gettysburg address?" with "Gosh, no! Is he still living there?" Then we meet young genius Thackery Van Thwerp, whose father is the town's billionaire, and Buster Bailey, who has trouble staying awake in class, much less learning properly. Lee shows how wise he is as a writer by not over-using the wacky kids. Instead, Miss Bliss and Donald Grant try to buy a used car in the hilarious fourth story before both decide riding the bus to work isn't so bad after all.

On the cover of #2, the principal says, "This is the only classroom where the children volunteer to stay in after school!" as Miss Bliss stands in front of three boys, who are apparently seeing their incipient hormones being a bit stimulated. But it's all in fun; at no time in the series is there anything suggestive.

The third story in #2 has one of the best lines, when Miss Bliss notices that Buster Bailey has a shiner, and he tells her when she asks about his opponent, "Tommy Brown.... But once he gets out of bed, he'll be as good as new!" When Miss Brooks responds, "Buster, you know what I think of fighting," he replies, "Natch! Who ever heard of a woman fighting?!!!" But at the end of the story, when Miss Bliss learns from Buster that he was defending the honor of the teachers at Centerville, she treats him to a strawberry soda.

The fourth story is the best in #2, when Miss Bliss takes a trip to Hollywood for a screen test and finds that cattle calls are not fun. She gets an earful when she hears film star Hedy DeVine—yes, that Hedy DeVine, whose Marvel series *Hedy of Hollywood* was cancelled in 1952—complaining bitterly and walking off the set. Miss Bliss promptly returns to Centerville Junior High, where she tells the folks, "I'm back where I belong ... where I'm happy!"

In the first story in #3 (September 1955), school board president Bigg Weel and his assistant tour Centerville High. The principal and teachers assume that the handsome, tall half of the pair is Bigg Weel and the balding small guy is his aide. So the teachers talk honestly to the little man about their fondness for their school and their students despite salaries smaller than those of day laborers and typists. When the little guy asks why they still want to work as teachers, Betty Bliss tells him, "Because teaching is important! The future of our nation depends upon our youngsters …" and Don Grant adds, "And their education depends on us! We couldn't quit teaching any more than a doctor could quit caring for his patients.... We're needed!" The teachers provide several other examples of dedicated teachers before the truth comes out. The real Bigg Weel tells the principal while pointing at the teachers, "As long as this nation has schools and teachers like these … we need have no fear for the future of our children!" This is a lovely piece of Americana and a heartfelt appreciation of education from Stan Lee.

The students appear in the second and fourth stories, which are wacky tales about what happens in drama tryouts and art class.

Oddly, none of the four issues has a number on the covers, only the month. Marvel must have done this on purpose, since it was commonly known that publishers and/or editors sometimes felt that a low number was not good for circulation expectations.

Music lessons and an outdoors field trip are fodder for funny stories in #4 (November 1955), but the third story is more touching than humorous. Betty decides to help a weary, discouraged Don grade papers and Don confesses that he would like to marry her. She demurs a bit with a sexy smile and he laughs while saying, "Just like a woman … make a man confess his feelings, and then deny hers!" But she still leaves him feeling like he has a chance, just as she does in the fourth story. It's a pity that the comic ended here, but we are definitely left with the feeling that Mr. Grant will find Bliss!

23

Henry Aldrich and the Dell Teens

Dell Comics always had a media connection of sorts for its teen humor titles, with none stronger than Henry Aldrich, whose name was likely more recognizable than Archie himself on the teen scene from 1950 to 1954.

In the early 1950s, when Henry made a 22-issue run with Dell, there were precious few potential readers of any age who had not heard of him. His radio show *The Aldrich Family* ran from 1939 to 1953, and few were more popular. His television show of the same name aired from 1949 to 1953. There were, of course, the 11 Henry Aldrich movies from Paramount in 1939-1944.

By 1954, *The Aldrich Family* had been cancelled on both radio and television and no new Henry Aldrich films had been made in a decade. That's why Dell (Western Printing and Lithographing) canceled the comic book with #22 (September-November 1954). By then Henry Aldrich appeared quarterly instead of bi-monthly, a sign of declining sales.

As Bill Schelly commented in his groundbreaking book *John Stanley: Giving Life to Little Lulu* (2017), "The *Aldrich Family* TV show, the prototype for teen-oriented situation comedy, debuted in 1949. Henry, an awkward teen, is best remembered for this opening exchange: When his mother calls 'Hen-reeeeeeeeeeeee! Hen-ree Al-drich!' he answers in a breaking adolescent voice, 'Com-ing, Mother!'" The radio show and the movies began the same way.

Schelly noted that Stanley, who became best known for his work on *Little Lulu*, wrote all but one (#3) of the first eight issues in his initial collaboration with the established humor artist Bill Williams, so Henry could not have had a stronger start. It's noteworthy that Henry did not have to spend any time on Dell's Four-Color list; he began his regular series right from #1, an April 1950 issue according to Dell's publication code on the first comic page but undated in the indicia. It was quite an honor at Western-Dell, who knew exactly what they had: Below the cover logo was a large box reading, "Coming, Mother! Right from radio and television to the comic book pages."

In the opening story of #1, Henry's father Sam is worried about Henry possibly going for a tattoo with buddy Homer. After ten pages of complications, Sam is gratified that Henry had the good sense not to get a tattoo but the next day Henry gives his mother, Alice, a pigskin wallet. "But notice the highly original feature—it's got a beautiful design with 'Mother' tattooed on it! I'll bet nobody ever thought of that before!"

In the second story, a 15-pager, Henry finds himself locked out of the house in the middle of the night. He talks Homer into helping him with a ladder but Homer says he needs help getting the ladder back home. Henry props open a door with a chair but his parents discover that and think a burglar may have been involved. Finding himself locked out again, Henry is forced to elude a police car and spends the night sleeping outside next to Homer.

As Dell boasted on so many covers, "52 pages—ALL COMICS!" *Henry Aldrich* was among the best entertainment bargains possible for a dime!

No matter how many complications Henry found himself involved in, Stanley had the unique knack of making them sound somehow plausible for a teen like Henry. Stanley was always a superb storyteller.

Williams not only drew some of the best interior art in any teen humor comic, but also consistently funny sight-gag covers. On the cover of #3, Henry and comic book girlfriend Geraldine are sharing two sodas as six boys say hello to her and Henry looks peeved. The cover of #5 found Henry and three friends standing outside a car, searching their pockets for enough money to pay for a gallon of gas. The cover of #10 (February–March 1952) shows a book titled *How to Confuse Your Neighbors* as Henry uses newspapers and a brush to make his shadow on the window resemble the outline of a shapely woman. On #16 (March–May 1953), Homer heads toward the refrigerator only to find a locked safe in its place as Henry laughs.

The Aldrich family was created by playwright Clifford Goldsmith for the 1938 play *What a Life!* and he retained the copyright on the characters. Jimmy Lydon played Henry in the 1939–44 series of 11 Paramount films.

Andy Hardy in the Comics

Western-Dell gave Andy Hardy a six-issue alternate comic book universe from 1952 to '54, well after the last of the Andy Hardy film series except for the 1958 reunion film. His parents, so important in the films, are not part of the comic series. Only girlfriend Polly Benedict and close friend Beezy are recognizable names, along with the town of Carvell.

The series is more than competent wild-and-crazy slapstick, about as far removed from the films as possible. The first issue, *Four Color* #389 (April 1952 by Dell's date code), includes a cute story in which Andy salvages a crazy haircut by playing an Indian in the school play. Andy appeared in three more *Four Color* issues—#447, 480 and 515—before earning what seemed to be the start of a regular series with #5 (February–April 1954). But #6 skipped four months and was dated September–November 1954 as the last issue.

Dell turned a series by *Little Lulu* creator Marjorie Henderson Buell into the *Blythe Four-Color* #1072 (February–April 1960), a cute title about a youngish teen, and Dell much earlier used a series by famed cartoonist and author Betty Betz to create the *Dollface and Her Gang Four Color* #309 (January 1951). Both appeared only once but were charming strips of young teen girls and how they dealt with both boys and girls. They are fun reads because the art is different and the cartoonists have pro-level talent.

Linda Walter's King Features Syndicate strip *Susie Q. Smith* was given *Four Color* issues #323, 377, 453 and 553 between 1951 and '54. As clever as the art was, the series never earned a regular Dell series, even though these characters richly deserved one.

In Susie's Dell debut in #323 (March 1951), she slaps a man, Sylvester S. Spookle, for trying to steal a kiss. The boy who has turned out to be her real secret admirer, Hutch Hopkins, rescues Susie when she tumbles into the lake. Susie, never shy about expressing opinions or emotions, begins to sob because her clothes and hair are drenched when Hutch drags her to shore. Hutch says, "Gee, don't talk like that, Susie! To me you're the most fabulous lookin' woman in the world!" setting up a nifty series of nicely rendered stories by Walter. Walter had a very appealing way of drawing all the teens in the strip, especially Susie and her friend Legs O'Hara. Legs, as her name indicates, is a glamour girl while Susie is the dreamer but highly attractive in her way. These Susie Q. Smith stories are fine Americana and well worth reading, incredible slapstick aside.

In "Some Men Are Mature and Some Men Are Just Plain Elderly"—Walter uses strip titles—Legs and Susie argue and won't speak to each other, but they come back to each other when they discover their handsome new teacher has a wife and four children.

24

Jetta, Teen-Age Sweetheart of 2052

Three of the scarcest 1950s comics in any genre consist of the all-too-short run of Dan De Carlo's *Jetta* from Standard Comics.

Fortunately, the Jetta stories aren't hard to find if you just want to read them—which you should if you care at all about one-of-a-kind titles. Famed comics historian Craig Yoe edited and designed a 2010 IDW reprint book of all three issues; he borrowed them from me, and they were scanned by Bob Carter.

Outside of the Archie Series, not many teen humor comics from the 1940s and 1950s have been reprinted, in part on the theory that few are all that memorable no matter how scarce they are today. But Yoe knew a classic series when he first saw it.

Jetta appeared in comics a decade before the Jetsons did on television and in Gold Key comics, so Jetta and her retinue were trailblazers, although these cute characters weren't marketed in any special way other than the banner line on the cover "TEEN-AGE SWEETHEART OF THE 21st CENTURY." There was no indication that Standard comics editor Joe Archibald—a standout pulp and teen readers fictioneer for many years in the fields of sports and airplane stories—realized just how different these comics were. However, he was familiar with the same publisher's Thrilling Publications science fiction pulps, including flagship titles *Thrilling Wonder Stories* and *Startling Stories*.

Dan De Carlo (1919–2001) drew thousands of teen humor and career girl stories for Marvel and Archie, beginning in the late 1940s and continuing for about half a century. But he somehow received the *Jetta* assignment from Standard. De Carlo signed most of his stories for editor Stan Lee at Marvel, which freely allowed artists to sign their work, but De Carlo did not sign the *Jetta* stories, likely because he was not a Standard employee.

His work on *Jetta*, while mostly inked by others, is easy to identify. De Carlo confirmed that he penciled all nine *Jetta* stories and the three covers.

How good are these? Yoe correctly quoted me in his introduction: "Three of the funniest comic books ever produced by the unforgettable Dan De Carlo."

And how good was De Carlo? Stan Lee told Yoe, "Not only does Dan De Carlo illustrate in one of the most attractive and cheerful styles imaginable, but his characters have a unique quality that seems to sparkle on every page. His drawings are so appealing, so crisp, so full of life and good humor, that just looking at them makes you want to smile."

The cover of #5 (December 1952) sets the tone for the series: Mini-skirted, V-necked, red-booted Jetta Raye and her sweetheart Arky (wearing a Neutron High futuristic jersey) are arm in arm as Arky says, "What d'ya say, Space Pigeon! Let's get the ol' hot saucer and beat sound to Nick's Blast-In." Jetta replies with the best phrase of the series, "Now you're cooking with super-atomic radiation, Arky!"

In the first story, "Man Trouble!," set in the year 2052, characters Biff, Gizmo and exotic newcomer Hilaria Hale are introduced. Gizmo, the teen genius, avoids paying off a $5 debt to Arky by creating a remote control, anti-gravity baton for the majorette contest. Everything goes awry when Arky can't control it and it's up to Jetta to soothe the Arky's wounded pride after Hilaria beats him with the runaway baton.

Everything is all about the future except for inflation, making Arky's $5 debt especially laughable when read from the standpoint of today's real 21st century world.

Jetta and the Jetmobile

In the second story, "Jet Jaunt," Jetta's mom ruins the family jetmobile, but her father calls the Mad Martian, his car dealer, and orders a replacement so Arky can take Jetta to the prom. When the car arrives, the teens are astonished to see a 1952 Oldsmobile (or so it seems). Turns out that dear old Dad explained, "I'm a member of the Old Timers Auto Club! … Isn't it a beaut?" Arky saves the day by installing an old helicopter propeller so the car can make it to the dance at the Flying Saucer Inn, high above the Earth, while a classmate yells, "Get a horse!"

Some things never change, as De Carlo and the unidentified writer knew all too well.

The third story, "My Cosmic Hero," opens with Jetta and Arky attending an old movie starring Humphrey Gocart, whom Jetta hero-worships and Arky mocks. But Arky is soon destined to encounter a "girl space bandit" and is kidnapped. He fools her into thinking he wants to join her and soon she drops her "ray gat" into space. Enough craziness ensues for the police to capture the femme fatale. But Arky can't win: On the visi-screen, Jetta saw him kiss the villainess.

The highlight of #6 (February 1953), the second issue, is "Pardon My Power," in which Arky and Biff are preparing to lead Neutron High in the championship space football game against Supersonic High. Biff deliberately miswires Arky's rocket belt and Arky finds himself on "space ship re-fueling station No. 416." But the gas jockey says he's an old Neutron grad and fills Arky with high-speed fuel, giving him more power than all the other players combined. The result finds Arky scoring 176 points in the last two minutes and winning the right to take Jetta to the victory dance. Arky comes down with a case of "rocket fuel radiation" and Biff dances with Arky after all, proving that good guys don't always win.

In #7 (April 1953), the third issue, "Act Your Age" finds Gizmo inventing a device for Arky that turns spinster instructor Miss Gorgon and Dean Foible younger with a "youthifying machine" after Jetta and Hilaria think Biff and Arky have made too much fun of the old faculty members. The girls are thrilled to see the young versions of Gorgon and Foible show up at the dance, but the effects of the machine wear off and Foible decides the only appropriate penalty would be to turn Arky into a toddler and force Jetta to babysit him. "Great shooting stars!" Jetta says. "All I wanted was more romance in life—and look what happened!" Little Arky tells her, "Aw thut up!"

The backup feature in all three issues is Zoomer, a younger version of Arky drawn by an unidentified artist. He, too, lives in the 21st century and, like Arky, finds futuristic ways to get into trouble.

Unfortunately for Jetta, Arky and their friends, their futuristic exploits apparently weren't enough to stand out on the comic book racks. There were nearly 6,000 issues published in 1952 and 1953 combined from more than two dozen productive companies—the most in any two-year period in the first 50 years of the modern comic magazine (through the mid–1980s).

Ironically, that most futuristic of postwar mass-market inventions—television—along with the critics of comics did much to cut the issue output by fully half by the end of the decade. Standard abandoned comics in 1959, by which time De Carlo had moved to Archie Comics full-time. Most of us never saw Jetta again until Craig Yoe unearthed her (pun fully intended!).

Junie Prom #1, Winter 1947, copyright Dearfield Publishing Co. This is one of the more obscure characters from one of the most obscure companies, but it reads well.

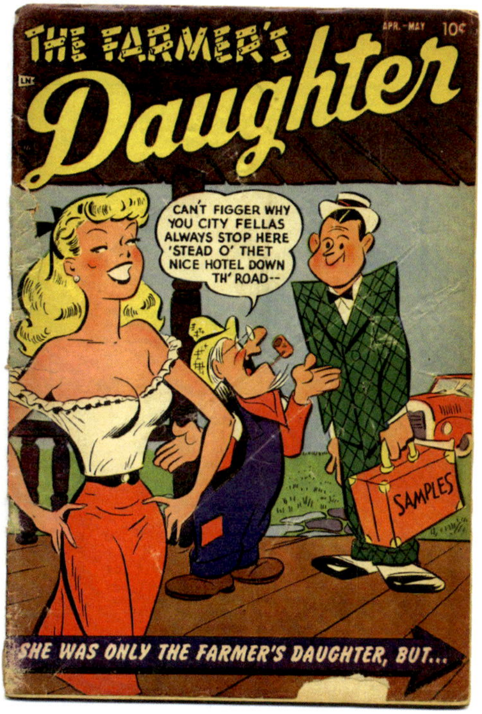

The Farmer's Daughter #2, April–May 1954, copyright Hal Seeger. Veteran cartoonist Seeger seemed to have fun with the wild antics in this four-issue series.

Patsy and Her Pals #1, May 1953, copyright Postal Publications, Inc. This was the fourth title to join the Patsy Walker stable, running 29 issues before the Marvel Implosion killed it in 1957. Cover by Morris Weiss.

Girls' Life #6, November 1954, copyright Broadcast Features Publications, Inc. Marvel tried to create a "Calling All Girls" type title using its biggest star, but it ran only six issues. This cover is by Al Hartley, who took over much of Patsy's art chores beginning in the mid–1950s.

Teena #21 (second issue), November 1949, copyright King Features Syndicate, Inc. Hilda Terry created a national comic strip favorite in *Teena*, but she lasted only three issues from Standard after three issues published by Magazine Enterprises.

Scribbly #6, June–July 1949, copyright National Comic Publications, Inc. Legendary artist/writer/editor Sheldon Mayer drew the boy cartoonist for several years before DC gave him his own title, but as funny as Scribbly was, he was nowhere near as successful as DC's Buzzy and Binky.

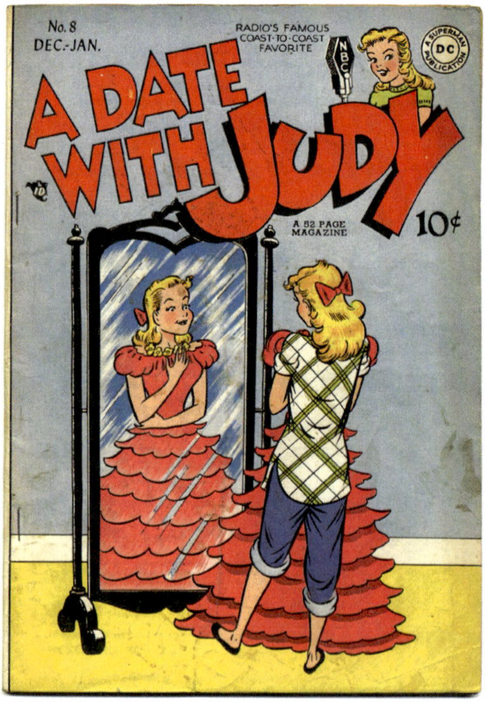

A Date with Judy #8, December 1948–January 1949, copyright Aleen Leslie. Other than the Patsy Walker series, no non–Archie female character was as successful as radio star Judy Foster. Cover by George Storm.

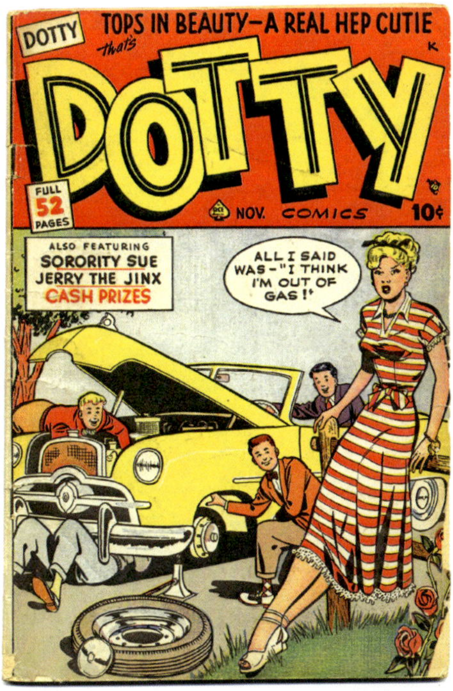

Dotty #37 (third issue), November 1948, copyright A.A. Wyn, Inc. Dotty was a cross between a working girl and a teen humor character, but she was still a teen. The title lasted only five issues before Ace turned it into *Glamorous Romances* with #40.

Hi-Jinx #3, November–December 1947, copyright B. & I. Publishing Co., Inc. This unique title of genuine "hep-cats" ran seven issues for the American Comics Group, but it was a funny seven issues.

Jetta #6 (second issue), February 1953, copyright Standard Magazines, Inc. This three-issue series by Dan De Carlo, including the covers, is among the most collectible of 1950s teen humor titles, what with its stories of teens 100 years in the future. Looks like current teens might be a bit disappointed in 30 years.

Ginger #7, Fall 1953, copyright Close-Up, Inc. Billed as the "Sweetheart of a Nation" by the Archie Series, Ginger was a longtime backup who deserved better than 10 issues.

Junior Miss #33 (tenth issue), March 1949. Copyright 1948 by Medalion Publishing Corp. Glamour girl Cindy Smith was among Marvel's most popular teens outside of Patsy Walker's crowd. Chapter 3.

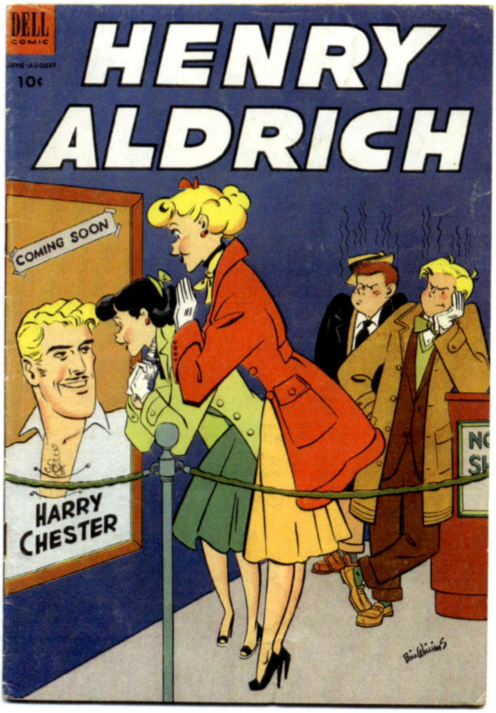

Henry Aldrich #17, June–August 1953, copyright Clifford Goldsmith. Henry and his buddy Homer aren't too happy on a date, which was nothing new. Cover by Bill Williams.

A Date with Judy #76, May 1960, copyright Aleen Leslie. Bob Oksner drew many of the most glamorous girls in teen humor comics, but the Comics Code still forbade two-piece bathing suits.

Tippy Teen #1, November 1965, copyright Tower Comics, Inc. With this title and *Thunder Agents* #1, Tower Comics was born with teams of teen-agers and superheroes. Skateboarding was relatively new for teens at this time.

25

The Mystery of *Candy* in the 1950s

After 13 issues between 1947 and 1949, *Candy* ran a stunning 51 issues from 1950 through 1956, when Quality Comics abruptly left the comic book business after nearly two decades and sold out to DC (then known as National Comics).

DC, however, decided not to continue with one of the most frequently published teen humor comics among all publishers during *Candy*'s final seven years. The question is: Why?

DC did pick up *Blackhawk* (Quality's best-selling comic for years); *GI Combat* (joining four other best-selling DC war titles); *Heart Throbs* (joining four other best-selling romance titles) and *Robin Hood Tales* (because the ongoing Richard Greene television series made the property hot).

During the same span, from 1950 to 1956, DC published the long-running teen titles *A Date with Judy*, *Buzzy* and *Leave It to Binky* on a regular basis (while cancelling three other much less successful teen titles in 1952 and 1954). But Buzzy and Binky were both suspended after their February 1957 issues and left the scene in 1958. Judy departed in 1960, while the war and love comics prospered in much of the 1960s, as did Blackhawk. (The *Robin Hood* TV show was cancelled in 1958 and so was DC's version of *Robin Hood*.)

The DC powers apparently felt that adding another teen humor title, even one as frequently seen as *Candy*, wasn't a good idea, especially because they may already have been thinking about suspending Buzzy and Binky. The fact that funny animal comics weren't doing as well as they once did for DC also may have entered into the thinking. *Candy*, drawn in a cartoony, often surreal style, also did not fit DC's more serious, more polished style in every genre.

Even so, *Candy* sure was given a good run and apparently earned it. After all, Quality had not been shy about cancelling a range of titles in the years that *Candy* was on the stands.

Check this out: *Archie* ran from #42 (January 1950) to #83 (December 1956)—42 issues in the seven-year span in which *Candy* appeared in 51! Of course, after *Candy*'s long-running backup strip disappeared when *Police Comics* changed format after #102 (September 1950), Candy appeared only in her own book, except for a handful of backup appearances in the short-run teen titles *Gabby and Jonesy* in 1953 and '54. Archie, in contrast, appeared in more issues than any other comic character except his pals and gals.

Look at this: Patsy Walker's eponymous title ran from #26 (January 1950) to #67 (November 1956)—42 issues! Of course, at one time or another during *Candy*'s run, Patsy appeared in five other Marvel titles. Likewise, Candy appeared more often than any of DC's *Big Teen Three* did.

So, did any teen title appear more often than *Candy* over those seven years? One: Marvel's *Miss America*! Though its numbering system was bizarre (see the chapter on *Miss America* in the 1940s and *Patsy Walker*), *Miss America* published 52 issues in those seven years. Even so, from a historical perspective, how could *Candy* go from good (if not great) to zero?

There is another hint: *Candy* #63 is dated May 1956 and #64 is July 1956. She exited stage right early. *Candy* was the first title Quality cancelled in 1956. Could it be that DC knew something about that oddity? It seems they must have. Maybe the disappearance of *Candy* isn't such a mystery after all.

Funny Covers

The *Candy* covers—which were all original, even in the last couple of years when Quality used story reprints—must have been standouts on the racks. The colors were vivid and the "action" was bold, brassy and often far-out. They did not have anything to do with the contents, but that was true of most teen humor titles. Many covers were among the most imaginative on the racks. Here are some of the best:

October 1950, #18: Candy sits atop a huge fish she has caught while Ted shouts, "Doggone it, Candy, your beginner's luck would have to show up today."

April 1951, #21: Candy is thrown off a horse as she approaches a sign reading "Full Stop" and complains, "Ted, why didn't you tell me he could read?"

December 1951, #25: Candy walks out of school with a robot toting her books as Ted says, "Candy, this is carrying your science course too far!"

August 1952, #29: Candy and Ted face each other on a couch while she says, "Ted Dawson, if you try to kiss me; I'll scream! But don't worry, there's no one home!"

April 1953, #37: Ted asks "Please, Candy, will you come to the dance with me?" and she replies, "You've got some nerve, Ted Dawson, asking me at the last minute! I certainly won't! What time will you call for me?"

September 1953, #42: Candy looks at a notice she has posted on a school bulletin board about her lost diamond ring and Ted says, "I didn't know you owned a diamond ring, Candy!" She responds, "I don't, Ted! But it's a swell chance to have my phone number posted in the main corridor!"

March 1954, #53: Candy answers the phone and says, "It's a proposal, Ted! What's your bid, before I make up my mind?" Ted's expression is priceless.

July 1956, #64: Candy complains, "Golly, Ted! Can't you ever talk about anything but baseball?" Ted replies, "Sure … that's not the only thing I can talk about! I can talk about football!"

Funny Business

In #15 (April 1950), Candy talks her father into buying her a $50 dress for the big dance to give rival Cornelia Clyde some competition, but only after he has broken a neighbor's window trying to show Candy how to use her softball bat. The neighbor is grateful because the broken window led to finding her missing necklace and she gives Candy a $50 reward because Candy has promised Dad that she would take the batting blame. As the story ends, Mr. O'Connor marvels, "And she still has a dress coming from me! Boy, this younger generation can cope with anything—and still come out on top!"

Television began showing up more frequently as a story factor, as a story in #21 (April 1951) demonstrates. Cornelia hatches a plot to film Candy in the arms of a handsome stranger on the program *We Catch You Off Guard* and then talks Ted into watching the program. But everything turns out all right when Tiny explains to a dismayed Ted what really happened. *Candid Camera*, which began in 1948, seems to have inspired this story.

In a human interest story in #23 (August 1951), Candy and Trish decide to tell mutual friend Tina that boys don't go after her because she needs to reduce her weight. Tina tries but it's too hard for her. Then look-alike but slender cousin Donna shows up to visit Tina. Ted, Candy and Trish see Donna heading into Madame Martha's Salon, but think she's a slimmed-down Tina. Donna and Tina decide to trick Tina's friends into thinking Donna is Tina at the sweet shoppe. The truth eventually comes out at the beach, where rotund Tina has found a boyfriend in newcomer Fats Jamison. "He likes fat girls!" Tina tells her friends, who go stag to the beach party while Tina has a ball.

When this story was reprinted in #61 (March 1956), the Comics Code Authority forced Quality to retouch all the panels with two-piece bathing suits to make them one-piece. The Code also took the cleavage out of Tina's appearance at the beach and out of a movie scene. In a panel with Donna in lingerie, what *was* a sexy two-piece became a modest one-piece. All of this was common for companies like Quality, Ace and Harvey, all of which published a multitude of romance comics in the mid–1950s and all of which draw reprints heavily doctored to eliminate any hint of sexiness and suggestiveness.

Ted is editor of the Hartwick High "Low Down" in #63 (May 1956) and finds himself at his wits' end because he has no photos. Candy and Cornelia snipe at him and themselves so much, he decides to take them both to an outdoor photo shoot. But Corny, as she's called, is accidentally caught plotting to unleash bees on Candy, then causing her to fall off a pier. Ted agrees not to print those photos, but Corny realizes that only Candy will thus appear in the paper, posing in a cute bathing suit shot taken earlier.

The girls make such cutting comments, it's a wonder the Comics Code left them in. For example, Corny tells Candy, "You couldn't make the cover of *Calling All Ghouls*—or maybe you could!" That comment was inspired when Candy told Corny of Ted's call for photos, "He's looking for a glamour-head! Not a hammer-head!"

The 1950s issues of *Candy* used a variety of traditional Quality backup teen strips, including Jitters, Will Bragg, Ezra, Jonesy and Gabby (who for some reason was dubbed Tabby in a reprint in #64).

But fate wasn't kind to Candy … she's one of the few examples of a leading character in her field simply vanishing forever with no notice.

26

The Amazing Mazie and Her Boyfriends

The only teen humor character to appear in four different comic book titles yet with fewer than 50 total issues was Mazie Dean, "The Hi-School Queen," as she was often called. Making her history even more remarkable, she was the only teen character with "And Her Boyfriends" appended to the logo of the final six issues of her flagship title. In addition, she and her retinue were also the only teen humor characters to appear in two distinctly different formats.

In 1950, Nation-Wide Publishing Corporation of Chicago debuted in comics with four 52-page titles in a digest format, each priced at a nickel. *Mazie* ran seven undated issues in 1950–1951, as did the western *Lucky Star,* the science fiction hero *Captain Atom* and the circus-themed humor *Do-Do.* Each issue of *Mazie* had an inside cover house ad with the commensurate numbers and cover images of the other three titles, though these comics were not dated except for the year of copyright.

Nation-Wide Comics was an obscure publisher. Ironically, the publisher apparently did not have had nationwide circulation, since of the 69 addresses from pen pals in *Mazie* #4–6, none were from states west of North Dakota. In #7, there were single addresses from Idaho, Colorado and Wyoming, but never from any West Coast state, nor any from Arizona, Nevada, Utah, Montana and New Mexico.

Mazie was the only one of the four nickel titles to continue in the standard ten-cent format with 36 pages (including covers), beginning with #8 (October 1952) from the "new" comic book firm Magazine Publishers, which had the same Chicago address as Nation-Wide. Magazine Publishers produced six issues of *Mazie* through #13 (March 1954).

However, Magazine Publishers added two other Mazie-related titles: the Archie Andrews knockoff *Stevie* with #1 (November 1952) and the Jughead Jones–like *Mortie* with #1 (December 1952). *Stevie* ran through #6 (April 1954) and *Mortie* ran through #3 (June 1953), to be replaced by the Reggie

Mantle knockoff *Flat-Top* #1, 2 and 3 (November 1953, February 1954 and May 1954), with all three titles under the Magazine Publishers indicia listing.

Mazie's titles even looked a lot like Archie's group. Even though Mazie was well done, accessible to readers of all ages and nicely illustrated, the series

Stevie #1, November 1953, copyright Magazine Publishers, Inc. When Harvey picked up the *Mazie* franchise in 1955, the firm opted to keep Flat-Top in his book but did not continue Mazie's main squeeze in his title.

seems to be closer to the Archie style than any other. I could imagine a parent picking up a *Mazie* and thinking it was an *Archie* Series comic—after the size became normal and the price was ten cents.

It was intriguing that Magazine Publishers chose to switch to standard ten-cent comics in 1952, which was the record-setting year with about 3160 different issues covering more than 600 titles in the first half-century of "modern" corporate comic book publishing, which began in the mid–1930s.

At no time did either Nation-Wide or Magazine Publishers feature a date on the covers, which was highly unusual. Apparently, the thinking was that some merchants would leave issues on the stands longer if they were not dated. All of the issues, which were published quarterly, did include numbers on the covers.

The Switch to Harvey

Harvey Comics, a long-established firm which picked up several titles from other publishers in the 1950s, began producing *Mazie* with #14 (February 1955), after nearly a one-year hiatus. That hiatus was not typical of Harvey, which earlier quickly began producing the likes of *Blondie*, *Dick Tracy* and *Little Audrey* after purchasing the rights.

Mazie #15 (April 1955) carried a large Harvey house advertisement with the image of *Flat-Top* #4 (March 1955) along with smaller images of the last two issues of *Stevie* and *Mortie* from Magazine Publishers. Harvey, which had long since published numerous incorrect house ads over the years, never did publish *Stevie* or *Mortie* titles, though the characters continued to appear in *Mazie* and *Flat-Top*.

Flat-Top lasted only four *Harvey* issues through #7 (September 1955) but *Mazie* ran all the way through #28 (September 1958). Mazie apparently ran into financial uncertainties, however, since there were gaps between #21 (April 1956) and #22 (September 1956), followed by a full-year gap until #23 (September 1957). Several Harvey titles of other genres ran into similar publishing gaps.

Harvey Hits, a title started in 1957 to feature characters without their own comics, had one Mazie-related issue, #5 (January 1958), which featured Stevie. At one time, collectors speculated this may have been material from the never-published Harvey continuation of *Stevie*, but *Harvey Hits* #5 actually reprinted stories from *Stevie* #6, which appeared nearly four years earlier. Indeed, most if not all of the stories in the final few issues of *Mazie* were reprints during a period when Harvey used numerous reprints in many titles. In all, Mazie appeared in 25 issues from Nation-Wide–Magazine Publishers and in 20 from Harvey.

None of the stories in any *Mazie*-related title were signed or credited to artists or writers. Nor is there any such information in the Overstreet Comic Book Price Guide or in *The Harvey Comics Companion* (2017) by Mark Arnold, the nation's leading expert on Harvey.

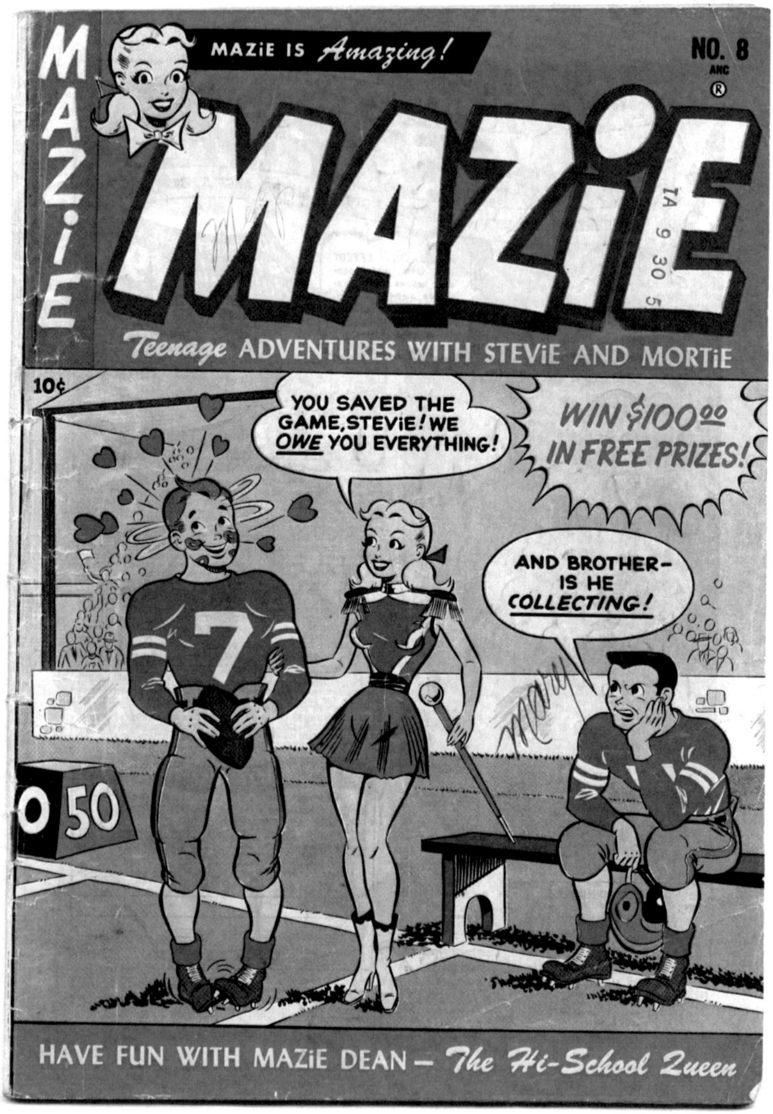

***Mazie* #8, October 1952, copyright Magazine Publishers, Inc. This is the first issue in regular comic book size after seven appearances as a 5-cent digest.**

Two other members of the Mazie crew, Mazie's best friend Laurie and the French girl Jeanie who was Mazie's rival, appeared on a regular basis, though never had their own titles. Unlike the high school faculty in the Archie Series, faculty members are Greenview High were not often spotlighted. The story themes—dances, sports, dating, classes, and so on—were similar to the *Archie* Series. Stevie even had red hair like Archie, while Mazie was a blonde like Betty Cooper and Jeanie was a brunette like Veronica

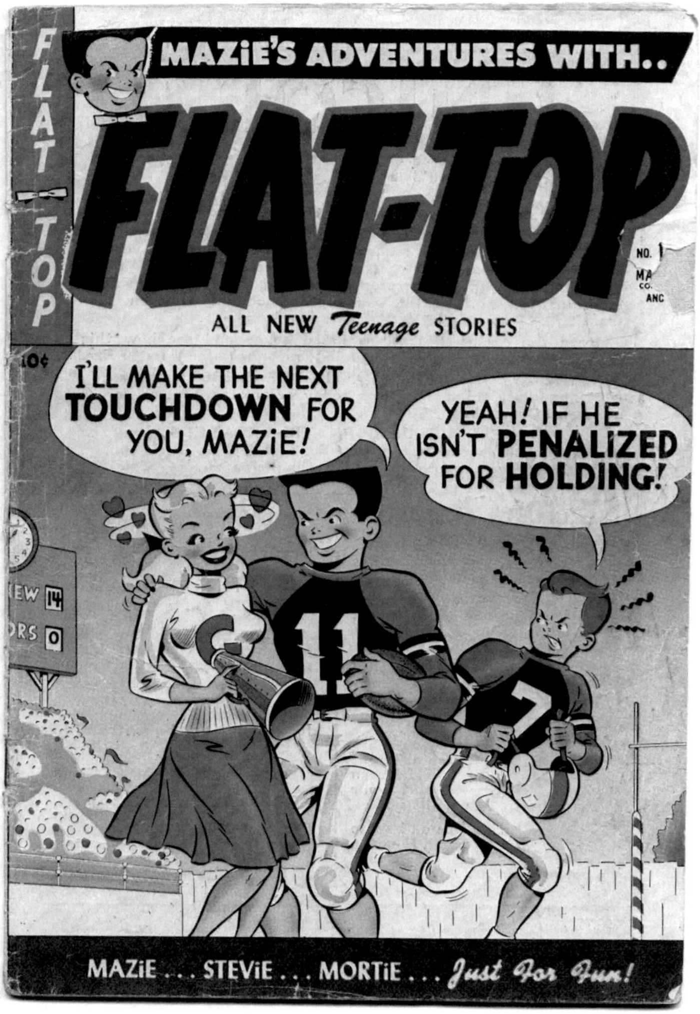

***Flat-Top* #1, November 1953, copyright Magazine Publishers, Inc. *Flat-Top* was the Mazie group's version of Archie's rival Reggie, but he lasted only seven issues in his own title.**

Lodge. I've always felt that the Mazie characters were basically marketed as an alternate version of the Archie gang.

As in the Archie Series, the *Mazie* titles all featured covers with clever (and sometimes obvious) jokes, along with many story titles with puns, both common and outrageous.

There were only three team sports covers, all with jokes that were original and not just Archie knockoffs. *Mazie* #8, the first standard-sized issue, showed a kiss-covered and dizzy football hero Stevie listening to sexy band

Mortie #3, June 1953, copyright Magazine Publishers, Inc. Mazie's friend Mortie was a genuinely nice early version of a nerd. He deserved more than three issues.

majorette Mazie telling him, "You saved the game, Stevie! We owe you everything!" while teammate Flat-Top mutters, "And brother—Is he collecting!" *Mazie* #19 has our heroine asking Stevie, "Is it true that Flat-Top is going to be a 3-letter man?" as Flat-Top catches a football when Stevie responds, "Yeah, if he can learn his 3-R's!" On *Flat-Top* #1, Flat-Top wraps his arm around cheerleader Mazie and tells her, "I'll make the next touchdown for you, Mazie!" as Stevie informs the reader, "Yeah! If he isn't penalized for holding!"

Outrageous Story Puns

Some of the story title puns would likely have gone over the heads of young readers. Among them were "All Fail the Queen" in *Mazie* #8, the illustrated "Screw-Ball" (with art of a softball and a screw) in #10 (reprinted in #19), "T.V. or Not T.V." in #13 (reprinted in #25), "The Face is Femm-iliar" in #15, "Beaches and Scream" and "Static in the Attic" in #22, "It's a Shoe Thing" in #25 and "Hoop-La" for a basketball story in #26.

Among the funniest *Mazie* covers: #16, on which Flat-Top asks, "Why the handkerchief, Mazie.... Do you have hay fever?" to which she replies as Stevie approaches, "No.... He fever!"; and #18, as Stevie says, "I've had this car for two years and never had a wreck!" to which Mazie responds, "You mean you've had this wreck for two years and never had a car!" For the swimming pool scene on the cover of #21, Mazie says, "Look Stevie—Our handsome swimmer [Flat-Top] is dripping!" to which Steve replies, "You mean our handsome drip is swimming!"

In a school library scene on *Mazie* #9, she asks, "What's a kiss, Stevie?" and he replies, "Proof that two heads are better than one!" as Mortie grimaces in pun pain. And for #13, Stevie is again kiss-dizzy in class as an angry Flat-Top says, "Hey, Mazie—Isn't this supposed to be an art class?" and Mazie replies, "Sure, Flat-Top.... Stevie was just trying out a new line!"

On the cover of *Flat-Top* #4, he says, "I want to thank you for not mentioning my grade in front of the class, Miss Little," as the teacher holds the page with a big red zero and says, "Oh, that's all right, Flat-Top. It was nothing—absolutely nothing!" For a beach scene on the cover of *Stevie* #3, Mazie asks him, "Do you prefer blonds, Stevie?" as Jeanie says in the background, "I'll simply dye if he says yes!"

27

Why Ginger Deserved a Better Fate

Ginger Snapp, the largely forgotten redhead with the cutest hairstyle among the teen characters in the Archie Series, definitely deserved better than only ten issues of her own title in the first half of the 1950s. She enjoyed several distinctions, but her title had to buck the busiest newsstands in the first 50 years of modern comics publishing.

Wilbur Wilkin, meanwhile, had become a well-established "second-string" version of Archie, though never involved in stories set in the Archie Universe. Entering the 1950s with a successful 28-issue history, "America's Son of Fun," as the firm bannered him, ran all the way through the 1950s before #87 (November 1959), the final issue of his bi-monthly run.

Ginger was the first teen girl to get her own eponymous ten-cent title in the 1950s, but she also had to wait longer than any Golden Age teen boy or girl to do so—eight years! Her debut in the mostly superhero anthology *Zip Comics* #35 (March 1943) made her the first teen girl with her own strip—Betty and Veronica were still seen only in the Archie stories in *Pep Comics* at the time, along with the then-new Archie title, although that gave them greater exposure.

Ginger ran in 13 stories, none of them long or noteworthy, through *Zip* #47 (Summer 1944), the last issue. She soon began serving as a backup in *Suzie*, beginning with #49 (Spring 1945), the first issue after the popular working girl title took over the numbering of the original *Laugh Comix.* (That odd spelling didn't became common until the undergrounds of the late 1960s.)

Ginger appeared regularly in *Suzie* for more than 30 issues, again with short stories that weren't featured on the cover or overtly publicized in any way. Then came *Ginger* #1, an undated issue with a 1951 copyright in the indicia. Ginger ran for ten issues, drawn mostly by the talented George Frese and published pretty much quarterly, through #10 (Summer 1954). During the 1951–1954 period—shortly before comics suffered severely with the combined whammy of the advent of the Comics Code Authority and the rapid growth of television—no fewer than more than 11,400 issues of corporately produced comics were published! Contrast this with the 1961–1964 period, when the four-year total was less than 6200 issues.

Unlike *Wilbur*, which was 52 pages (including the covers) between 1950 and 1952, *Ginger* was always what soon became the standard 36 pages (with covers) for all but the most popular comics. That afforded her fewer opportunities to impress readers, although the first five issues were not dated and the indicia offered no mention of the application for second-class mailing privileges. That meant *Ginger* #1–5 did not need to run either backup comic strips of different characters and/or text pages.

The Archie Series folks apparently intended *Ginger* to run continuously, since #6–10 were dated quarterly—from Summer 1953 through Summer 1954. The indicia did run an application notice for mailing, so subscriptions were planned, but *Ginger* ended before the application was improved.

Ironically, the long-running *Pep Comics* little girl backup strip *Li'l Jinx* two years later took *Ginger*'s place in the lineup. *Li'l Jinx*, like *Little Archie,* started with #1 late in 1956, then oddly switched to #12 (January 1957) during a six-issue run. Apparently the Archie Series record-keepers forgot they had a defunct title with numbering they could hook onto. When *Li'l Jinx* was cancelled, the four-issue run of *Little Archie* in *Animal Land* (#1, 17–19) ensued in the same odd way.

Ginger Was Far from Typical

Ginger was billed as "America's Typical Teen-Age Girl" on the cover of #1 along with "Sweetheart of a Nation" as part of her logo. Comic book publishers were shameless in their boasting, whether an issue was #1 or #100. Archie was often called "America's Typical Teen" and that seemed to work for him, although one wonders why a reader would choose "typical characters" over those ostensibly more unusual, such as the lamentably short three-issue run of famed artist-creator Dan De Carlo's *Jetta* from Standard Comics in 1952 (see the chapter on Jetta).

Some of the *Ginger* cover jokes were cute, such as #1: A handsome young history instructor asks, "Ginger—What do you consider to be the most outstanding developments in history in recent years?" to which she replied, "The history teachers!" By #7, the history teacher was female and she pointed out, "Ginger, you've overlooked a very important date in history! Ickky.... Can you tell us what date she's forgotten?" To which the kind-hearted nerd responded, "The one we were supposed to have last night!"

The cover of #1 ties in with the feature story "Smellbound," when Ginger falls for her young history teacher, Mr. Thompson, but must turn down a $40 perfume (more than $400 in today's dollars). Instead, she buys Royal Mounted from a five-and-dime store. (Its motto: "Always Gets Your Man!") When the teacher asks, "Good heavens, Ginger! What's the idea of coming to class smelling like that?" she invites him to the prom! She totally misunderstands when she interrupts him as he says, "As a matter of fact, I'd love to, Ginger … but you see, I need a girl to …" and she blurts, "A girl! What's the matter with me?? I'm a girl!! I'm ALL girl!!" He also misunderstands and ultimately Ginger appears at his house with a babysitting job as Mr. Thompson takes his wife to the prom. In today's society, no comic strip creator would dare even make a joke about a teacher taking a teen to the prom. But such was not the case in the infinitely more innocent '50s.

There's also a heartwarming story in #1, "Saved by the Belle," in which Ginger lets the bully Monk take her out when he threatens a guy she really likes as a friend, the sweet little nerd Ickky. (Ginger alternates between clean-cut, handsome Tommy and the ever-so-nice nerd.) She pretends to be so fickle that Monk begs Ickky to take her back, and of course he does, much to the relief of Ginger's father.

The Ginger stories are cartoony, unlike so many of Patsy Walker's tales at Marvel, but there isn't much slapstick. Ginger is all plot-driven and sheer fun. (Some male collectors have noted that Frese drew Ginger with two overly large attractions—the "headlights" of yore—and thus she is especially easy on their eyes.) Not that Ginger always comes across as perfect. The cover of #4 (undated but with a 1952 copyright, as are #2, 3 and 5) has Ginger telling classmate Biff, "No, Biff, I'm not going to the prom with you—I'm going with Ickky because he's such a gentleman…. So noble, so sweet …" followed by Ginger's thought bubble and an image of Ickky's snazzy car in which she thinks, "And because he just got a new, sleek, red convertible!"

Some of the jokes made by Ginger's female competition are downright clever. When Ginger sports a fashionable spring green dress in #6, Tommy tells Bunny, "Wow! That was Ginger! She looks like a million bucks!" Bunny gives Ginger's back side the evil eye and responds, "Yeah, in Confederate money!"

It wasn't long before Ginger's title was discontinued. Issues of *Ginger* are much harder to find than those of other Archie Series titles, so she apparently did not sell enough to warrant continuation. Likewise, *Archie's Rival Reggie*, as he was billed, also was discontinued after a 14-issue run from 1949 to 1954. But bad boys had their day in the 1960s and 1970s. When Reggie resumed with #15–18 in 1963–1965 and then became *Reggie and Me* with #19 (August 1966), his title ran all the way to #126 (September 1980). But then, Archie and Me ran 115 issues and *Betty and Me* lasted 107.

Ginger wasn't done. She would pop up as a backup in various titles.

Wilbur Lasts a Decade Longer

Until the blond practical joker finally ended regular publication with #87 (November 1959), Wilbur rivaled Archie and Patsy Walker as the longest-running eponymous title. He appeared in anthology titles as well. He probably was portrayed in high school scenes far more often than most comics teens, many of whom had misadventures with parents and other adults.

Linda and Laurie were rivals for Wilbur's attention right up to the end of the run. But then, there were girls of one sort or another on Wilbur's covers, where the jokes were always gently suggestive. On the cover of #40 (December 1951), Wilbur lugs a football out to practice and asks admiring Linda and Laurie, "Would you girls like to see me throw a few passes to the boys?" Linda comes right to the point: "I'd much rather see you throw a few passes at the girls, Wilbur! Especially me!"

Wilbur, unlike some teens, was in his share of sports stories (he was neither shy nor small). His buddy Red tells Linda on the cover of #52 (December 1953) as they head out to football practice, "I'm tired of always being a substitute! I'd like to be on the first team with Wilbur!" A discouraged Linda, seeing how taken Wilbur is with Laurie on this fall day, responds, "So would I, Red! So would I!"

Wilbur #57 (November 1954) skipped the usual October issue and began a series of "odd" month publication instead of "even" months. Issue #57 also began nearly two years of multiple panel cover jokes, ending with #67 (July 1956). These were unusual for teen comics but the Archie editors decided to use such covers for most issues during that period.

Beginning with #80 (September 1958), Archie changed the logo to "The New Wilbur" although the indicia title remained Wilbur Comics, and that's how everything was presented for the last eight issues. By this time, Linda and Laurie had modern short hairstyles, but there was really nothing new about the title.

The cover jokes were just as good. For #80, the English teacher has written on the blackboard, "Define the words *misfortune* and *catastrophe*." Linda stands up and the teacher tells her, "You say if Laurie fell into the river it would be a misfortune! Then what would you consider a catastrophe?" To which Linda claims, "If somebody pulled her out" as both Laurie and Wilbur look astonished.

Given the uneven but generally successful history of the Archie Series, it's hard to say why *Wilbur* ended regular publication with #87 in 1959. The slightly more than 1500 comics published that year were by far the fewest in the 1950s, although the Archie Series had published 100 issues for the first time, according to the year-by-year and title-by-title information compiled by comics historian Dan Stevenson. The number of significant companies producing comics dropped to only seven with even as many as 40 issues published (or averages per month of from 33 issues from leader DC Comics, with a total of 382, to three per month from the American Comics Group [total 40]).

Archie grew slowly but steadily in the 1960s, reaching a decade-long peak of 164 issues in 1969, which ranked sixth behind the only other five remaining giants of the industry: DC, Marvel, Gold Key (Western), Charlton and Harvey. There were slightly less than 1500 comics published in 1969—about the same as a decade earlier.

But the non–Archie characters did not do well in the wake of the Funny Fifties. After *Wilbur*, the next long-running comic that the Archie Series cancelled was *Super Duck* with #94 (December 1960), which like *Wilbur* started in 1944. *Katie Keene* was the next big name to go, with #62 (October 1961), after starting in her own title in 1949. She debuted in *Wilbur* #5 in 1945.

In one of the more inexplicable publishing moves in comic book history, *Wilbur* returned with three one-shots: #88 (September 1963), #89 (October 1964) and #90 (October 1965). But the 1950s were over, and so was *Wilbur*. When *That Wilkin Boy* began a 52-issue run in 1969, he was Bingo, not Wilbur.

28

The First Kathy and Company

The only teen humor title that served as a true bridge from the Golden Age superheroics of the 1940s to teenage antics in the 1950s for a significant company was the unusual Standard Comics title *Kathy*.

Kathy #1 (September 1949) appeared on the stands not long after the last of the company's numerous superheroes vanished that year. She was published continuously for only four years, essentially on a quarterly basis, but the colorful redhead was a harbinger of the many Standard humor comics of the 1950s, including *Dennis the Menace*, *Super Mouse* and *Little Angel* after the firm discontinued its romance, horror, war and crime comics in the wake of the establishment of the Comics Code Authority.

Kathy debuted as a backup strip in the company's flagship title, *Thrilling Comics*, ironically in #64 (February 1948). That was the last issue with Doc Strange, the company's longest running superhero, who began in *Thrilling* #1 (January 1940). *Kathy* continued in *Thrilling* #66 through #74 (October 1949).

As common as the name Kathy was in real-life America, Standard (also known as Better Publications, Nedor, Visual Editions and other sub-publishers) was the first company to use it on a teen humor character. The second and last would be Marvel, with its 27-issue run of *Kathy* from 1959 to 1964. (The larger companies tried hard to avoid duplicating title names during the era of teen humor comics.)

Most of the *Kathy* strips were signed by Clark Haas, an obscure cartoonist who drew them with a competent yet heavy line that looked like an old Sunday newspaper reprint (it wasn't). *Kathy* #1 opened with a page introducing readers to Kathy Crane's family and friends. They included "No. 1 boyfriend" Hank Stevens; "most loyal pal" Fanny Farnsworth; kid brother Mickey; Mom and Dad; and Aunt Lucinda. As the writer said: "Oh, yes—let's not forget Gyp, Kathy's dog!" (Gyp was often drawn winking—and how many dogs have ever done that?)

Kathy ran steadily through #16 (September 1953) and oddly reappeared once in the Comics Code era with #17 (September 1955). Since that last issue carries no advertising except on the covers, it's possible it's filled with art that had been paid for yet had definitely never been published. Like most issues in the run, #17 carried the top-of-the-cover banner "America's Most Lovable Teen-Ager!"

The cover of #1 set the tone for many jokes seen on the covers of numerous teen comics. Hank watches Kathy walk by with her lunch in a diner as the waiter asks him, "What dish will you have friend?" (None of the covers were signed.)

An Original Cover

Perhaps the most original cover has Kathy telling a female friend, "Hank's promised to help me read my lines tonight!" as a wall sign nearby notes a meeting of the dramatic society. Her friend responds with the subtle (for comics, anyway), "What do you think he's doing now?"

What made the consistently wholesome Kathy unusual was the fact that most stories heavily involved family members and/or friends but seldom actual rivals for Hank's affection. Fanny was a hearty, heavy-set type, in no way a rival. But, as *Kathy* showed often, there were an unlimited number of plots that depended on genuine, if usually wacky, humor.

In the first Kathy story in #1, the tone for the series was set when Kathy won $38,000 in radio contest merchandise (worth more than ten times that much in today's dollars). There was something for everyone, but everyone soon realized that what they won took away from some aspect of their lives. Kathy was only too glad to see everything taken back when she was informed that she had been given the wrong prize-winning question. In the other Kathy story (several shorts were devoted to family members), Fanny is surrounded by boys at a picnic because she's the only girl who made large box lunches.

The funniest story in #2 (December 1949) was the debut of a backup starring the oddly named teen Speedy Hopper. (In ensuing issues through #6, his name was Chester.) In "Clothes Make the Man," Speedy and his high school classmates are upset that girls are wearing pants instead of dresses to school as well as other spots. The boys decide to wear skirts, but they chicken out a bit and wear Scottish kilts. That seems like a bad idea until Speedy's girl, Ginger, introduces Speedy and the boys to Ginger's father's boss. It turns out he's from Scotland and is delighted to see the kilts—so a wild dance ensues, with all the girls in pants and all the boys in kilts.

There is a great in-joke in *Kathy* #3 (April 1950), when a town gossip says she has a story about the Crane family that is "Amazing, Fantastic, Startling,

Exciting and Thrilling!" *Amazing* and *Fantastic* were the names of the rival Ziff-Davis science fiction pulp magazines and *Startling*, *Exciting* and *Thrilling* were used on numerous titles of Standard's pulp arm.

In *Kathy* #4 (July 1950), her bodybuilding cousin Rowena totally wears out the family until Gyp saves the day by convincing Rowena he's a mad dog. It's an amusing story, and there's an even funnier tale in #5 when Kathy and Hank inadvertently run into a band of counterfeiters during "Love Your Neighbor" week.

Kathy #4, July 1950, copyright Visual Editions Inc. Running 16 issues from 1949 to 1953 and a single final issue in 1955, this was Standard's most successful teen humor title. Cover by Clark Haas.

New backup stories arrive in #7 (May 1951) with Bingo, the woman-hating nerd from Standard's *Leroy* title, and Myrtle Mudlark, a dumb but good-hearted blonde type. Bingo stayed for most of the rest of the fun, but Myrtle was funnier with her inability to handle words with double meanings.

The Kathy stories were well-plotted but they weren't always logical. For example, in "Pardon My French" in *Kathy* #8 (August 1951), she dates her French teacher only to find he's a selfish cad. What is a high school girl doing dating a teacher, even in teen humor comics? (In the last panel, she's thinking of the handsome new Spanish teacher!)

There's that same lack of logic in "The Basketball-Brawl Game" in *Kathy* #10 (February 1952). Kathy has distracted hoops star Hank to the point where he is unable to play, so the coach tells Kathy she has to save the game because "you're a terrific player." She proves it in the final minutes and leads Colfax High to a win over Pinhead Prep. In what world, especially in 1952, would a girl play in a boys' game?

In *Kathy* #16, she disguises herself as a newsboy for a truly hysterical story in which she is taught to throw papers on both sides of the street with both arms. Her mother also needs money and wants to try the same thing, but one fake newsboy in the family is enough for Pop, who gives Mom the money she needs.

There is an oddity in *Kathy* #5 (October 1950), in which there is a full-page house ad on the inside front cover for that very *Kathy* comic! The same ad was used in *Leroy* #6 (November 1950), the final issue of that title, so there must have been some confusion. Comics companies seldom wasted money with full-page ads for the issue in which they appeared!

Leroy Loomis

Standard tried a companion to *Kathy* in *Leroy*, which ran for a year from #1 (November 1949) through #6 (noted above). *Leroy*, for which all the art was unsigned, had its moments, but it wasn't as distinctive as *Kathy*, since most of the stories involved competition for Janey by Leroy and his nemesis Jasper.

Leroy was among the few Standard Comics in the late 1940s and 1950s that started with #1; most began with #5 or #11, ostensibly to fool news dealers and customers into thinking such titles were more established than they really were.

In a very funny story in *Leroy* #4 (June 1950), Leroy causes all kinds of chaos when he chases a windblown paper airplane he has created from a note in his principal's "incoming" box. When Leroy finally grabs it, the note reads: "Dear Dean Underwood, It gives me great pleasure to report that Leroy

***Leroy* #2, January 1950, copyright Visual Editions, Inc. Leroy was an original character but ran only six issues from Standard.**

Loomis has kept out of trouble for two weeks. Therefore, I recommend him for the good conduct honor roll. Yours truly, Miss Ghastly." This story made me laugh a lot because I couldn't help but recall when I threw a paper airplane out of the library window on the second story of my high school and it hit the principal on the head. Fortunately, nobody told on me!

Rodger Dodger and Ricky

In the Golden Age, one-shots were not all that rare, for many reasons, but teen humor comics were almost always given at least a minimal chance to succeed. But that wasn't true with the only issues of *Roger Dodger* (August 1952) and *Ricky* (September 1953), both listed on the covers as #5.

Roger Dodger was a backup strip in *Exciting Comics* #51 (September 1946) through #67 (May 1949). But most readers were likely unfamiliar with him by the time his own title appeared on the crowded newsstands of 1952, when approximately 3,160 corporate issues set a single-year record for the first half-century of the modern comic book (1935–1985).

A clever cover joke introduced Roger in 1952, when his teacher tells him, "In this composition, Roger, you need a comma after [the words] 'that girl'"; Roger responds while he eyes a sexy passerby, "I'd rather make a dash after her!"

In the first story, Roger tries to solve the old dilemma of making two dates on the same night by rushing from seat to seat in a theater. The girls realize what he has been doing, and he ends up in bed telling the reader, "Oh, well, at least I'll get a chance to read my book!" He bought the book from a store with a sign saying, "We take orders for the Book of the Month, the Book of the Week and the Book of the Day."

There are Leroy and Ginny backup stories, likely left over from the short run of *Leroy*, along with a funny final story in which Roger is responsible in his role as school gossip columnist for seeing a pair of teachers elope.

Ricky was an undistinguished title dealing with a young teen's dating problems in slapstick stories. The character may not have ever been used by Standard earlier and certainly wasn't seen later.

In the late 1940s, Standard also had another teen character in a backup role, but Jefferson Jones did not appear in his own title after running in *Startling Comics* #44 (March 1947) through #53 (September 1948) and in *America's Best Comics* #29 (January 1949).

Standard also started four teen humor titles in the late 1940s that reprinted newspaper strips: *Boots and Her Buddies, Etta Kett, Freckles and His Friends* and *Teena*. These are fodder for a different chapter.

29

Lucy, the (All Too Soon) Real Gone Gal

St. John Publishing Company, sometimes one of the better second-tier companies of the later Golden Age, tried only one significant teen humor comic book, or at least it was a comic with a teen humor character in the title.

The phrase "real gone" predates the beatnik era of the late 1950s and early '60s, but was seldom seen in earlier comics. That didn't prevent St. John from trying *Lucy,* subtitled "The Real Gone Gal"—and the title had nothing to do with *I Love Lucy*, the TV sitcom that was fabulously popular during St. John's run of *Lucy* from #1 (June 1953) through #4 (February 1954).

In this case, "The Real Gone Gal" referred to the teenager's wild ideas. In the first issue, the only elements of an origin were these words on the first splash page: "You are now entering Centertown, U.S.A. … Population 50,000 … Including Lucy!!!" as she dreams of three elaborate dress designs for the mid-summer formal. She finds that she can't soften up her dad for something new to wear, so she tries her younger brother, whom she addresses as "ghastlier than I." This story is actually a re-purposed Kitty story originally by Lilly Renee from the one-shot *Kitty* title in 1948 (see chapter 15).

He's no help, either, and then the phone rings: It's raven-haired rich girl Wanda Farr, "the solvent siren," as Lucy calls her. Wanda just wants to rub in the fact that she has a "divine green" outfit for the dance. More determined than ever, Lucy tries charging a dress at Stacey's … only to be told that charge accounts have been discontinued. Spotting a "Sales Girl Wanted" sign, she takes the job, only to be caught hiding when Wanda wanders into the store. But all is not lost: She sells $300 worth of dresses and her father is so excited that he offers to buy her a new formal to reward her newfound ambition. She confesses that she sold the dresses to herself, but her dad owes only $270 because of her ten percent discount. Then she calls Wanda to rub in the fact that "I have several new formals. How? That's a trade secret!"

In the second Lucy story, boyfriend Wally drops a book and Lucy finds a note inside that opens "How do I love thee?" Irate, Lucy tells Wally to get lost. Desperate for a date, she connives to convince dull-but-dependable Rodney Bookmark that she wants him to take her out. After a suitable period of boredom, Rodney pulls a book out of his library to express his feelings: "How do I love thee? Let me count the ways ..." and tells her it's a poem by Elizabeth Barrett Browning. It doesn't take Lucy long to snatch Wally away from Wanda.

The rest of #1 consists of a silly slapstick one-shot strip named *Ginny*, along with the only appearances of Rita, a scheming adult, and Jelly Bean,

Lucy #4, February 1954, copyright St. John Publishing Corp. This cute sight gag appears on the cover of the last issue from a company that didn't have much luck with teen humor.

a teen girl who finds a way to get screen tests without the glasses she needs, only to be given glasses after she's hired. Rita tries three unsuccessful ways to land a handsome fellow: with her personality, her intelligence and her glamour … only to see him rescue her from a fall, leading her to think in the last panel, "I keep forgetting that woman's strongest point is … helplessness!" Well, this was long before Women's Liberation.

Lucy #2 includes three new backup characters: the forgettable teen strip *Kenny* and the equally lackluster *Private Thistlewait* and *Trudy*, a man-chasing woman unnecessarily worried about her weight. But there are two Lucy tales and they make the issue worthwhile. In the first, confusion over a fraternity pin is resolved with Lucy and Wally together and Wanda the odd person out. In the second yarn, Lucy develops a crush on the new high school gym teacher, who asks her "to come out to my house tonight and meet the family …"—which turns out to be his wife and children, much to Lucy's surprise. Properly chastened, she retreats to Wally's arms.

Lucy #3 has a cover signed by Mort Drucker and, like the other issues, has unsigned Lucy art that may be by Dave Berg. The highlight of the issue is another one-shot character, this one a clever teen named Peggy, and deals with the hysterical developments when everyone in Peggy's family tries the offer of a free one-week trial of a television set from three different stores.

The best of the three Lucy stories finds her getting a modeling agency job, only to learn that she "is supposed to be the unfortunate teen-ager whose mother doesn't own a whizzo automatic floor scrubber" and thus is photographed mopping floors. "Just think! You get ten bucks for the job!" the cameraman tells her … which would be well over $100 in today's dollars for a quick but humiliating job!

Except for the third of the unmemorable Kenny short stories, *Lucy* #4 is all Lucy, with three longer and three one-page Lucy stories. The cover is the best of the four issues, with Lucy emerging from a tailor shop with a dollar sign on her chest as two fellow cheerleaders wear the proper "S." The three stories are all amusing but the best is the last Lucy story, with our heroine fooling Wanda by wearing a wig and thus winning a role promised by visiting movie star Lana Grable.

Meet Miss Pepper

Alas, that was the end of Lucy, the Real Gone Gal. In her place, for only two issues, came the teacher humor title *Meet Miss Pepper* by Joe Kubert, Norman Maurer and Bob Bean. *Meet Miss Pepper* #5 (April 1954) and #6 (June 1954) were mostly wild slapstick career girl comics with high school student and faculty antics. It would have been nice to see more issues from

Meet Miss Pepper #6 (second issue), June 1954, copyright St. John Publishing Corp. This title ran only two issues, taking over from _Lucy the Real Gone Gal_, but featured funny art by Joe Kubert.

Kubert and Company, if only to find out if the three capable artists could have made the comic better.

What makes these six St. John issues fun is not only the wild ideas the characters cook up, but how different they are from the far more successful and comparatively far more logical contemporary Patsy Walker and Archie titles.

30

Oh, What a Brother!

Teen humor reached an attractive new level with the five-issue run of *Oh, Brother!* in 1953.

Teen humor was almost entirely the realm of top-tier and strong second-tier comic book firms when the genre began in the 1940s. But in the first half of the 1950s—before the expansion of television and the advent of the Comics Code Authority began to badly hurt the field—several tiny companies tried to crack the teen ranks.

Among them was tiny Stanhall Publications, a part of Trojan Publications, which released 38 comics in 1953 and 55 in 1954, of which five were *Oh, Brother!* in 1953 followed by four issues of *The Farmer's Daughter* in 1954. All of them are scarce today, indicating they didn't last long despite their quality.

Creator Hal Seeger's *Oh, Brother!*, illustrated by the talented Bill Williams, was an intelligent venture, dealing with the always amusing antics of high school freshman Brother Blair and older sister Ellen, who dated college men and was often frustrated by her younger brother. We don't learn Brother's real name is Bertram until #3 (May 1953), but it doesn't matter, because no one calls him that, not even his parents when they shout in frustration. There were several successful titles involving little kids and many more related the adventures of teenagers and glamorous 20-something "working girls," but in 1953, putting a high school freshman in the comic book spotlight was unusual, especially a boy.

Seeger and Williams focused on telling genuine plot-driven stories rather than on slapstick antics. Like so many teen humor titles, *Oh, Brother!* #1 seemingly appeared out of nowhere, with no origin story or appearances in any other media.

In the first story, Brother's father asks him to return a box to Mr. Stevenson, a bank president in Newtown. Brother's precocious eighth-grade friend Babs (who has a crush on Brother) can't resist peeking inside the box and finds a hat. Brother: "That could mean only one thing—Mr. Stevenson's bank has run out of money!" (Brother is too young to remember the Great Depression, but bank collapses had a huge mental effect on the population.)

Babs asks her mother to contribute to the Stevenson family, thereby setting off a chain reaction that results on a run at Stevenson's bank. "That's wonderful, Babs!" Brother says when they see the crowd rushing the bank. "That means business is picking up at the bank!" Brother is wrong, but the banker assures people the bank is okay, so Brother and Babs decide to turn over everything to the Helping Hand Society.

Oscar Blair, Brother's father, thus is forced to buy back the hat he borrowed, so he can return it to Stevenson. But because, as he tells Brother, "You've got a good heart," nobody is too agitated. Until the last panel, when Brother confesses he has donated his father's shoes and suits! This gentle story is typical of the entire series.

A Funny Football Story

The second story is much funnier: Brother tells Babs he has received a promise from the freshman football coach that he will get a chance to play. On his way to the locker room, he spends ten cents on a voice-throwing device, saying, "I'll bet I can have fun with one of these in the locker room." And so he does, but his teammates don't think it's so funny when they go to a lot of trouble "rescuing" someone from being trapped in a locker, only to have Brother tell them it was all a voice-throwing joke.

When a teammate accidentally traps Brother in a locker, everyone thinks it's just more funny stuff and Brother can't get out in time for the start of the game. Babs comes to the rescue and Brother enters a tie game with two minutes left, as the coach says, "A promise is a promise!" Brother uses the voice-throwing device to make the Truman High ball-carrier think the ball is talking to him: "Please don't hold me so tight! I'm only a little football!" He fumbles into Brother's arms and Brother runs for a game-winning touchdown.

Brother tells the befuddled Truman team that the ball-carrier is right when he says the ball seemed to talk to him. The would-be goat slaps Brother on the back in gratitude and he swallows the device. In the last panel, it's an "Oh, Brother!" moment for the coach, when Brother tells him, "Coach, I want to thank you from the bottom of my heart … even though it's coming from the pit of my stomach!"

The "Oh, Sister!" story finds Ellen in an identity switch with her youthful-looking mother, who knows more about how to handle boys, but Ellen's date knew it all along. It's not a bad story, but nowhere near as funny as "Oh, Brother!" tales.

Not all the stories in the series are wildly funny, but at least one tale in every issue is laugh-out-loud amusing. In #2 (March 1953), it's the tale of how Babs wants a lock of hair from movie star Guy Dearing on his visit to Newtown. After much finagling involving a hotel bellhop friend, Brother discovers the star is bald and wears a wig. But that doesn't stop him from getting an autograph for Babs while also using his good heart to salvage the star's pride. In #3, Brother inadvertently leads police to bank robbers and gets a

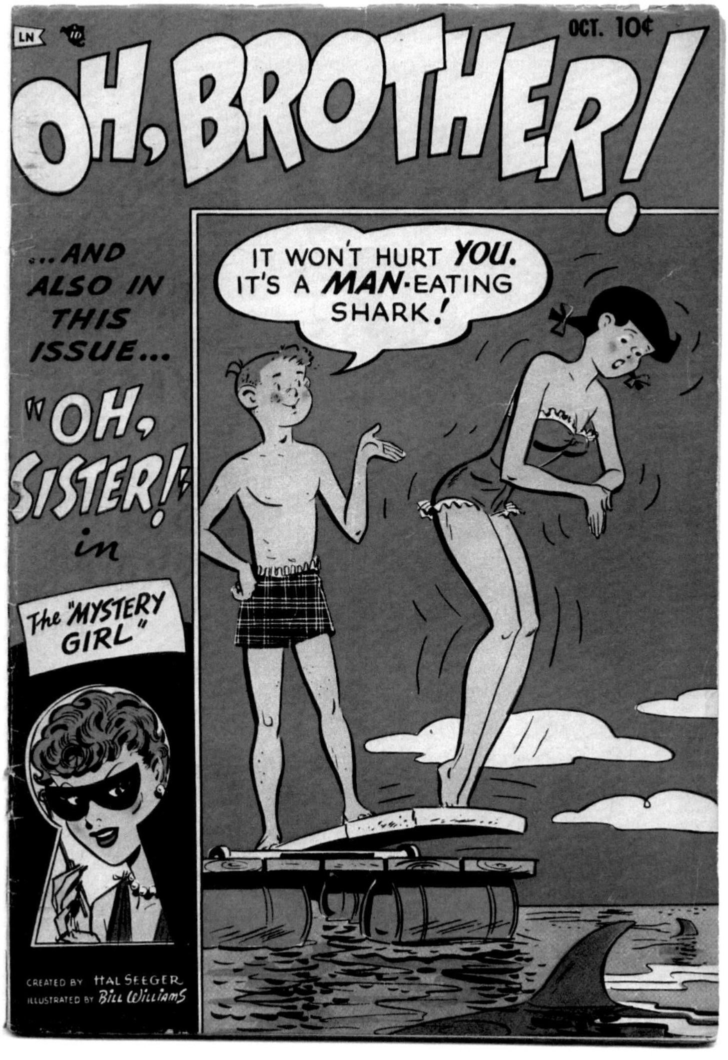

***Oh, Brother!* #5, October 1953, copyright Hal Seeger. This series was often genuinely funny and deserved a better fate with tiny Stanhall Publications. Cover by Bill Williams.**

$25 reward, which he gives to Ellen. When she asks him why, he answers, "Because—the next time I find a man for you and tell him you're loaded, I want it to be the truth!"

Williams' covers for the last two issues are especially clever. For #4 (July 1953), Brother brings an apple to class and tells the teacher, "Since you're only a substitute teacher, I brought you half an apple!" The cover of #5 has Babs unwilling to dive off a pier with a shark in the water, only to have Brother tell her, "It won't hurt you. It's a man-eating shark!"

"Oh, Sister!" in #5 features Ellen disguising herself as an exotic visitor in town so she can "date" boyfriend Ollie during his crusade to make Ellen jealous. Newspaper photos taken at a dance club show Ellen has lost a shoe, so Ellen can't tell Ollie she was his mysterious date. "Everyone in town will know I wear as much as a size 8 shoe!" Ellen tells her friend. Today, size 8 is common in shoe stores!

The Farmer's Daughter

One of the few pre–Comics Code teen humor titles that would not have passed the Code was Stanhall's risqué "The Farmer's Daughter." The fourth and final issue was dated October 1954 and was likely still on some racks when the Comics Code Authority was founded by most members of the comics industry in September 1954. The Code symbol began appearing on comics dated February 1955 (at the earliest). By May and June issues, all corporate newsstand comics except those from Dell, Gilberton (the Classics titles) and the Canadian publisher Superior carried the Code symbol.

The Farmer's Daughter was another Hal Seeger creation, as indicated in the indicia, but the unsigned art was definitely not by Bill Williams. In fact, the totally unorthodox art was neither signed nor credited on the covers, as it was on *Oh, Brother!*

Except for lovely Amy Dingle, who appeared to be about 18 years old, all the characters were drawn in remarkably exaggerated, cartoony ways and the stories were the ultimate in slapstick. The plots, if they can be called that, involved a whole lot of double entendres along with Father Dingle's attempts to protect his daughter from visitors to the farm such as traveling salesmen, men who want to purchase the farm, hired hand Orville (who was also protective in his own way) and more.

Stanhall publicized the *Farmer's Daughter* debut with a full-page house ad for #1: "GET HEP … She's the newest sensation! The gayest and most tantalizing comic book on the stands today. Sparkling with fun and frolic from cover to cover. Find out what really happened when she met the Traveling Salesman. She'll steal your heart from the first page on." The ad continued at the bottom of the page, "This doll is terrific! Make a date with The Farmer's Daughter. Give yourself a real treat … get a copy from your news dealer today and you'll agree that she's a honey!"

For *The Farmer's Daughter* #1 (February–March 1954), a scarce title, the cover featured tall, blonde, full-figured Amy day-dreaming along the fence as a traveling salesman approached on the path, wildly chased by Father Dingle, who looked a lot more like a grumpy grandfather. Amy was usually pictured almost falling out of her blouse. Since the Comics Code did not allow cleavage to be portrayed for any genre—for example, pre–Code romance reprints were always retouched—Amy's two big features would not have been allowed any exposure.

The cover theme on all four issues was "She was only the farmer's daughter, but …" inscribed on an arrow pointing inside. Issue #2 (April–May 1954) has Mr. Dingle telling a leering salesman, "Can't Figger Why You City Fellas Always Stop Here 'Stead O' Thet Nice Hotel Down Th' Road …" as Amy flashes a come-hither smile.

None of the stories are memorable, but the last story in #4 does have a great last line. The title is "What Happens When the Baby Arrives" but that refers to the toddler with whom a couple, Harold and Kathy, are traveling when they stop to inquire if the Dingle farm is for sale. Amy tells them there is one for sale 20 miles up the road and volunteers to look after the child. Much confusion ensues when the kid says "ma ma" and both father and Orville go ape, threatening a shotgun wedding for Amy when Harold returns. Oddly, Harold thanks Mr. Dingle when the truth comes out, because Kathy realizes she wants to keep Harold happy after trying to convince him to become a gentleman farmer.

In the last two panels, Harold says of Kathy's shyness, "Can't blame her, though! When folks ask what I do, she's too bashful to say!" Amy asks, "Why? What do you do?" And, as the title recedes into the mists of comic collecting history, Harold replies, "I publish comic books!"

Stanhall and Hal Seeger tried one other humor title involving men and women, *Broadway Hollywood Blackouts*, which ran from #1 (March–April 1954) through #3 (July–August 1954). There was a good share of cleavage in numerous short joke stories, but the humor did not involve teenagers.

31

The Most Obscure Teen Humor Comic Book

The only comic book produced in the first half of the 1950s by the Green Publishing Company of Wilkes-Barre, Pennsylvania, was also somehow connected with some of the worst teen humor art ever released by any corporate publisher.

The identity of the artist involved in the two scarce 1950 issues of Fox Comics' teen humor title *Romeo Tubbs* will likely forever remain unknown. That's probably just as well, because the only aspect of this title worse than the art is the writing. Likewise, it's not known how the 1952 issue of *Romeo Tubbs* from Green came about, or who worked on it.

Romeo Tubbs began out of nowhere with #26 (May 1950) after Fox killed *My Secret Life*, a sleazy romance comic that is listed in the *Romeo Tubbs* indicia as the former title. There was some bookkeeping confusion, since *My Secret Life* accurately ended with #26 (March 1950), so the first issue of *Romeo Tubbs* should have been #27.

Fox was notorious for picking up new titles from Fox's other totally unrelated titles to try to save on postage permit costs. Sometimes Fox got caught and had to renumber a new title.

The second and seemingly final issue of *Romeo Tubbs* was #28 (July 1950), which is scarce enough that it was not listed or pictured in the *Gerber Photo Journal* in 1989. Fox's headquarters were listed in Wilkes-Barre in the Fox indicia listings of the time.

But ... and in the case of the strange Fox company, there's often a but ... a third *Romeo Tubbs* popped up with a December 1952 date and listed as #27. The cover's logo style and the banner "That Lovable Teenager" (with Teenager spelled as one word) were exactly the same as the Fox issues and so was the home office city: Wilkes-Barre, although no street address was listed as it was in the Fox issues.

The format of the Green issue was exactly the same as that of the two Fox issues: three Romeo Tubbs stories and one tale with the logo of his love interests, Hildegarde and Daisy. Thus, the Green personnel—whoever they were—apparently acquired an unpublished Fox art stash for the never-Fox third issue.

Except for a handful of one-shot issues in fall 1951, Victor Fox ended his often-controversial line of comics late in 1950 after 11 years on the newsstands. But not, however, before trying to cash in on the 1949–1950 romance comics craze. Fox started 21 romance titles, all but two of which started with *My*… Three titles died outright and 18 had numbering picked up by non-romance comics. Some of the title changes are amusing today: *My Desire* became *Murder, Inc.*; *My Intimate Affair* morphed into *Inside Crime*; and *My Love Affair* emerged as *March of Crime*!

The Romeo Tubbs stories were characterized by an endless series of mixups and slapstick antics. There were no fashion tips and not much in the way of sports at Centerville High; it was just Romeo Tubbs (no, he was not heavy) conspiring with his sleepy buddy Beanie to find a way to beat out the ostensibly better looking Byron in order to date Hildegarde and sometimes Daisy.

Faculty members like the biology teacher Mr. Punctilious (the only staffer in the first two issues) and Miss Grizzly were drawn in the most less-than-complimentary styles possible. But then, except for Romeo and his two sweethearts, who definitely were no threat to Archie, Betty and Veronica, nobody looked good in this comic book.

What makes issues like this worthwhile is their sheer scarcity and oddity.

Zoot Turns to Teens

Fox's *Zoot Comics*, a Golden Age title that began with funny animals and finished most of its run with jungle heroes and heroines, turned to never-before-seen teens (and never-after-seen teens, for that matter) for issues #5 (January–February 1947) and #6 (March–April 1947). Both issues are exceptionally difficult to find.

The only noteworthy feature is the ten-page introduction of *Honey* in #6. The logo has a message ("Starting a new strip") and the introduction is as follows:

> Meet Miss America!! No, she hasn't won any beauty contest and she's not striking (enough) for a movie contract (although she's thought about it). But she is Miss America. Sure, you know her. She dresses in the latest style—sloppy slacks and her brother's field jacket. How old is she? Well you know women, they never tell their age. So let's say she's teenish!—That's right, she lives around the corner (she stands by a street sign with 'Main Street U.S.A.')—She's everybody's kid sister!

It was thus ironic that a second-tier comic company introduced the only appearance of a character with more fanfare than most companies began the adventures of far more commercially successful teens.

Honey's boyfriend is a hot-shot hot rodder named Chester (and only Chester). The art is, to put it kindly, surreal at best, especially the dance scenes. *Honey*, like all the other teens in *Zoot* #5 and #6, is not signed.

Fox did have three 1940s teen comics that were well done in their own frankly sensual way: *Junior* and *Sunny* (original comics characters) and *Meet Corliss Archer* (based on the long-running radio character). (They have their own well-deserved chapter.)

32

Junior Hopp and the Hopp Rod

Although one could debate the accuracy of the scarcity index listings in Ernie Gerber's two-volume *Photo-Journal Guide to Comic Books* (1989–1990), one has to admire just how many Golden Age comics are listed and photographed. About half of the covers of the approximately 38,000 comics published in the 1934–1959 era are included (along with a number of key early 1960s issues) and the vast majority of them are listed. Since this was three decades ago, when much remained to be learned about comic book publishing history, there are numerous errors, but few comics are left out of the listings entirely.

That brings us to the scarce three-issue run of *Junior Hopp Comics* in 1952 from the then-fledgling company operated by Stanley P. Morse (known as SPM in the *Junior Hopp* indicia listings). They aren't listed in the *Photo-Journal* at all, which made *Junior Hopp* one of the few comics with more than one issue that were not listed.

It is possible that Gerber knew of them but thought they were a Canadian publication, since the indicia of all three issues read PRINTED IN CANADA, but they were nonetheless primarily an American publication. The publisher's office was in New York City, all the ads were for firms with addresses in the United States, and all 26 names of letter writers printed on a Junior Hopp Club page in #3 (July 1952) were likewise from addresses in the U.S. (two were from Hawaii, then a U.S. territory). The Morse company, linked to several small imprints, began publishing comics in 1951 with six issues across two titles and became best known among collectors for their grim and grisly horror and crime comics, which are included in the *Photo-Journal*.

The cover of #3 was signed by future *Mad* magazine artist Dave Berg, along with one Junior Hopp story in that issue. Otherwise, the work is all unsigned and uncredited. On the pages listing opportunities to join the Junior Hopp Club (an obvious knockoff of the Archie Club), no creators or editors were mentioned.

The cover of #1 (January 1952) introduced Junior Hopp and his rotund buddy Chuck in the Hopp Rod, which had a wooden bumper with the inscription "Imagine Running Into You!" Junior tells Chuck, "Y'say the ol' Hopp Rod has no pick-up Chuck? Watch this!" while about to offer Myrna a ride.

The opening page offers a map of Highvale, Junior's hometown, complete with Highvale High and the uniquely named Fountain of Youth (the name of this teen hangout was the most creative aspect of *Junior Hopp Comics*). Junior is bannered as "The Keenest Teen in Town" and the others portrayed are girl friends Myrna and Peggy, best buddy Chuck, rival Lester, Mom, Pop and Gramps.

The stories were almost entirely illogical slapstick and drawn that way. They were seldom more than six pages long, but then character development was not a factor in *Junior Hopp Comics*. Junior was always portrayed with an odd hat with a button in front and a feather in the back. (Why he wore a feather was never explained.)

In the first story, Highvale High principal Mr. Twiddle lets Junior know his bubble gum chewing is not acceptable, but after chewing the gum himself he refuses to punish Junior. The teen hero himself comes off as a hero to Myrna, a Southern belle who conked Mr. Twiddle on the head with a thrown shoe but gave credit to Junior for not telling on her. The second story was even wackier, with Peggy and the soda jerk at the Fountain of Youth conniving to have Junior spray Myrna with water instead of perfume, thereby leaving Junior to the clutches of Peggy for the big dance. Another story was the funniest of the six in #1, what with Chuck's pet aardvark saving a picnic by eating all the ants.

In #2 (April 1952), Junior conks Lester on the head with a vase worth 98 cents after Lester concocts a plot to make Junior think he has gone to great slapstick lengths to save a valuable Ming Dynasty vase. In another story, the school superintendent is called "the commissioner," and Mr. Twiddle hides in a garbage can after Junior has left exploding cigars on the principal's desk and he gives them to the commissioner.

Dave Berg draws a funny, creative story in #3 involving the hijinx of Junior and Chuck for the police faculty softball game. Mr. Twiddle runs afoul of a police officer who flunked Twiddle's English course when he was a teacher. Junior and Chuck help their principal break out of jail in time to win the game with a pinch-hit home run, but Mr. Twiddle finds himself back in jail and begs Junior not to help him break out again.

A *Junior Hopp* reprint from #1 mysteriously appeared in *Algie* #2 (February 1954), part of a poor three-issue teen humor series from tiny Timor Publications, which may have been affiliated with Morse. *Algie* #1 is pictured in the Gerber *Photo-Journal*, but that's about all the publicity this raggedly drawn, even more raggedly *written* series deserved. *Junior Hopp* and

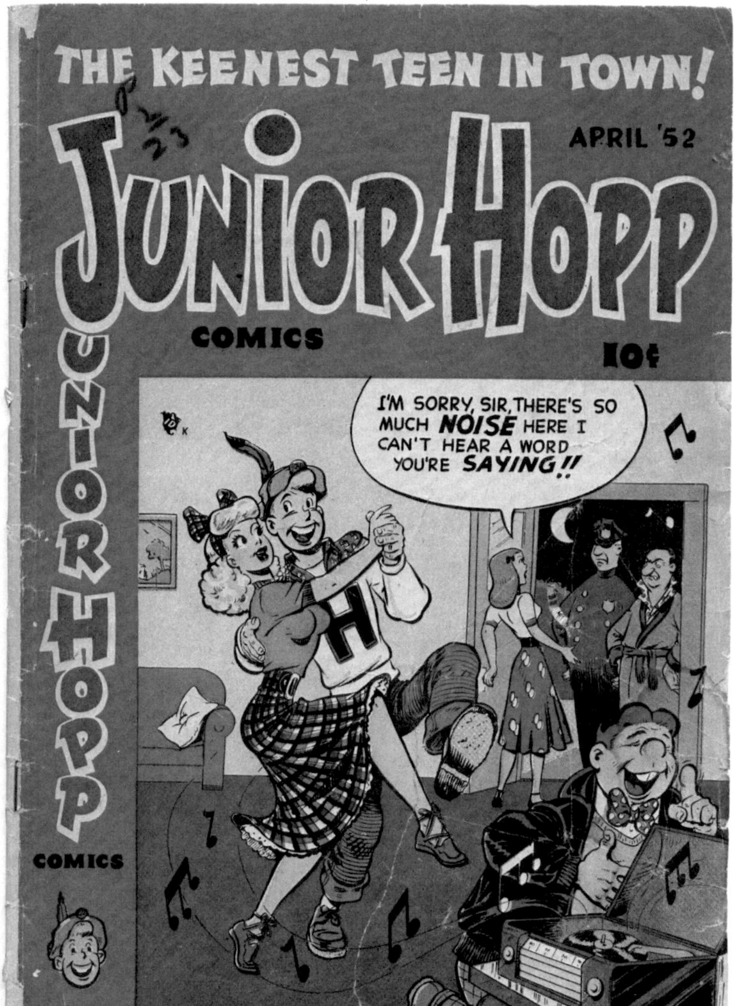

Junior Hopp #2, April 1952, copyright S.P.M. Publications. S.P.M. stands for Stanley P. Morse, who had a number of interconnected companies in the 1950s. This title ran only three issues.

Algie, with three issues apiece, were typically unsuccessful titles from small publishers.

Although the large companies Marvel, DC, Archie, Quality and Dell did not succeed with every teen humor title they tried, they also produced the vast majority of the most memorable and financially successful titles. Of the many small companies that produced only a few dozen comics apiece of any kind—at most!—only one teen title ran as many as seven issues in the 1940s or 1950s. That was *Junie Prom* from Dearfield Publications, detailed in Chapter 14.

Hector Comics

Junior Hopp was not the only character bannered across the top as "The Keenest Teen in Town." So was Hector in the short run of *Hector Comics* #1 (November 1953) through #3 (March 1954) from tiny Key Publications. That was no coincidence, since Key was one of the firms operated by Stanley P. Morse and Hector was a basically a reworked Junior Hopp.

These weren't noteworthy efforts, but the unsigned cover of #2 (January 1954) is hilarious and creative, showing Hector and girlfriend Mona stranded on the rocks in a boat with Mona complaining, "Well, Hector! At least this time you didn't say that you ran out of gas!"

Almost all the stories in these three issues are signed by Ben Brown, whose style of drawing teenagers was surreal, to say the least. Everything, especially heads, was shaped in a weirdly cartoony fashion. But the art is so different, some collectors might like it. It certainly doesn't look like anything done even a few years earlier.

In *Hector* #3, the story "A Tisket, a Basket" involves a scheme by Dextor, Hector's rival for the affections of Bonnie and occasionally Mona, to prevent Hector from taking Bonnie to the dance. "I'm the captain of the team—and I just decided I need him badly!" Dextor tells Bonnie, who had agreed to date Hector because he wasn't playing in the basketball game.

Hector is thrilled to get the chance to play but finds he can't shoot well. Bonnie tells him she's captain of the girls' team and gives him pointers. That's when Hector tells Bonnie that the point leader between Hector and Dextor will have the most dances with newcomer Harriet Honeybun. Dextor's best effort to score the most points fails, but it all works out well with Hector because he realizes he'll dance with Bonnie.

The logic of this story, even in the surreal world of Hector, does not pass muster. There would never be a situation where the team captain picks the players (although no coach is shown); and how would Hector not have earlier realized that Bonnie was a basketball star?

33

The Short-Run Guys in the Not-So-Nifty '50s

Ironically, the first two fellows who received their own teen humor comics, *Archie* and *Wilbur*, were the most successful. A few others who started in the 1940s did well, but the guys whose eponymous titles began in the 1950s were almost entirely duds instead of comic book studs like the first two.

Of the teen boys outside the Archie Universe whose own titles ran only in the 1950s, only Dell's *Henry Aldrich* (22 issues) and DC's *Here's Howie* (18 issues) enjoyed even a modicum of success. It's actually somewhat astonishing that the other titles did not even reach double-figure publication numbers. Some of the boys, of course, were seen more often in girls' comics and as backups in anthology and adventure titles. Then there was a relative success story like Charlton's *Freddy*, which was birthed in 1958 and lasted 36 issues into 1964.

In this chapter, we're talking about five characters from the 1950s: Quality's *Gabby* and *Jonesy*, Toby's *Meet Merton*, Lev Gleason's *Dilly Duncan* and Charles Biro's *Jim Dandy*. The rest are covered elsewhere.

But just to show how futile most of the '50s fellows really were, check out this alphabetical list: *Algie, Andy Hardy, Dilly Duncan, Everything Happens to Harvey, Flat-Top, Freckles* (Argo edition), *Gabby, Hector, Homer Hooper, Jim Dandy, Jonesy, Junior Hopp, Leroy, Meet Merton, Mortie, Oh, Brother!, Ricky, Rodger Dodger, Romeo Tubbs* and *Stevie*.

Those 20 titles, combined, ran for a grand total of only 89 issues!

Comic book publishers and editors of the 1950s were well aware of this, if only on an instinctual, gut level. Only one of these titles, the science fictional three-issue run of *Jim Dandy* in 1956, began publication later than 1954. None made it into 1957 in his own title.

The most successful, at least in terms of volume, were the little two bow-tied teens from Quality, Gabby and Jonesy, both of which had been backups until surprisingly being given their own titles. Surprising, that is, in retrospect, since they both took over from two of Quality's better action-adventure titles. *Gabby* began with #11 (July 1953) after ten issues of the noir-oriented detective Ken Shannon, and *Jonesy* started with #85 (August 1953) after 22 issues of *Crack Western*, which itself was spun off from 62 issues of the superhero title *Crack Comics*.

***Jonesy* #5, April 1954, copyright Comic Favorites, Inc. This title took the place of Quality Comics' wild and wooly *Crack Western*, but *Jonesy* had its own share of slapstick action.**

Quality had long been running teen humor characters as backup strips but only Candy had held down her own book (see her chapter). Her boyfriend Ted Dawson thus appeared in hundreds of stories. So why did Quality decide to hit the trail, er, stands, with *Gabby* and *Jonesy*? Perhaps it was because only *Blackhawk*, *Plastic Man* and *G.I. Combat* survived Quality's purge of action-oriented comics in 1953. Quality dispatched *Dollman* with #47 and cancelled *Police Comics* with #127 (both October 1953) after giving up on *Ken Shannon* with #10 (April 1953) and *Crack Western* with #84 (May 1953). All four had become comics with intense themes involving violence, and there was plenty of that left in *Blackhawk*, *Plastic Man* and *G.I. Combat*. The rights to all of them were purchased by DC when Quality discontinued comics at the end of 1956.

The folks at Quality, which was among the largest and best of the Golden Age companies, continued *Gabby* with #2–9 (September 1954) and *Jonesy* with #2–8 (October 1954) to finish with nine and eight similar issues, respectively. Both titles were slapstick-oriented and exceptionally cartoonish, featuring six stories in most issues, all running four to six pages.

Neither *Gabby* nor *Jonesy* was focused primarily on high school life the way the Archie and Marvel teen characters were in the 1950s. All of their stories would immediately introduce a plot point and follow it to its usually wild conclusion. Neither bothered to introduce the cast of characters in the first issue. Quality figured that "Hey Kid It's Gabby Louder and Funnier" and "For a Laugh a Minute Jonesy Wits and Half-Wits" would be the cover blurbs. The banner across the bottom for *Gabby* was "Gabby Hyatt … the Teen-Age Laugh Riot" and the banner across the top for *Jonesy* was "Gags and Gals and Teen-Age Pals."

None of the stories or covers was signed or credited to the artists, all of whom were more than competent in the high-caliber Quality way. The covers were nothing special, although the joke on the cover of *Gabby* #3 (November 1953) wasn't bad: A waiter asks, "How did you find your steak, sir?" and Gabby replies, "I'm just lucky! I happened to move the potato … and there it was!"

Jonesy was involved, if that's the word, with brunette Carol and blonde Mary Jane and his timid buddy Weepy and their frenemy Jeepers. Jonesy was always getting into jams like the cute story in #5 (April 1954), "The Voice Is Yet to Come," when Carol plays a love song as Jonesy walks by and he thinks she's a great singing prospect. True to the ethos of the series, a pie-throwing comic act breaks out as planned by an impresario who offers Carol the chance to warble before a crowd at a studio. Jonesy ends up alone at home, listening to his heartthrob Rosemary Rooney on a platter.

Jonesy, who dressed well and always wore a hat, was often part of a surreal scene. In #8, for example, Carol forces him into a track and field meet, only to have Jeepers unleash a nest of hornets on Jonesy's backside. On the last page of the story, Jonesy proceeds to set school records in the 100-yard dash, the low hurdles, the high jump and the discus throw while trying to shake the hornets. With Jonesy, everything happened in an alternate universe!

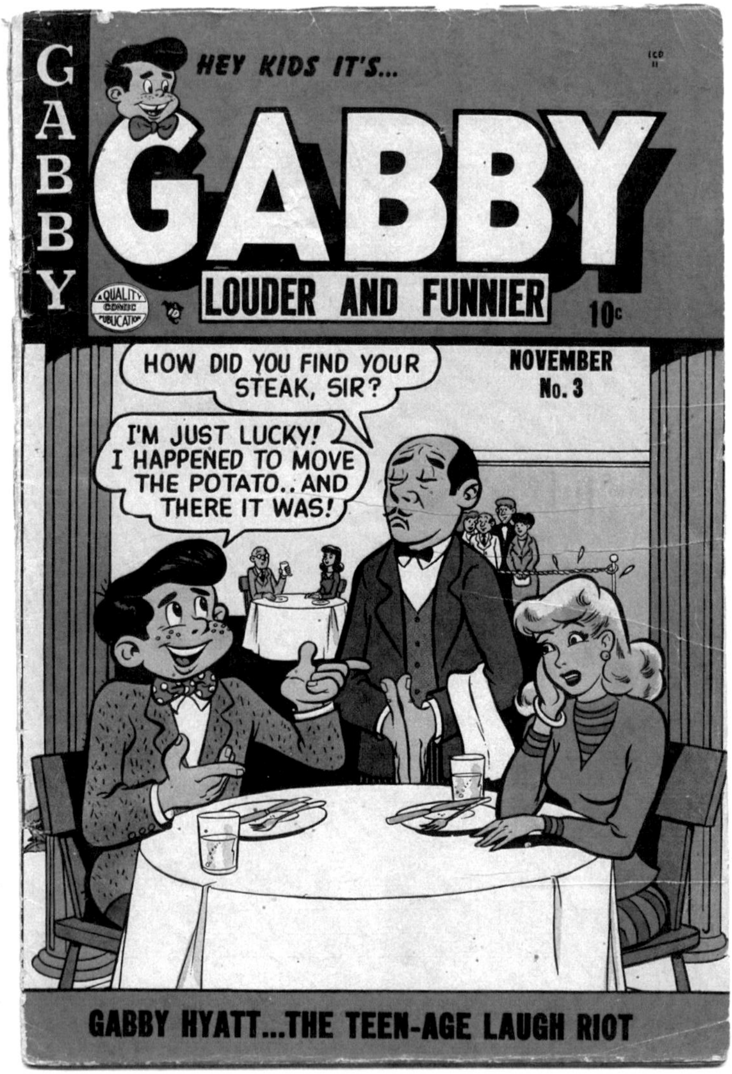

Gabby #3, November 1953, copyright Comic Favorites, Inc. Gabby, a fat, talkative little guy, ironically took the place of hard-boiled detective Ken Shannon in Quality's lineup.

Gabby also had a fat little friend, the well-meaning Peahead Wilson, plus their nerdy friend Algy Duckworth. There were two beautiful girls in the boys' lives, the blonde Taffy O'Toole and the redhead Rusty, who often liked Peahood for his mild-mannered nature. (The percentage of redheads in teen humor comics was far higher than real life, partly because red is one of the primary colors.) Like Jonesy, Gabby was not an athlete or ruffian, but rather a well-dressed idea man.

Gabby's ideas, though, often didn't pan out, such as his attempt to work in a laundromat in the story "Clothes Spin" in the first issue. The result, a riot with several women involved, was a truly funny story that finished with Gabby and Peahead keeping the girls away from the dance while they try to iron matters out (pun fully intended).

In *Gabby* #2 (September 1953), Gabby takes Peahead's suggestion and they hire out as babysitters. It's looking grim with little Chester when the baby's glamorous Aunt Doris shows up and entertains the boys. Gabby dances with her while saying, "This must be a dream! Nothing works out this good except in comic books!"

Gabby, again like Jonesy, was not an athlete, unlike the likes of Archie, Wilbur and Patsy Walker's boyfriend, Buzz Baxter. But when Gabby goes on a fox hunt on horseback, he catches the fox—and makes friends with the critter! The boys and girls end up at a picnic—with the fox, of course—after telling everyone else, "Yeah, he went that way!"

In "Beauty vs. Duty," Gabby is terrified to be judging the high school beauty contest, with four lovely girls all set to convince him, but it turns out perfectly for him when the girls batter and bruise each other in the dressing room following a series of verbal onslaughts. The winner: Miss Prunepit of the faculty! But when Gabby treats a bandaged Taffy to a soda, she asks, "Why do you keep saying everything worked out fine," and he responds, "Maybe some day I'll explain it to you, Taffy!"

Gabby's rival, the tall, athletic but slimy Smedley, is the star of "Convenient Arrangement #9" (September 1954), the last issue. Smedley sabotages the instruments of Gabby and his band, the High Hatters, but it works out well when the strange music that results turns the kids on at the school dance. They look like early rock'n'rollers and Smedley winds up "playing" the drums—with his head!

Meeting Merton

One of the teen boys' comics that deserved a better fate was the four-issue run of *Meet Merton* from second-tier publisher Toby Press by soon-to-be *Mad* magazine regular Dave Berg. He did the covers and Merton stories from #1 (December 1953) through #4 (June 1954).

***Meet Merton* #4, June 1954, copyright Toby Press, Inc. Future *Mad Magazine* great Dave Berg drew all four issues and covers of *Meet Merton* and showed the ability that made him a star with the "Usual Gang of Idiots."**

The adventures of Merton Muddle, his rotund buddy Calories Casey, and his love interests, the blonde Marcia Thorndyke and the raven-haired Jo Ann, plus fittingly named scheming rival Chris Cross, are among the funniest of that teen humor era. Berg had a way of drawing facial expressions that can't help but make a reader laugh out loud at times.

In "Crazy Disk Jockey!" in #3 (April 1954), Merton and Calories plot to plant a recorder in the girls' locker room so they can listen to what the girls really think of them. Not only does Merton get trapped and exposed in girls' clothes, but later the girls discover the recorder and pretend to be insulting Merton and the boys. Guess who learns his lesson?

The football story in #2 (February 1954), "The Eyes Have It," isn't bad in the humor department, either. Marcia plants post-hypnotic suggestions and Merton runs off with the only football available for the boys to practice with. The result at Marcia's house is hilarity when Merton and his teammates catch Marcia in her mother's "beauty mud."

One of the best stories is "Anything for a Laugh" in #4, in which Marcia wants to edit and publish a school fashion magazine and Merton wants a humor magazine. The school vote ends in a tie and the principal rules that the magazine will feature both types of content. Merton shows his chauvinist side when he tells Marcia, "I hope you don't think I'm going to take orders from a mere girl! I'll show you that running a magazine is a man's job!" Marcia retorts, "Why you conceited male! I was going to let you have a few pages at the back of the book, but …" All along, though, the principal didn't want to let either of them edit the magazine. So he picks himself and, in the last panel, as he tells himself, "Heh! Heh! Pretty clever, if I do say so myself!" Marcia tells a smiling Merton, "We've got to stick up for our rights!" and Merton responds, "For once, you're right! Shake!!"

And that is the last panel in the annals of *Meet Merton.*

Jim Dandy Is Incredible

Each issue of *Jim Dandy*—billed as "The Incredible Jim Dandy" on the covers—features Jim and his gals and pals, who can't see his friend Cup, a visitor from the planet Zikalug. Cup and his flying saucer are visible to Jim but to no one else.

The comic book ran with May, July and September 1956 dates and each issue had a 20-plus–page story of the adventures of Jim and Cup. Longtime Lev Gleason editor-writer-artist Charles Biro did the covers and most likely put together the entire book for Dandy Magazines, which has a different New York City address than Biro's longtime comic book employer, Lev Gleason Publications.

Cup's always teaching lessons about life and capabilities to the smallish Jim, who looks younger than he is. If you can totally suspend your disbelief about a lot of wacky activities, you might enjoy this. But it's badly dated now and is more of a fantasy comic than a teen humor series.

When Gleason left the comic book business late in 1956, so did Dandy

Comics, so there must have been a circulation connection. Jim Dandy is a lot tougher to find than any of the Gleason comics of the period.

Dilly Duncan: From Backup to Bust

Three years before Biro published *Jim Dandy*, he tried his first teen humor comic with the title *Dilly*, sub-billed as "Dilly Duncan of Daredevil Comics." Dilly began as a backup in the popular Lev Gleason hero title *Boy Comics* in #57–71 (September 1950 through November 1951) After the Little Wise Guys, who had long served as the Lev Gleason costume hero Daredevil's group of young heroes, took over the title with #70 (January 1951), Dilly became a member of Daredevil's lineup.

The publisher retained the Daredevil title until the series ended with #134 (September 1956). The colorful hero himself reappeared in #79 and #80 before departing for good.

Dilly Duncan of Dorset High was bannered as "America's Funniest School Hero" in all three issues. Indeed, all three covers were humorous and drawn by Biro, but the stories were more like "brave teen tackles tall task and proves his mettle." The stories had a lot more serious moments than light-hearted fun.

Dilly was thus among Gleason's few failures. Biro and Gleason teamed to produce several other long-running Golden Age titles, including *Crime Does Not Pay, Crime and Punishment, Boy Loves/Meets Girl, Lovers' Lane* and the masked western title *Black Diamond*.

Biro, a longtime pro, wrote an introduction to *Dilly* at the top of "The Big Dance," the first story in #1 (May 1953). It reads:

> Meet Dilly Duncan, the only kid who can do everything wrong and still come out on top! And his arch enemy, Gruesome Jones, a big hunk of muscle with a brain to match! Marvin Montmorency, educated in England but catching on fast! Hoppy Hopkins, slow, fat and a little helpless, and Dilly's girl, Carol … a cute little number who's a lot brighter than you might think, and all the rest of the gang at Dorset High. We think you'll enjoy getting to know them!

Notice the only character without a last name is Carol! But, alas, women's lib was nearly two decades away.

In the first story, a ten-pager typical of Biro's dense writing, at least for comics of the time, Dilly helps solve his family's financial problems and catches a couple of scammers to boot. Things don't end so well in the second story, "Gruesome Gets the Girl," when Carol dumps a pail of water on Dilly for paying attention to someone else.

Snooty rich boy Ellsworth Edgerton joins the high school gang in #2 (July 1953) in "To Jump or Not to Jump." Dilly saves him from drowning dur-

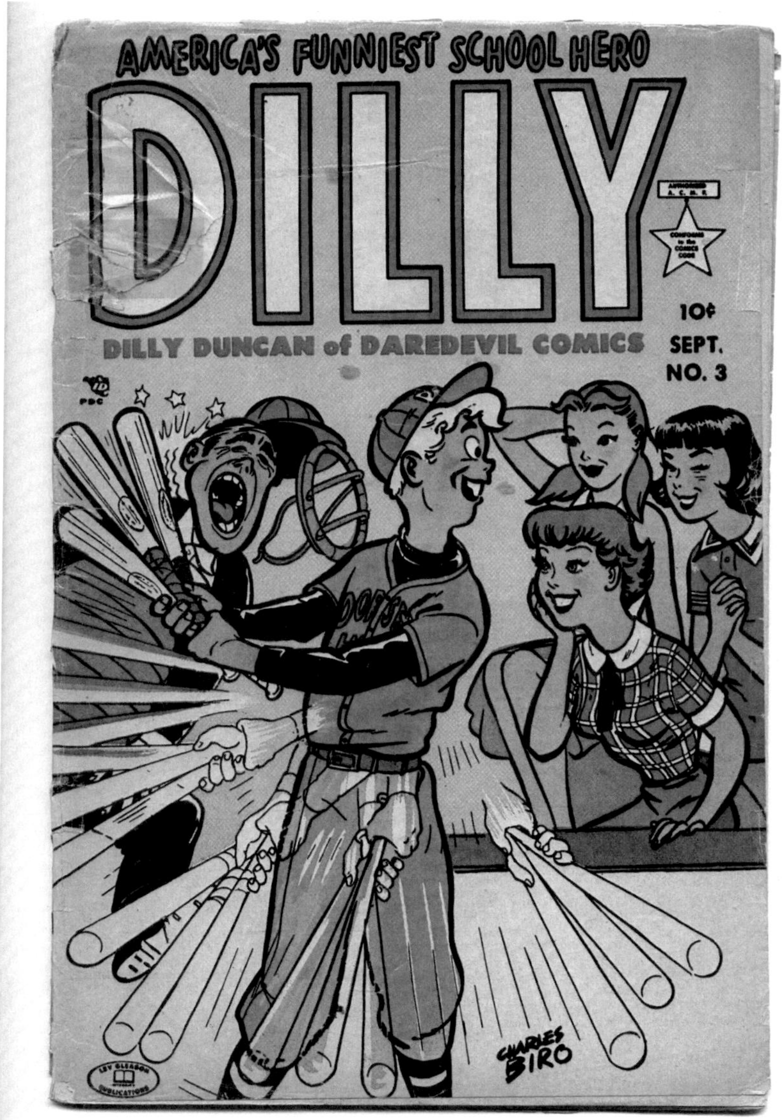

***Dilly* #3, September 1953, copyright Lev Gleason Publications, Inc. This is the last issue of *Dilly*, which was a successful backup in Gleason's Boy Comics and Daredevil Comics but a flop on his own. Cover by Charles Biro.**

ing a canoe race but then lays him out with one punch when he complains about Dilly paying attention to Carol, whom Ellsworth figured had become his girl. In the second story, "The Moth-Eaten Musketeers," Dilly inadvertently saves his father's job.

Dilly #3 (September 1953) featured "The Carnival Queen Kidnapping," in which Carol is frustrated by Dilly, and "The Baby Sitting Service," in which Dilly ends up being on good terms with his father when it seemed he wouldn't.

The backup strip in all three issues, *Betty Campus of Suburban High*, was a series of muddled tales involving Betty and Bob, the guy who receives her favorable attention in the final story after much frustration throughout.

Section III

Introduction: The 1960s and 1970s

The 1960s featured only three long-running survivors from the 1950s from outside the Archie Universe, but several newcomers to the teen comic scene provided a much-needed dose of fun and a collectible aspect.

The total number of non–Archie teen humor issues in the 1960s, fewer than 300 in comparison to a little more than 1,000 with the Archie characters, provided a unique genre contrast.

Marvel's *Patsy Walker*, entering the 1960s with a third or perhaps fourth generation of readers (many publishers considered a comic book-reading generation to be from five to seven years in length) ran from #87 (January 1960) through #124 (December 1965) for 38 issues. Longtime sister title *Patsy and Hedy* lasted even longer—from #68 (February 1960) through #110 (January 1967) for 43 issues.

In contrast, DC's once hugely popular *A Date with Judy*—having started in 1947 only two years after *Patsy Walker* #1—had long since left radio and television and thus lasted only six issues into 1960, from #74 (December 1959–January 1960) to #79 (October–November 1960). Even so, she was the last of the original DC teen humor comics.

The only new Marvel teens in the era were the reasonably successful *Kathy* #1–27 (1959 through 1964)—billed as "The Teen-Age Tornado"—and the short-lived *Harvey*, whose six-issue run in 1970 and 1972 after skipping 1971 made him the last of the multitude of Marvel teens.

What saved the Sixties from the standpoint of interest were three new titles that ran more than 20 issues, which is better than most teen humor start-ups did in the 1950s.

One of the finest teen humor comics of all was the New Dell's *Thirteen... Going on Eighteen* by John Stanley, the phenomenally talented artist-writer. The title ran from #1 (December 1961–January 1962) through #25 (December 1967), with reprints of the first four issues and covers running at #26–29 sporadically in 1969–1971. This was one of the first titles published by Dell after its split with Western Printing and Lithographing, which had produced Dell's comics since 1940. Western became Gold Key and took the majority of its licensed characters with it, such as those from Disney and Warner Brothers. Outside of comics, Dell had been publishing a wide variety of its own magazines and paperback books for many years.

Thirteen.... Going on Eighteen had never received much attention until accomplished Eisner Award–winning comics biographer Bill Schelly wrote Stanley's 2017 biography *John Stanley: Giving Life to Little Lulu* (the character he is best known for), published by Fantagraphics. The firm Drawn and Quarterly earlier drew some welcome attention to *Thirteen* when it reprinted the title with commentary from the creator known as Seth.

Tower Comics, a publisher of superheroes that emerged in 1965, also did well with old-style humor comics starring Tippy Teen (sounds like the name of a Chester Gould villain in *Dick Tracy*) and her friends Go-Go (a girl) and Animal (a boy). Tippy was actually tied with the superhero title *Thunder Agents* as Tower's first comic, both with #1 (November 1965). *Tippy Teen* ran through #25 (December 1969).

Harvey Comics, a major publisher whose only flirtation with teen humor occurred with the Mazie family of characters in the 1950s, decided to make the teen scene again with *Bunny* #1 (December 1966) through #20 (December 1971) followed by a one-shot final appearance dated #21 (November 1976).

Of course, teen humor powerhouse Archie, by now a comic book publishing icon, came up with what many collectors consider one of the best teen humor comics of all: Dan De Carlo's *Josie*, a character named after the stellar cartoonist's wife. The title was *She's Josie* from #1 (February 1963) through #16 (October 1965), then became *Josie* with #17 (December 1965). With #45 (December 1969), the title became *Josie and the Pussycats* in honor of her band and ran to #106 (October 1982).

Lee Holley's cute and appealing newspaper cartoon *Ponytail* found a home at the New Dell with #1 (July–September 1962) though #12 (October–December 1965) and eventually was picked up by Charlton with #13 (November 1969) through #20 (January 1971). DC had success with two titles that were quasi–teen humor, *The Many Loves of Dobie Gillis* (26 issues) from 1960 to 1964 and the Beatles-inspired *Swing with Scooter* (36 issues from 1966 to 1972).

Once again, just as happened so often in the 1950s, the boys also got the short end of teen humor luck in the 1960s with short-run titles *Dunc and Loo* (by John Stanley, with eight issues from Dell, 1961–1963); *Fast Willie Jackson* (seven issues from Fitzgerald in 1976–1977), *Henry Brewster* (seven issues from MF Enterprises in 1966–1967), *Wally* (four issues from Gold Key in 1962–1963), *Cool Cat* (three issues from Prize in 1963) and *Seymour* (two issues from the Archie Series in 1963).

34

John Stanley's Masterpiece: *Thirteen*

John Stanley was already an accomplished comic book professional when he wrote and drew possibly the best of all teen humor titles. *Thirteen* was definitely the most literate and subtle, and surely among the most unusual.

Thirteen's subtitle was "Going on Eighteen"—a phrase from an earlier era but still understood in the 1960s—and that tells you so much of what you need to know about petite blonde Val and the initially heavyset Judy. They are surely the most well-characterized 13-year-olds in comic history.

Possibly the best description of Stanley's career was applied by famed comics biographer Bill Schelly in *John Stanley: Giving Life to Little Lulu*, his perceptive 2017 book. The same could be said for the way the great *Little Lulu* artist-writer Stanley made Val and Judy spring to vivid emotional life in the 25 original issues of *Thirteen* in the 1960s.

There was no formula at all for *Thirteen*, which in itself was pretty much unique in teen humor. Stanley was given as many or as few pages as needed to tell his tales of teen angst, confusion and occasional joy. Veteran cartoonist Tony Tallarico drew the first two issues, Schelly notes while also pointing out that #3 was the first issue Stanley both wrote and drew for the New Dell.

In the first panel of *Thirteen* #1 (November 1961–January 1962) for the New Dell following the split of Dell Publishing and Western Printing and Lithographing, we see Val's 17-year-old sister Evie finding her in tears in the bedroom they share. Val tells her in "Beginner's Luck," "Even elephants have a secret place to crawl away to when they want to die!"

Answering a question about bawling from Evie, Val responds with dialogue probably never before or seen in a teen humor comic: "I wasn't bawling! I was weeping softly!"

Those two comments by Val told me, as a 13-year-old reader in the fall of 1961, that this was like no comic book that I—as a budding collector and historian—had ever read. Or probably ever would read. *Thirteen* touched some readers, including me, to the core.

Thank you, Mr. Stanley!

Schelly nailed the ethos of *Thirteen*: "The series is basically about an awkward thirteen-year-old dealing with the difference between how she thinks her life should be versus its much more prosaic reality."

Val had been upset because her mother (her father was never seen or mentioned) would not let her wear lipstick, but Evie got permission for Val

***Thirteen* #3, May–July 1962, copyright 1962 Dell Publishing Co., Inc. This was John Stanley's first cover in a unique teen series about two 13-year-olds for which he wrote all 25 issues.**

… and to use mascara, too, but only around the house. Val invites a couple of boys over but when she greets them at the door, with lipstick and mascara applied … well, way too generously! … the boys burst into laughter. "Kind of early for Halloween, isn't it, Val?" asks one. The other says, "For a second there, I thought they rented a room to a lil' ol' weirdy midget!" Val closes the door and flops on the floor face down, leaving facial evidence of her humiliation. In the last panel, Evie says, "I can't imagine how those stains got on the rug, Mother! Say, it looks like some kind of horrible face!" Mother responds, "Feels very damp. It should come out easily …" I doubt if there has ever been a more touching and effective story of emotional teen humiliation.

With more than 125 stories of Val, Judy and the spunky child Judy Jr. (either a younger version of Judy or perhaps another girl), it's not possible to do each story justice here. But here are a few highlights:

The cover of #3 (May–July 1962) is brilliant, with a boy in the background and Judy and Val saying simultaneously, "Notice the way he looked at me?" Understated doesn't begin to describe Stanley's genius.

"Judy's Twist" in #4 (September 1962) has Judy taking Val's next-door neighbor, Billy Wilson, aside because he hasn't asked Val for a dance all evening. "Ow! Oo! Ee! Ow! Oo!" are the sounds from the next room. When Billy comes out of the room, he cheerfully asks Val to dance. Bill's erstwhile partner asks Judy what she was doing with Billy, and Judy replies, "Oh, just twisting, Donna.… Arms, Donna, just arms!"

In "First Kiss" in #6 (February–April 1963), Val is thrilled to have a date with Paul Vayne, "the handsomest boy in the whole school," but she tries to hide when he appears to stand her up. She had no idea he did some modeling jobs for a photographer and she spots him and another girl in the park. The photographer soon realizes that Val is the image of the girl he wanted. In the last panel, he says, "I've got to get at least a dozen shots before the light begins to fade …" as Paul leans over to kiss Val over and over and over!.

This is the issue in which Stanley permanently takes a lot of weight off Judy. (Judy, like Val, never had a surname.)

Stanley's cover of #13 (November 1964–January 1965) shows Val telling a boy in full football face gear, "Oh, Billy, I just adore you in a football uniform … er—you are Billy, aren't you?"

Val moans and groans for three pages in #16 (August–October 1965) about how Billy hasn't called her in the ten minutes since he returned from vacation in "Welcome Home." On the final page, Billy knocks on her door and says, "I'm glad to be back, Val, because I sure missed …" after an interruption he finishes with "…playing basketball with the guys every afternoon! That's where I'm heading now!"

The last original issue, #25 (December 1967), offered "Strange Girl," in which Val changes her hairstyle and inadvertently fools Billy into thinking she's a new girl in Val's house. When Billy dresses up and confronts her and realizes it's Val, he says of her hair, "It looks terrific, Val!" Val responds, "I couldn't care less what you think of it, Billy! Evie was absolutely right about you! You wouldn't get all dressed up like that for poor me." Billy says what he thinks is logical: "Val, if I liked another girl better than you and the other girl

***Dunc and Loo* #8, October–December 1963, copyright Dell Publishing Co., Inc. Bill Williams shows how the little kids take on lanky free spirit Loo in the last issue of John Stanley's series of stories about two urban teens.**

turns out to be you, too, what's the difference?" "It shows you're fickle, Billy!" Needless to say, there's no date for them that day!

Thirteen's original run ends with #25, but #26–29 reprinted the first four issues and covers in 1968–1969. The circulation legal statement in #7 read an average of 269,940—not bad for a new title—but by #23 the circulation average for the previous year has fallen to 139,108. In those days, that meant likely cancellation.

Stanley's first signature on a comic book cover was on *Thirteen* #12 (August–October 1964). He signed every ensuing original cover except #15.

Around the Block with Dunc and Loo

Stanley's vibrant writing and Bill Williams' polished art on *Around the Block with Dunc and Loo* #1 (October–December 1961) highlighted one of the first comics the New Dell published. The theme was the slapstick-packed misadventures of two city boys, debonair Dunc and slapdash Loo. The title ran through #8 (October–December 1963), but it became simply *Dunc and Loo* with #4.

This was a solid teen humor comic, but I feel that limitations on the dialogue of teen boys prevented the feelings expressed so well in *Thirteen*.

Loo always worse a strange-looking hat, leading a kid to say, "Foul! Foul! No Stompin' on Loo's Hat" as they fouled him all over his body in a nutty basketball game on the cover of #8, which was drawn by Williams. He was the cartoonist Stanley worked with on seven 1950 and 1951 issues of Dell's *Henry Aldrich*.

35

Patsy and Hedy: A Novel Approach in the 1960s

Marvel editor Stan Lee, who wrote most of the Patsy Walker stories in the late 1950s and 1960s, tried a much different approach to this classic teen humor series toward the end of its run.

He and others wrote almost nothing but 18-page stories for the last 10 issues of *Patsy Walker* and the final 16 issues of *Patsy and Hedy*, beginning with issues for the summer of 1964. Although some of the dialogue was humorous, they actually turned the stories into soap opera–style dramas similar to much of the long groundbreaking superhero work Lee began writing with *Fantastic Four* #1 (November 1961).

It was also in 1961 and 1962 that he began using cover-featured story titles for the two remaining Patsy Walker titles while they were still running multiple stories, all short, to go with shorts and pin-ups. He did this right from the start with his superhero stories. This was quite a shift from Marvel's teen humor policy of the 1940s and 1950s, when the cover quips and sight gags usually had nothing to do with the inside contents.

In *Patsy Walker*, his first cover-featured title was in #97 (October 1961), with "Patsy Walker a Bride?" This was the story of Patsy's dream about marrying Buzz but being disappointed by his lack of attention. Buzz, having been verbally assaulted at the door after Patsy wakes up in a sour mood, asks her father, "What's she angry about, Mister Walker?" Patsy's father replies in typically 1960s sexist style: "She doesn't need a reason, my boy! She's a female, isn't she?"

Patsy's second crossover with *Millie the Model* occurred in #98 (December 1961), when Patsy acquired a blonde wig in order to portray Millie at a masquerade. As a caption puts it, "The long arm of coincidence reaches out, and look what's happening right outside of Patsy's home …" Millie's car gets a flat tire and she takes a taxi to avoid being late for a modeling job in Centerville. After fixing the tire, Millie's boyfriend Clicker sees Patsy in "Millie drag" and thinks she's Millie. When he arrives at the photo shoot with her, the real Millie sees Patsy looking like her twin. The girls quickly decide to play a trick on Clicker, who mutters, "Why didn't I become a test pilot or something easy?" At the masquerade, Hedy puts a typically snarky capper on the story when someone tells her that Patsy is dressed as Millie: "'Millie the Model?' Don't make me laugh! There isn't the least resemblance at all!"

Lee came up with another short but sweet crossover in #99 (February 1962) when Patsy Walker and her friends meet Linda Carter, Student Nurse, who was in the middle of a nine-issue run at Marvel.

In "Patsy Walker Fan Club" (*Patsy Walker* #100, April 1962), Patsy is invited to a meeting and, instead of the expected compliments, hears a litany of complaints: "We want more fashions! More pages! More stories! More magazines!" Then Lee snuck in an in-joke: "Bring back My Girl Pearl!" (which had recently been cancelled for the third time!). Hedy is so unimpressed that she turns down an invitation to a meeting of her fan club, unaware that the members had prepared gifts and a trophy. When Hedy fails to show up, a club member says, "Oh well, let's get our money back and start a Millie the Model fan club!"

Some of the cover-featured titles on #101 through #114 provide a hint of Patsy's preoccupations in high school, "Patsy Becomes a Millionairess!" (#101), "The Blonde Tempest Twins!" (#102), "Her First Fur Coat!" (#105) "The New Patsy Walker!" (#107), "When a Doll Needs a Date!" (#108), "Patsy's Troublesome Twin!" (#109), "Patsy's Summer Job!" (#110), "Patsy on TV!" (#111), "The Teen-Ager and the Heart-Stealer" (#112), "Somebody Has to Lose!" (#113) and "An Engagement Ring for Patsy!" (#114).

The Patsy and Hedy series began using titles with "Patsy and Hedy Enter the Wonderful World of Fashion!" (#83, August 1962). This was followed by "The Rage of the Roaring Twenties!" (#85), "Patsy and Hedy Try to Become Cover Girls" (#88), "Her Dude Ranch Romance!" (#90), "Everybody Loves a Party!" (#91), "Patsy and Hedy Split Up!" (#92) and "Hedy's Romantic Trap!" (#93).

In "Patsy and Hedy Split Up!" (February 1964), the two agree to go their separate ways but eventually Nancy can tell how much they miss each other and cleverly gets them back as friends by coaxing Hedy to admit how much she misses her rivalry with Patsy. Buzz sums it all up this way: "I can't figure out if they're friends who hate each other, or enemies who love each other??!" To which a girl ends the story, "You're not supposed to understand! You're only a male!"

The Long Stories Begin

Both *Patsy Walker* and *Patsy and Hedy* were published bi-monthly with the same dates in 1964, instead of alternating them so that one of their titles

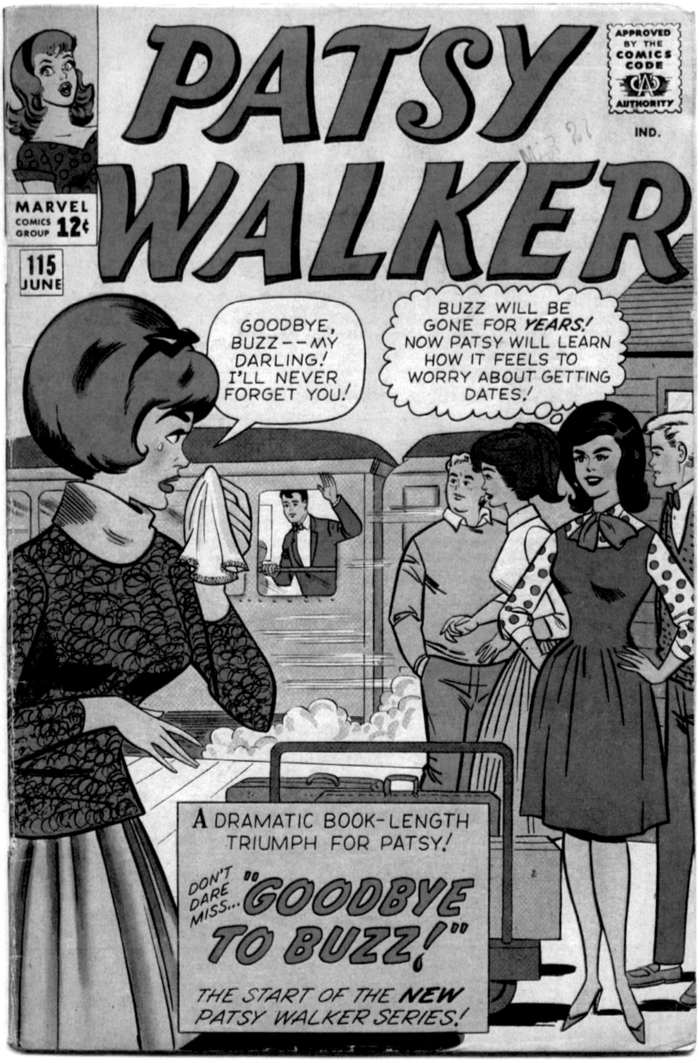

***Patsy Walker* #115, June 1964, copyright Bard Publishing Corp. With no notice in any previous issues, longtime boyfriend Buzz Baxter joined the U.S. Army shortly after high school graduation, in an 18-page story by Stan Lee. Cover by Al Hartley.**

would always be on the racks. When the long stories began (all the titles and issue dates are listed below), there was some confusion, because the story in *Patsy and Hedy* #95 (August), "Patsy's Graduation Day!" (cover titled "Patsy and Hedy Graduate"), should have run in *Patsy Walker* #115 (June), which instead featured "Goodbye to Buzz!" with the shocking development that he joined the Army! That story takes place shortly after graduation day. In the graduation day story published two months later, Buzz says nothing about joining the Army and instead muses about what he'll do next. That must have confused readers greatly!

The plot of the graduation day story centered on who would be announced as valedictorian. Both Patsy and Hedy figured they had the best chance, but the honor went to Nancy Brown. At many schools in those days, there was only one student chosen as valedictorian, even if there were multiple straight-A students. But what seemed strange was that neither Patsy nor Hedy considered Nancy and her scholastic accomplishments until the announcement was made, even though the girls were constant companions. At any rate, Nancy thanks her family, faculty and friends, especially Patsy and Hedy, who show the expected emotions. "Greatest speech I ever heard!" Hedy says. Patsy says, "I'm prouder right now than if I had made the speech!" The story ends with the girls in arms in their gorgeous gowns and Patsy saying, "Let's go to the soda shop and cry up a storm!"

Patsy and Hedy #95 thus can be considered the last teen humor issue of both titles. Beginning with *Patsy Walker* #115 and *Patsy and Hedy* #96, they essentially become romance comics, although enough of the dialogue contains sarcastic and snarky elements to finish in the humor category. "Patsy and Hedy Career Girls" was the logo beginning with #96.

"Goodbye to Buzz!" in *Patsy Walker* #115 not only appeared out of sequence, but seemingly out of the blue. There was no mention of Vietnam; when the story was written and hit the stands in March 1964, the U.S. bombing of North Vietnam and a huge troop build-up was still a year away. But what seemed strange was that there was no mention of Buzz considering a service academy, even though he was a standout student, citizen and athlete in the series. The military draft, however, did scoop up many young men who did not attend college.

Buzz appeared in uniform in #117, 119, 120, 122 and 123. The news of his being shot twice in the leg and evacuated from Vietnam appeared in #122 (August 1965), which coincided with the real-life ramping-up of the conflict. The news reached Patsy in an odd way: Her landlady (Patsy and Hedy had become roommates while working on the Centerville newspaper) showed Patsy the front-page news in the paper! At first, Buzz decided to lie and told Patsy he no longer loved her while he recovered at home. He didn't want her to suffer if he was seriously injured in his upcoming return to Vietnam.

Buzz changed his mind, however, after much soap opera–style conversation. In *Patsy and Hedy* #102 (October 1965), he tells Patsy he does love her. At the end of the story, readers were promised: "Next month, Buzz must leave for Viet Nam! You will want to be on hand to witness the most tender parting two young lovers have ever had! You will want to hear their vows of love to each other! …" But that did not occur in *Patsy and Hedy* #103 (which portrayed only a letter from Buzz in Vietnam).

Instead, that story was told in *Patsy Walker* #123. In his last appearance in comics after 21 years in more than 1,300 stories, Buzz told Patsy, "I love you," and passionately kissed her goodbye in #123 (October 1965). Then, in the last issue of her own title, the only mention of Buzz is when Patsy writes a letter to him in #124. At the end of #124, Patsy becomes editor of the society section and Hedy becomes beauty columnist in their hometown paper under editor Ted Trent, who sought Patsy's affection but eventually realized that he could not compete with her love for Buzz.

Patsy and Hedy #104—the first issue to appear in 1966 after the cancellation of Patsy's flagship title at the end of 1965—featured Nancy's engagement party in an entertaining story written by young Roy Thomas, a Marvel newcomer. After the long stories had begun, Nancy became a nurse and fell in love with Don, a doctor who was serving an internship. Also in #104, Hedy received the news that her latest love interest, 26-year-old reporter Mike Herald, was recovering well after what Nancy called "only a mild heart attack."

In the hospital, Mike introduces Patsy and Hedy to his kind, elderly mentor in journalism, publisher Saul Morris of *The New York Star*. Near the end of the story, Morris tells the girls that they deserve his support as promising journalists. "Discovering exceptionally talented young journalists is my business. It's always a thrill when I discover two as talented as you…. I'd like you two gifted young ladies to tour the U.S.A. on your own, sending back to the *New York Star* a weekly column on 'Young America.'"

The stunned girls, not yet out of their teens, immediately accept. Patsy says, "It'll keep me busy while Buzz is away …." That sets the stage for a series of adventures with surfers, actors, musicians and the like in #105–110 in what turned out to be the final issues of *Patsy and Hedy*, beginning at the epicenter of American youth culture: the West Coast.

Patsy Walker

The long stories, all in the last ten issues:

#115, June 1964: "Goodbye to Buzz!"—18 pages
#116, August 1964: "After Graduation, What?"—18
#117, October 1964: "Soldier's Sweetie"—18
#118, December 1964: "The Wrong Man for Patsy!"—18
#119, February 1965: "Patsy's Secret Boy Friend!"—18
#120, April 1965: "What Will We Do About Nancy Brown?"—18
#121, June 1965: "Another Spring, Another City, Another Love!"—18

#122, August 1965: "No Greater Love!"—18
#123, October 1965: "Don't Leave Me, My Love!"—18
#124, December 1965: "The 3 Faces of Patsy"—three linked six-page stories

Patsy and Hedy

The long stories, all in the last 16 issues:

#95, August 1964: "Pasty's Graduation Day!"—18
#96, October 1964: "Patsy in Love!"—18
#97, December 1964: "The Girl Between Them!"—18
#98, February 1965: "Marry Me, Patsy!"—18
#99, April 1965: "Trust Me, My Love!"—18
#100, June 1965: "When a Girl Becomes a Woman!"—18
#101, August 1965: "I See My Love Again!"—18
#102, October 1965: "So Much Love, So Few Kisses!"—18
#103, December 1965: "Love's Finest Hour!"—18
#104, February 1966: "No More Tears!"—18
#105, April 1966: "Hello, Hollywood!"—18
#106, June 1966: "Ski, Sea and Sweethearts!"—18
#107, August 1966: "When a Star Is Born!"—18
#108, October 1966: "Treasure Hunt a Go-Go!"—18
#109, December 1966: "Surf-Side Spies!"—18
#110, February 1967: "Patsy and the Prince!"—14

36

An Early '60s Bright Spot: Marvel's Teen-Age Tornado!

Teen humor comics outside the Archie Universe had reached their absolute nadir late in 1959 when Marvel made what in hindsight was the unusual decision to create Kathy Carter, a new character who was bannered on all 27 issues of *Kathy* as "The Teen-Age Tornado!"

Writer Stan Lee and artist Stan Goldberg signed almost every story, all of which were short and loaded with teen action and jokes, although only Lee had his name on stories in #1 (October 1959). They were pretty much knockoffs of the Archie Series, but they were never boring and were often creative. Since Lee had an extensive background writing humor throughout the 1950s, in retrospect it was no surprise that he added a companion title for *Patsy Walker* and *Millie the Model*, both of whom had two remaining titles heading into 1960.

In 1959, Marvel was in the second full year of its restrictive printing and distributing contract with DC Comics and Independent News. Though the number of issues gradually increased in the 1960s, Marvel had to kill a title to bring in *Kathy*. That ill-fated comic book was either *Strange Worlds* or *World of Fantasy*, both science fiction. Marvel also produced the second run of *A Date with Millie* beginning with #1 (October 1959). It later became *Life with Millie* and then *Modeling with Millie*.

When *Kathy* debuted, the only significant comic book publishers left were Dell, DC, Charlton, Harvey, Archie and Marvel. Archie at the time had clearly won the battle for teen dollars: the only non–Archie teen titles remaining at the beginning of 1960 were DC's *A Date with Judy* (destined to expire that year), Charlton's *Freddy* and the two devoted to Patsy Walker.

Blonde pepper pot Kathy's friends and frenemies were typical: Ricky Brown was her boyfriend and Ace Arnold often wanted to be, though more often than not Ace wound up with the lovely scheming brunette Liz Hilton. The supporting cast included plump Fanny and goofball Speedy, who often dated each other since they had no chance with the Fab Four. The faculty of

Midville High featured Principal Fluster and Miss Agony (their school was Midtown High in #1).

The Teen-Age Tornado certainly earned her nickname, when she drove her father nuts in a familiar plot in "The Stay-at-Home" in #1. Dad repeats

Kathy #1, October 1959, copyright Zenith Publishing Corp. Billed as "The Teen-Age Tornado" right from the start, hyper-active Kathy was Marvel's first new teen character since the firm's 1957 financial implosion. She ran 27 issues into 1964. Cover by Stan Goldberg.

what he read in a magazine: "A girl needs to spend more time safely nestled in the heart of her home!" So he tells Kathy to stay home instead of dating Ricky. She first cuts out an ad for "the darlingest dress" in the sports section of her dad's newspaper. Then she plays Fabian on the radio so loud that her father misses out on sports scores. Then she plays "fantastic progressive jazz discs" and finally her father gives up and takes her to Ricky at the malt shop.

There were constant quips, such as in "Kathy at the Movies" in #2 (December): Ricky asks an usher at a crowded theater, "Do you have seats inside?" and the usher replies, "Naturally! You don't think we'd keep 'em out here, do you?"

Just as he was building his ever-burgeoning line of superhero comics in the 1960s, editor Stan Lee was not afraid of teen crossovers. But the one in *Kathy* #14 (December 1961) was wonderful, titled "A Visit to Patsy Walker" but not featured on the cover! The six-page story opens with an unusual reference to a specific comic, when Kathy is excited because *Patsy and Hedy* #79 (actual date also December 1961) has arrived on the stands. Kathy, having replaced her ponytail with an up-to-date bouffant, gets even more excited because the issue used her fashion design and, as was the custom, gave Kathy credit. When Liz decides to take a bus to Centerville in order to protest these developments in person to Patsy, Kathy and Franny decide they must go, too.

The first person the three girls run into is Patsy's rival Hedy Wolfe. Hedy tells Kathy, "You're even more of a square than Patsy is," and Liz responds, "Something tells me we're going to get along fine!" No sooner do they knock on Patsy's door than her longtime boyfriend, Buzz Baxter, makes a four-panel cameo, immediately noticing the two visitors with a "Hubba Hubba! When did this happen?" Liz responds with typical snark, "Sixteen years ago! So put your eyes back in your head, kiddo!"

Buzz asks Kathy, "Is she always that grouchy?" and gets the answer, "You kiddin'? This one of her pleasant moods!" On the way out the door, Buzz asks Kathy, "Wowee! How come you aren't in a comic mag of your own?" Patsy has her hands full with Liz's accusation that she is playing fashion favorites as Kathy's thought bubble says, "Poor Patsy! As if she doesn't have enough trouble with Hedy Wolfe!" But Patsy preserves the peace by telling Liz her fashion credit "is in *Patsy Walker* #98 [also dated December 1961 and featuring a crossover with Millie], which will be on sale soon!"

All told, it's one of the most subtly funny stories of 1961 but was lost in the historic wake of *Fantastic Four* #1 (November 1961), which featured the first of Marvel's new line of superheroes. By the time *Kathy* bowed out with #27 (February 1964) just a little more than two years later, Stan Lee had created or co-created four superhero teams, plus separate adventures of ten popular superheroes.

Before the Teen-Age Tornado bowed out, however, she had a nine-page crossover with *Millie the Model* in #26 (December 1963) in "Kathy Becomes a Model" in which Millie Collins visits Midville. Kathy boldly knocks on Millie's hotel room door and Millie decides she would be ideal for a photo shoot with Millie's staff, which includes Kathy's artist Stan Goldberg! Liz, however, convinces Millie and her people that Kathy can't stay long. When Kathy and Liz return home, Kathy depresses Liz by telling her Millie had planned to use her, too, if only she had stayed longer.

Marvel published 152 comics in 1964 and 104 of those featured Lee's increasingly beloved superheroes—a publishing pace not seen by any company since the Golden Age of the early 1940s. One of them, *Daredevil*, replaced Kathy on Marvel's production schedule and ultimately become one of the company's favorites.

After *Patsy Walker* ended in 1965 with #124 and *Patsy and Hedy* bit the circulation dust with #110 (January 1967), only one other teenager ever again headlined a Marvel comic. His name was Harvey.

Harvey's Short Runs

One of the last characters Stan Lee created at Marvel was Harvey Hooper, who debuted in *Harvey* #1 (October 1970). Harvey's the new kid at Midville High, as an eight-page introductory story makes clear. He meets gorgeous Raven and Wendy, the Reggie Mantle–like Duke, and the hippies Goober and Raquel.

By this time, however, Marvel wasn't giving readers many comic pages for their money. *Harvey* #1 had 11 ad pages out of the still-usual 32 pages (plus three more full-page cover ads), in contrast to the six-plus pages readers received for a penny only 30 years earlier in the standard-sized 64-page comic books for a dime.

(Today, readers pay more than a dime per page for most 32-page comics.)

Harvey #2 (December 1970) was the last issue until the series wound up with *Harvey* #3 (June 1972) through #6 (December 1972), by which time Lee had left his editor's job at Marvel.

By *Harvey* #4 (August 1972), which continued to feature Henry Scarpelli's art, the cost was nearly a penny a page, with 21 pages of comics for 20 cents. In that issue, Goober's uncle, a television journalist, invites Harvey and Goober on a trip to China with President Nixon. There a lot of laughs packed into five pages.

In that same issue, the lead story features on early Marvel African-American character, the physical education teacher Dewey Neebenz. Harvey and Goober discover that their teacher sang in a '50s trio named Dewey and the Doo-Wops and they convince them to sing their old songs at the school dance. Their lyrics are a hit and in walks Alan F. Reed, who tells them he is promoting "rock'n'roll revival concerts" and offers them $1,000 for a one-stand performance in Hoboken. This inspires the kids to try doo wop on the street outside Reed's window and he finishes the story with "They're going to have to do something about noise pollution in this city."

Alas, even though they weren't bad, Harvey and his gang didn't last, just as almost all teen humor titles started in the 1950s and 1960s with featured boys fizzled after short runs.

Little Luck for the Boys

Other than a handful of non–Archie characters from the Archie Series and DC Comics, few titles outside the Archie Universe named for boys succeeded or were even attempted in the 1960s and 1970s. Overall, from the 1940s through the 1970s, of the 57 titles named for boys, 37 ran fewer than ten issues. Only 12 ran more than 20 issues and eight of those began no later than 1950. None of those reached 100 issues, as Archie Comics did in 1959.

Cool Cat from Crestwood Publishing (known for its logo reading "Prize Comics") was typical of the bad luck the teen boys encountered, although *Cool Cat* was by no means a typical teen humor comic. In fact, it featured one of the few beatnik characters in comics, likely inspired by Maynard G. Krebs on the *Many Loves of Dobie Gillis* TV program.

Cool Cat ran three issues—from March to April 1962 (Volume 8, #6, picking up its numbering from the weird-story title *Black Magic*) through July–August 1962 (Volume 9, #2). In fact, other than *Young Romance* and *Young Love*, both sold to DC in mid–1963 without missing an issue, *Cool Cat* was Prize's last comic book.

Cool Cat's unsigned art was primitive and every story featured a situation beyond ridiculous, but the three issues were nonetheless moderately amusing. The last issue cover-featured the banner "You, too, can talk hip! See inside," and the story title was "For Squares Only." The three-page story translated the following hip talk:

Words: pots (carburetors); a short (a car); threads (clothes); windows (glasses); back seat Bingo (necking in a rear seat); a flip-flop (a convertible); doughnuts (tires).

Phrases: Cobs are really old folks; Bread is really money; Beatsneaks are really tennis shows; a Bake is really a party; Smash Your Brains is really studying; an Ankle Biter is really a child; Fig is really old-fashioned; I Was Shot Down is really I failed the examination; a Cube is really a normal person; a Tube is really a TV; Let's Put It in Orbit is really let's go; a Fream is really a square; an Axe is really a musical instrument; Fuzz really means cops; Hacked is really bugged; Bugged is really bothered.

Did you learn something?

Four years later, magazine entrepreneur and artist Myron Fass tried a "jumbo size" (as it was bannered) teen humor title simply named *Henry*, with six bi-monthly issues in 1966 and a seventh dated September 1967 and numbered Volume 2, #7. Published by MF Enterprises, Henry's indicia publisher was Country Wide Publications. The title sold for a quarter but it was the smallest quarter comic around—square bound but only 48 interior pages, which less than two decades earlier was still the standard size for the most popular comics.

Most of the *Henry* art was done by Bob Powell, one of the most talented artists of the 1940s and 1950s but not usually a teen humor artist. *Henry* was drawn in an exaggerated style with numerous distorted faces. This was among the last art Powell did for comics before he passed away in 1967.

The stories revolved around redheaded Henry Brewster, who was always accompanied by a gang of friends *à la* Archie. The wording was dense and likely could not have been well understood by someone younger than 11 or 12. The stories presented a problem for the gang to solve. In #4 (August 1966), for example, the problems involved cheating in a bathing suit contest, dealing with a teenager from South Korea, weight loss for girls, martial arts mastery and a vintage car contest.

Fast Willie Jackson Is the End

The first and only African American teen humor comic of the original era, Fitzgerald Periodicals' *Fast Willie Jackson* was candidly described as "Archie in blackface" by the 2003 edition of *The Slings and Arrows Comic Guide*. That was unkindly correct, but it's still a title worth looking at.

Bertram Fitzgerald was the publisher of a series of black history comics called *Golden Legacy*, which originally ran at least 15 issues from 1966 to 1972. He published *Fast Willie Jackson* during the era now remembered for "blaxploitation" in commercial media. *Fast Willie* ran from #1 (October 1976) to #7 (August 1977).

Fast Willie Jackson #1 featured cover art by G. Lemoine of a dance scene involving Fast Willie and seven other teens seen in the series. The artist's splash page was bannered "They're cool, bad, fast and together! They're the brothers and sisters of Mocity USA!" and it introduced the major characters with Fast Willie in the middle: Dee Dee Wilson, Frankie Johnson (the Reggie Mantle of the piece), Jo-Jo, Hannibal and Jabar (holding his usual Black Power sign). Of course, Officer Flagg, an obviously at least institutionally racist white cop but with a good heart, is dubbed "The Man."

The first story, "Finders Keepers," sets the tone for the entire series. Officer Flagg orders Fast Willie to "pick up a gum wrapper before I run you in for littering." Not exactly stop-and-frisk, but this was 1976. When the crowd goes into the Spanish Main—a chocolate shop run by Latino Army veteran Jose Martinez—Fast Willie realizes he has lost his five dollar bill. When the fellows go back to look for it on a street full of litter, they explain to Officer Flagg that they're just trying to clean up. "Well, I guess my lectures on law and order are getting through to you guys!" he responds.

In "Don't Thread on Dee Dee," our girl tells Fast Willie she'll go to the movies with him if he dresses like Flashy Frankie, but when he shows up on her doorstep, she tells him to split. This impresses her father, who decides she may be mature enough for the clothes she has told him she wants. The story closes with Dee Dee winking at the reader and hugging her father while telling him, "Oh, you're outasight, Daddy! You sure know how to handle women!" He responds, "Yeah! I haven't had forty years experience for nothing!"

This was the last new teen humor title of the 1960s and 1970s era. *The Slings and Arrows Comics Guide* was hard on this series: "Coming from a company that established itself by promoting black heritage and dignity, it's nothing short of deplorable." But, for better or worse, it is now a vintage period piece.

37

Judy, Dobie, Freddy and the Early '60s

Perhaps the best teen humor art of the 1960s was by DC staffer Bob Oksner and it never showed to better example than in later issues of *A Date with Judy* and in most of the four-year run of *The Many Loves of Dobie Gillis*.

For the first time in his distinguished DC career, Oksner received an unexpected regular chance to draw beatniks, who were all the pop cultural rage in the late 1950s and early 1960s era before hippies began to dominate the free-thinking aspects of American culture.

A Date with Judy would have been DC's last teen humor book—or so it seemed when the title was cancelled in 1960 after a 13-year run—had it not been for the unexpected emergence of Dobie Gillis.

It's hard to believe that Judy Foster's comic book was cancelled, considering how beautifully Oskner drew most of the later covers and interior art. Judy truly held forth in one of the best-looking comics on the stands of 1960 in #74–79, her final six issues.

The focus of the stories may have seemed dated, though. The majority dealt with Judy's never-ending jealousy whenever she saw Oogie Pringle in the presence of another girl, though in all cases the confusion—always a key plot element—was ultimately resolved.

The title received a new character in #74 (January 1960) when a high school beatnik who called himself Nervous—his real name was Norman—turned up on Oogie's doorstep as his new next-door neighbor. Nervous played big roles in #74, 75 and 76 and much smaller roles in #77, 78 and 79, so perhaps DC received complaints about having such an unorthodox character in such a clean comic book. But there was nothing unsavory about Nervous, who obviously had a keen eye for girls.

And his lingo was far out indeed. For example, when Oogie tells Nervous he has a date with Judy at 7 p.m., several hours away, Nervous responds with "Seven? That's off in the dim, man! You've got plenty of ticks to spare!"

When Nervous wants to unlock his huge collection of sound equipment, he shrugs and says, "Man! I forgot the twister to the slammer!" and Oogie translates accurately when he says, "You mean the key to the door?"

Oksner's ability to draw beautiful women was unmatched at DC, so Judy's last five cover appearances featured her ability to appear on the beach in fashionable one-piece bathing suits. Believe it or not, the then–five-year-old Comics Code Authority would not allow Judy or any other female to appear in a two-piece! The Code also continued to proscribe cleavage in its first decade or so.

The cover of the last issue, credited to *Mad* legend Mort Drucker, was subtle but funny. Judy carries Oogie ashore and tells him, "Next time don't be such a big hero, Oogie!" and he asks, "But Judy, why did you yell for help if you didn't want it?" as a muscular lifeguard smirks alongside them.

Dobie Arrives Late to TV and Comics

The Many Loves of Dobie Gillis was a half-hour CBS television comedy, first shown September 29, 1959, based on vintage magazine stories by Max Shulman collected in *The Many Loves of Dobie Gillis* (1953) and *I Was a Teen-Age Dwarf* (1959), the title of which parodied the American-International drive-in hits *I Was a Teenage Werewolf* and *I Was a Teenage Frankenstein.*

Dobie was an instant hit, what with Bob Maynard stealing so many scenes as Maynard G. Krebs, television's most famous beatnik. Dwayne Hickman played Dobie, the humble girl-loving son of a grocer, and future film star Tuesday Weld, then 16, portrayed Thalia Menninger.

The first season was more than halfway over when *The Many Loves of Dobie Gillis* #1 (May–June 1960) hit the stands in March 1960. The 20-page Dobie-Maynard story set the tone for the book-length stories that distinguished the humorous series. In "Miss Grocery Queen of 1960!" Thalia cops the crown but Dobie and Maynard are arrested for disturbing the peace, parading without a permit and numerous other infractions in the story-ending parade. Thalia tells a distraught Dobie, "My folks don't want me to see you any more! They don't want me to go out with an ex-convict!" Maynard provides consolation in the last panel when he tells Dobie, "Don't take it too hard, man! I'll stand by you even if it does ruin my reputation!"

The TV series ended in September 1963 but Dobie's comic book lasted a year longer. Dobie and Maynard became involved in wild fantasies, such as their outer space trip in #25 (September 1964) and the craziness created by a witch in their lives in #26 (October 1964).

That seemed to end DC's teen humor titles, but the company persisted, albeit without success. They even re-worked Dobie and Maynard with reprinted plots in *Windy and Willy* #1 (May–June 1969) through #4 (November–December 1969) after an appearance in *Showcase* #81 (March 1969).

DC brought back Binky Biggs and his friends and family with four funny and beautifully drawn Oksner stories of *Leave It to Binky* in the tryout title *Showcase* #70 (September–October 1967), nine years after what had seemed to be their last appearance. DC responded by bringing back *Leave It to Binky* with #61 (June–July 1968). The title ran 21 issues through #81 (October–November 1971), followed six years later by #82 (Summer 1977). The title became just *Binky* with #72 (April–May 1970). The company also published *Binky's Buddies* #1 (January–February 1969) through #12 (November–December 1970).

Binky sometimes featured one-page jokes of an African-American child named, believe it or not, Li'l Leroy. Talk about the era of blaxploitation!

DC published *Date with Debbi* from #1 (January–February 1969) through #17 (September–October 1971), followed a year later by #18 (October–November 1972), along with *Debbi's Dates* #1 (April–May 1969) through #11 (December 1970–January 1971).

DC thus tried to take advantage of the emerging rock and youth culture of the late 1960s. But apparently the titles struggled in the increasingly iconoclastic early 1970s. *The Slings and Arrows Comic Guide* accurately describes the situation this way with regard to *Date with Debbi*: "This freckle-faced, red-haired teenage klutz looks even more like a female clone of Archie than Josie did." Stories inevitably revolved around "love-hungry Debbi's social and physical clumsiness ruining her chances for happiness, with allegedly hilarious results."

DC's *Swing with Scooter* #1 (June–July 1966) through #35 (August–September 1971), followed by #36 (October–November 1972), was more rock-humor than teen humor, benefiting from a strong start in #1–11 thanks to the covers and art by the always underrated Joe Orlando. Scooter and his guitar were basically a metaphor for the Beatles, the British Invasion and a whole lot of British influences on American rock.

Freddy Lasts Longer Than Expected

Charlton published many thousands of genre comics in the 1950s, 1960s and 1970s before disappearing slowly in the 1980s, with an emphasis on romance, westerns and war titles after experimenting with nearly everything imaginable in the 1950s. But the genre in which Charlton least participated by far was teen humor.

The one exception was the original title *Freddy*, which appeared out of nowhere with #12 (June 1958) while picking up from *My Little Margie's*

Boyfriends #1–11. *Freddy* inexplicably lasted 36 issues to #47 (February 1965). Not that Freddy wasn't fun but he was about as generic as possible, although nicely drawn by Jon D'Agostino.

Charlton published an introductory page, with Freddy describing himself as "The guy that lives next door! I go to your school, play the same re-

Freddy #12 (first issue), June 1958, copyright Charlton Comics Group. Freddy, an original Charlton creation and the only successful teen the company had, had more of a 1960s sensibility and ran 36 issues into 1964. Cover by Jon D'Agostino.

cords, and do all the rest of the things you do! So even though this magazine has my name on it, and tells about my gang, it's for you and about you! The whole thing is for fun, so let's begin.... Come on, kids, turn the page!"

Freddy's gang includes girlfriend Peggy, bandleader Horace, best pal Stuff, rival Rip, school superintendent McHazy, and next door neighbor Mr. Tantrum, who calls Freddy "a noisy kid." In the first story, the kids take their pets to school, with chaotic results. The stories are about as basic as could be, likely helping to explain Freddy's longevity. Grade-school kids must have loved him, because no teen character of the late 1950s and 1960s was more accessible.

From June 1966 to October 1967, Charlton published a parody teen comic, *Go-Go*, with the theme "We're So In, We're Out" for nine issues. One of the wacky characters was Miss Bikini Luv, who actually wore some two-piece swimsuits! It was a mishmash of fact (?) and fiction, with nothing memorable but still fun.

38

Tippy Teen's Surprise Appearance

Throughout the 1960s and 1970s, the vast majority of mainstream corporately published comic books appeared from only six primary publishers, unlike the much greater variety of producers in the 1940s and 1950s, which were the first full decades of the modern comic magazine.

Marvel, DC, Charlton, Harvey and Gold Key (the imprint Western Printing and Lithographing created in 1962), however, were not heavily into the teen humor market following the 1950s. The sixth primary publisher, of course, was teen humor titan Archie, which was a solid No. 3 with regard to the two-decade total of circulation from 1960 to 1979, behind only Marvel and DC. While Charlton, Harvey and Gold Key gradually faded out in the 1980s, Archie remained a solid economic and pop cultural entity.

In the early 1960s, the New Dell popped up on newsstands and racks following the 1962 split with Western, which had published all of Dell's comics. The New Dell published a handful of teen titles (see separate chapter) along with a variety of other types while operating directly as Dell Publishing and thus could claim a distant seventh in overall circulation and influence.

By 1965, when Tower Comics and *Tippy Teen* surprisingly emerged at the end of the year, the never-large American Comics Group (known for its AGG logo) was near the end of its double-decade run, which came in 1967. The Hallden logo represented only the popular *Dennis the Menace* titles, which were distributed by Fawcett. Gilberton ended publication of the *Classics Illustrated* series late in the 1960s. Crestwood (Prize) was gone by mid–1963.

Tower was the only new publisher in 1965, beginning with the November issues of *Tippy Teen* #1 and *Thunder Agents* #1, a superhero team that tried to take advantage of the immense mid–1960s success of Marvel and DC in the superhero market.

Tower got off to a good start, publishing 30 issues in 1966 and 24 in 1967, as enumerated in comics historian Dan Stevenson's year-by-year, issue-by-issue lists. But Tower quickly faded with only 11 issues in 1968 and 13 in 1969, then abruptly left comics.

Tippy Teen and her teen circle, who appeared in comics seemingly designed for grade school and junior high school readers, thus had only a short but meaningful four-year run. The last issues were *Tippy Teen* #25 (October 1969), *Tippy's Friends Go-Go and Animal* #15 (October 1969), *Teen-In* #4 (Fall 1969) and the one-shot *Tippy Collector's Edition* (November 1969). These teen titles made up 45 of Tower's 78 total issues, so Tippy's temporary influence cannot be dismissed.

Tippy's unsigned art and unsigned stories were essentially Archie knock-offs, but that doesn't mean they were bad. They were actually often highly amusing, and easily understood by younger readers. They were as wholesome as could be; they were nothing any parent needed to worry over.

Tower Bargains

Tower Comics were the only comics of their era that all sold for 25 cents, but they were nonetheless among the biggest bargains in comics at their start. *Tippy Teen* #1 (November 1965) gave readers 64 interior pages, the same jumbo page count that almost all comics of the 1935–1943 period gave readers for a dime, until World War II paper restrictions forced a permanent reduction (with few exceptions) to 48 and/or 32 pages. A dime in 1940 was worth more than a quarter in 1965, regarding inflation. It wasn't long until Tower Comics reduced their interior page count to 48, but they remained square bound publications.

All of Tower's teen tales were titled, beginning with "Great Skate" to open *Tippy Teen* #1, which made no introductory remarks except on the cover, where Tippy moved toward the reader on a skateboard and "all the teeners" had headshots: Go-Go West, the guitar-playing brunette; Animal, the athletic blond giant; Tommy, the red-headed Archie type who was Tippy's main squeeze; and Peggy Fleagle, Tippy's blonde rival.

Tippy's first words in comics were "Doing the slalom on a skateboard is just like doing it on skis!" and Go-Go's first utterance was "One small difference, Tip! There's no soft snow to land on!" She spoke those words of wisdom as Tommy crashed to the sidewalk. (At this time, skateboards were fairly new to teenagers.) Go-Go and Animal soon also needed medical help from Tippy before Principal Phogg halted the "stunt riding trophy" competition with harsh words for Miss Snodgrass, the teacher running the contest. Mr. Phogg, inadvertently standing on a skateboard, much to his dismay, did a great "shake" exhibition, grabbed onto a tree limb, did a vault-like gymnastics move, and finally landed on his rear end. He not only won the teens' admiration, but also the trophy for the best stunt!

This highly improbable but amusing little epic pretty much set the tone for Tippy along with the second story, "Runaway Romance." In it, Go-Go sang her first tunes with her guitar: "Far away on distant shores, they are all

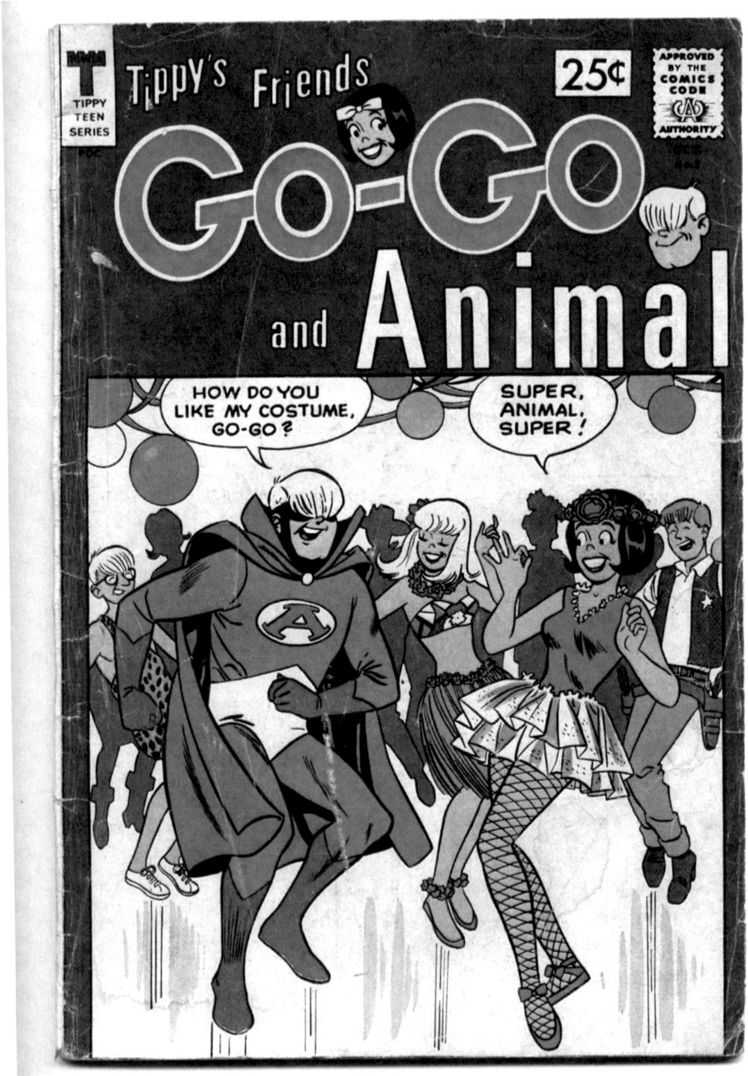

***Tippy's Friends Go-Go and Animal* #2, October 1966, copyright Tower Comics, Inc. The enthusiasm for go-go dancers and super heroes in the mid–1960s is captured.**

involved in wars, international affairs, are giving all of us gray hairs! What kind of troubles have you found? Our economy is sound, seems that everyone's employed … so you should be overjoyed!" Not a bad summary of the mid–1960s!

Tippy complains that she can't be overjoyed because Tommy is so wrapped up in "that second-hand car of his." But Go-Go warbles this advice: "If you want to get your man, you must worship his sedan, make him think his car is great, then you'll surely get your date, it's your one and only chance, to get him to the dance!" Tippy gets it: "The mutual interest routine!" But knowing nothing about cars, she removes the brick stabilizing his car—"I saved his tire!"—and the car goes on a truly wild driverless ride. Go-Go sums it all up on the last page: "Oh … this is a tale that's really sad … of a gal and a lad she almost had, 'till fate played her a dirty trick, with a brakeless car and a misplaced brick …"

The story "Chemical Warfare" is a direct swipe from other teen comics, with Tippy falling for her new science teacher and winding up babysitting for him while the teacher and his wife attend the big dance. There was even a "Dear Tippy" advice page. I wonder how many readers considered the fact that the "letters" were supposedly mailed even before Tippy ever hit the comics. There were also fashion tips, pin-ups, a movie star page, nail care advice and more.

Tippy Teen #2 through 10 all appeared in 1966, with Tippy symbolically celebrating her first "birthday" on the cover of #10 (December 1966). But Tippy appeared only seven times in 1967 and quarterly in 1968 and 1969. *Tippy's Friends Go-Go and Animal* debuted with #1 (July 1966), which appeared in conjunction with *Tippy Teen* #6, so Tower apparently must have though Tippy Teen was off to a great start. *Go-Go and Animal*, in which Tippy usually appeared, appeared twice in 1966, five times in 1967 and quarterly in 1968 and 1969. By the end of the series, Go-Go had the cover title to herself, but Animal was also featured on the covers, as always.

Teen-In, filled with advice during the era of Vietnam War protest sit-ins, was mostly a reprint title in its four-issue run. *"Tippy Teen" Special Collectors Edition* was all reprints, including the newer cast regulars Ashley (tall, dark and handsome) and Egghead (one of many early comic book nerds).

By the way, Teen was actually the family's surname! Mr. and Mrs. Teen made appearances.

Tippy as Vicki

Tippy was gone by the end of 1969 but not entirely forgotten. Atlas Comics, founded in 1975 by people who originated with Marvel Comics, published

65 issues that year before going out of business before any 1976 issues could appear. They were mostly fantasy and hero comics but *Vicki* #1 (February) through #4 (August) was an unusual exception.

Vicki published Tippy reprints. The only change was that whenever the name Tippy appeared in the text, it was replaced by Vicki. All the other characters kept the same names. The unsigned covers, though, were original. The last issue had both "4th fun-filled issue!" and "No. 4" on the cover. Not since Fawcett once stated "More pages of action!" on covers had there been anything like that.

Bunny Soon Follows Tippy

Perhaps inspired by the early success of Tippy Teen, Harvey Comics tried its hand at a different sort of teen humor with *Bunny* #1 (December 1966), always bannered "The Queen of the In Crowd!" In this case, the in-crowd was older teens and twenty-somethings, since Bunny Ball was a cute young model and not a student. For the regular series through #20 (December 1971), her below-the-logo plug always said, "She's Hip! She's Mod! She's Boss!"

Harvey had a long history of erratic publication of the final issues of many titles over the years. So it was with the mysterious *Bunny* #21 (November 1976)—five years after #20! By this time the interior page count had declined to 48 from 64 and the price had increased from 25 cents to 40 cents. Harvey's editors apparently felt "hip, mod and boss" were already too dated, so Bunny's logo read "She's Foxy! She's Cool! She's Dyna-Mite!"

The stories were all original in #21, as reflected by Bunny's comment to bearded artist Marc on the first story's splash page: "So this is your floating studio, Marc! Zoovy!" Now *there's* a word that may never have appeared in another comic book.

Some of the funniest *Bunny* stories were those of her blonde kid sister Honey, a high school student who wasn't nearly as confident as Bunny. In "A Cheerful Scene" (#21), Honey turns out for cheerleader to catch the eye of basketball star Jonathan Jumpkins (now there's a name). It turns out that Jonathan is a super-serious player who wants no part of cheerleaders—at least until Honey turns to be, well, a real honey of a cheerleader. After a poor start in the big game, Honey's cheers finally get to Jonathan and his shooting perks up in the second half. He wins the game with a long last-second shot and tells his teammates he needs to be carried off with Honey.

Harvey had tried teen humor only once before, when the firm purchased the Mazie franchise from obscure Nationwide Publishing so that Harvey could print the adventures of "The Teen-Age Queen" Mazie, red-headed boyfriend Stevie, scheming rival Flat-Top and nerdy good guy Mortie from 1955 to 1958.

By keeping her out of college, Harvey could use Bunny wherever she was needed to make a nutty story even nuttier and funnier. For example, in #2 (April 1967), Bunny joins secret agent Ossimer O. Heaven, "my favorite secret agent from A.U.N.T.," in their search for "The Ultrazaric Decodifier," as the story is titled. They find the weird machine in a two-part laughfest but all Bunny is thinking about is taking the heavenly Mr. Heaven dancing.

In the second story in #2, "Guests from England," Bunny meets the four Beagles and receives an invitation to their concert. The third story involves Bunny's rival Esmeralda, who tries to keep her from meeting her heartthrob, the hip poet William Wordfellow. But Bunny inevitably dances with Wordfellow, one of the many handsome men who hold her in their arms during the series.

Bunny's unsigned covers usually involved all sorts of young people at all sorts of parties. Among the locales of the covers are beaches, a circus, swimming pools, hot-air balloons, a castle, a celebration of Native American dancing, parachuting, a bullfight, a skating rink and more. Truly, this was not your typical teen comic.

For more on *Bunny*, see the ultimate book about Harvey Comics by the ultimate Harvey historian, Mark Arnold's *The Harvey Comics Companion* (2017). The book credits Warren Harvey (the son of Robert Harvey) with scripts and Hy Eisman with the art in #1–6, plus the covers to #7 and 8 and Hy Rosen for the art in #7–20 and the covers to #9–20.

39

Josie, Pussycats and All

Dan De Carlo, pretty much the master of teen humor and career girl comic book art during its height, was the only cartoonist to create a teen title in the 1960s that ultimately ran 100 issues.

Josie—proudly named for De Carlo's wife—ran 106 issues for the Archie Series across nearly two decades after almost all other teens had vanished from comic books in the wake of the Archie Universe's almost total domination. There were three title incarnations: *She's Josie* #1–16, *Josie* #17–44 and *Josie and the Pussycats* #45–106. After Josie debuted in the 25-cent quarterly comic *Archie's Pals and Gals* #23 (Winter 1962–63), *She's Josie* #1 (February 1963) immediately followed but there was a six-month gap until #2 (August 1963). The popular title became *Josie and the Pussycats* with #45 (December 1969) when her band was created, and ran through #106 (October 1982), bolstered in the 1970s by the Saturday morning cartoon.

Josie was a red-headed female version of Archie, although that is not necessarily what De Carlo (1919–2001) intended, since he was already on the way to becoming the best of all artists who portrayed Betty and Veronica in the hundreds of issues of the various titles bearing their iconic names. When you say "Betty and Veronica" to the majority of Americans, they know who you mean, just as they know Superman, Batman, Spider-Man and Wonder Woman.

It's intriguing how Josie is approached by comics historians. She wasn't as important as multimedia figures like Judy Foster in *A Date with Judy* or Henry Aldrich in *The Aldrich Family*—both of which were part of radio, television and films—or comic book icons like Marvel's Patsy Walker, much less the Archie gang. But she received more space in encyclopedic-type books like *The Slings and Arrows Comics Guide*.

Josie stories were not only well-drawn, but often amazingly funny, if readers can suspend their disbelief in the fantasy aspects like the teen witch Alexandra Cabot. But then, one of the most popular TV sitcoms of all time is *Bewitched* from the 1960s.

Josie's boyfriend Albert and BFFs, clever Pepper and stunningly gorgeous Melody, were the core characters, soon followed by wealthy twins Alex

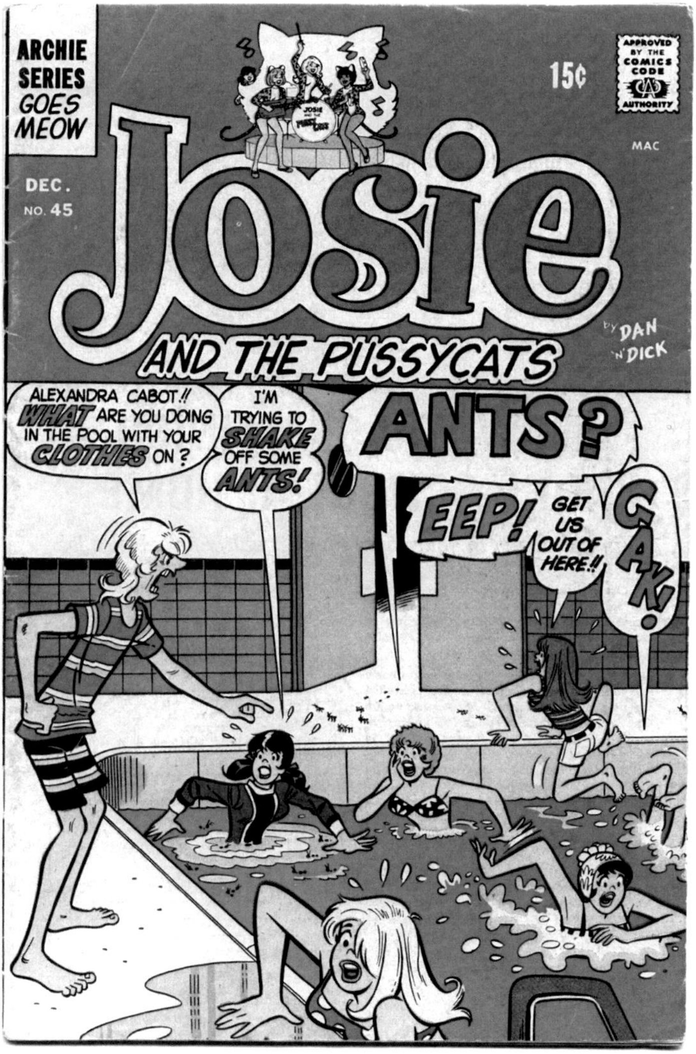

***Josie and the Pussycats* #45, December 1969, copyright Radio Comics, Inc. The title changed from "Josie" with this issue in which Josie and her friends formed their band. Cover by Dan De Carlo.**

and Alexandra Cabot. Stories such as "Over Dated" in *She's Josie* in #11 were typical. Josie calls it "a simple oversight" when she explains how she has a date with both Albert and Alex for a dance. But Josie, Pepper and Melody cook up a plot that actually works and neither Albert or Alex suspects a thing after many laughs.

Melody comes in for this evaluation from *Slings and Arrows*:

> The traffic-stopping blonde bombshell Melody was the closest to a sex symbol one could have in a Comics Code-approved comic. The chaos caused by her inability to grasp facts was equaled only by the disasters that occurred when her startling figure was seen by drivers, traffic cops, or just about any male, who developed a sudden inability to focus on what he was doing. Hugely popular with readers of both sexes, she gave the book such a boost that a proposed Melody spin-off was rejected, for fear Josie would lose too many readers!

In *Josie* #20 (June 1966), the emerging Women's Liberation influenced "Rebellion," in which Josie, Pepper and Melody create picket signs to protest the actions of men, who had lately been particularly frustrating. Older women took over the signs and picket lines and shoved the teens aside. The upshot was that Albert, Sock (Pepper's guy) and Alex flee to Josie's home, screaming, "The town is full of wild women!" and "They tried to tear us apart!" Josie's father is impressed by the care the boys receive from their girls, ending the story with this: "It's good to see that the younger generation is not as nutty as their mothers!" In the same issue's "Video Virus," Melody takes ill and finally finds that a private hospital room is the only place she can watch her beloved soap operas in peace.

The first issue of the retitled *Josie and the Pussycats* features a battle between Josie and Melody—Pepper is now gone—and the snooty Alexandra, who insists their band be called Alexandra's Cool Time Cats. (It just doesn't have the same garage band ring, does it?) The battle takes up the entire issue, which has become a treasured collectors' item among older Baby Boomers who grew up not only with the comics but the TV cartoon. Alexandra is infuriated when brother Alex introduces a new voice to play with Josie and the Pussycats: Valerie, an African American guitarist. *Slings and Arrows* calls Valerie "only about the fifth black person seen in Riverdale."

Seymour and (Briefly) *More Seymour*

One of the oddest comic book developments in the 1960s was the totally unexpected appearance of *Seymour My Son* (September 1963) by De Carlo from the Archie Series. It's a unique, 30-page, partly slapstick story of a teen's life largely told in captions by his father, who is not named.

The editors included a full-page letter to readers asking for their reactions to this unusual comic, offering $5 for the best letters (more than $40 in today's dollars). They asked if readers wanted more of Seymour, but they had already prepared *More Seymour* #1 (October 1963).

"More Seymour," which is a 30-page story devoted primarily to Seymour's hysterical trip to the beach, contained no note from the editor or letters from readers, as promised in *Seymour My Son*. Whether the $5 awards were ever sent, we will never know. All we have is 60 pages and two covers of Seymour, all by De Carlo and a seldom-seen must-have for collectors of De Carlo's consistently fascinating fiction. De Carlo had a lot more success with his creation *Sabrina the Teen-Age Witch* for the Archie Series, but that title more properly belongs in the fantasy genre.

The Archie series had some success with *That Wilkin Boy*—Bingo Wilkin, not Wilbur Wilken—which ran basically quarterly from #1 (January 1969) through #52 (October 1982). But, to provide context as to how unmemorable this series was, #1 is valued at $4 in "good" condition in the 2019–2020 *Overstreet Comic Book Price Guide*. That's typically the price of a modern comic, not the current value of issues that are 50 years old!

Ponytail in Two Versions

Lee Holley's newspaper strip *Ponytail* from King Features Syndicate appeared in comic book form from the New Dell as *Ponytail* #1 (July–September 1962) through #12 (December 1965) and from Charlton as #13 (November 1969) through #20 (January 1971) as the only teen humor title Charlton published at the time.

Ponytail appeared in several short stories each issue, so that plot points were always tightly focused. For example, in "Brace Yourself" in #1, Ponytail's friends convince her that all teens need braces on their teeth to fit in with the crowd. She talks her parents into the braces, only to tell them she wants to take them off for her date with Donald. Her parents steadfastly refuse, so she wears an exotic veil on her date. When a dance results in foot pain for both of them, they discover they both have braces. "I guess we were made for each other!" Donald says as they walk outside, presumably for a kiss over the moon in the last panel.

The New Dell struggled financially through much of the 1960s after Dell Publishing's 1962 split with Western Printing and Lithographing. By 1973, the company published its final ten comic books and left the field.

In the 1950s and 1960s, Charlton purchased titles from numerous companies, not to mention creating many dozens of its own. One of them in 1969 was *Ponytail*, which was among many newspaper strip type comics the firm acquired.

Holley's style was the same in the Charlton issues. If anything, the stories became shorter, although the one-note jokes were still fun. Holley's cartoony feature actually fit in well in the late 1960s, an era when impressionistic comic art was coming into full flower. There were lots of wacky humor strips and

Ponytail #4, October–December 1963, copyright King Features Syndicate. Ponytail's boyfriend Donald scores a touchdown and knocks her down in the process. Lee Holley brought his newspaper strip to original stories for Dell Comics #1–12 and Charlton #13–20.

very few finely rendered adventure strips such as were dominant in the 1930s and 1940s.

Ponytail probably could not have appeared in the 1920s and 1930s, but strips like Hilda Terry's *Teena* in the 1940s helped pave the way for stick-figure teens.

Wally Was "The Most"—for Four Issues

When Gold Key became the logo for Western Printing and Lithographing in 1962, the first and really only regular teen humor title the new imprint tried was *Wally*, subtitled "He's the Most!" in early '60s teen lingo.

Many Gold Key titles were aimed at the grade-school market just as many Dell Comics of the 1940s and 1950s were, with an endless lineup of funny animals and western heroes, all done with professional polish. By 1962, the market was changing, and young readers had become far more interested in television shows than comic books. *Wally* lasted only from #1 (December 1962) to #4 (September 1963). Wally Brewster, whose antics and adventures were always unsigned, actually deserved better. Most of the stories were genuinely funny and more than a little creative.

The first story in #1, "Operation Stopwatch," is a vivid example. Wally and his buddy Hippo, along with featured girls Jackie and Pam, are dismayed to see the new principal of Beachdale High, Fulton Klearmont, has cut the period for changing classes from five minutes to two minutes. In real life this would have been utterly absurd, but Klearmont declares, "If man can orbit the Earth in 90 minutes, he can surely travel from English to biology in two!"

After 12 pages of amusing complications, "Benedict Brewster"—as his classmates have dubbed him—was given an award by the principal, who then instructed Wally to show the student body his running form on the track. The students sarcastically support Wally in the last panel as one yells, "Tomorrow, we go back to five minutes between classes!"

In "Twist Now, Pay Later," Wally gets the bright idea to introduce the students to the Twist at the Paper Straw, the local teen hangout. It's a big moneymaker until the school board chairman visits and declares the new dance "positively indecent." The principal is forced to ban the Twist, but soon the adults take it up and the dance is restored. The big hitch in Wally's plan is that the kids have all moved to the malt shop because, as Hippo tells Wally, "They say the Twist is for square ball elders!"

"Physically Fit to Be Tied" in #3 (June 1963) tells the tale of how the principal declares that students are in such bad shape that they all must walk to school. (President Kennedy's National Physical Fitness Award was a big deal in those days.) This spoils Wally's plan to make 50 cents per student driving them to school. Eventually cars are restored but Wally is pelted by kids in other cars when he decides to keep walking.

40

A Word on the Working Girls

I hope I have not frustrated too many readers by excluding what are called the career girls or working girls comic books in the humor field. They really deserve a book of their own since there were so many of them.

In their heyday of the 1940 and 1950s (only a handful survived into the 1960s), they were also called glamour girls comics and even included as girls' romance comics. They were always called girls in the argot of the pre–Women's Liberation era.

Titles like *Millie the Model* and *Tessie the Typist* are often mixed with teen humor and/or romance comics in the stock of vintage comic book dealers at conventions and in stores. Boxes are often labeled "teen humor," "romance comics" or "comics for girls." Beginning in the 1970s, some collectors and dealers also began to label them as "good girl art" or "GGA."

Trina Robbins, always the pre-eminent historian of female creators and characters in the comics, did her usual thorough job of including the likes of Millie and Tessie in her comprehensive 1999 overview book *From Girls to Grrrrlz: A History of (Female symbol) Comics from Teens to Zines* from Chronicle. I refer readers to this volume, which is fun-filled and informative.

Millie the Model will forever be remembered as the queen of the career girls. Or maybe it should be Katy Keene, although Millie far surpassed Katy in total number of issues of all titles with Millie's name in the title. Television fans who did not see the comics in the 1950s would perhaps nominate *My Friend Irma*, who was also a successful Marvel comic.

Marvel produced by far the most comics for girls—in the pre-1960s days before superheroes took over the venerable firm—and surely the most glamour girl and working girl comics. Robbins cites one list of 49 titles in a mid-century Marvel comic and 27 were published for girls! That is exactly right. What that says is that girls were far more often seen at the newsstands of the 1940s and 1950s than they were in the first two full decades of the comic book stores in the 1970s and 1980s.

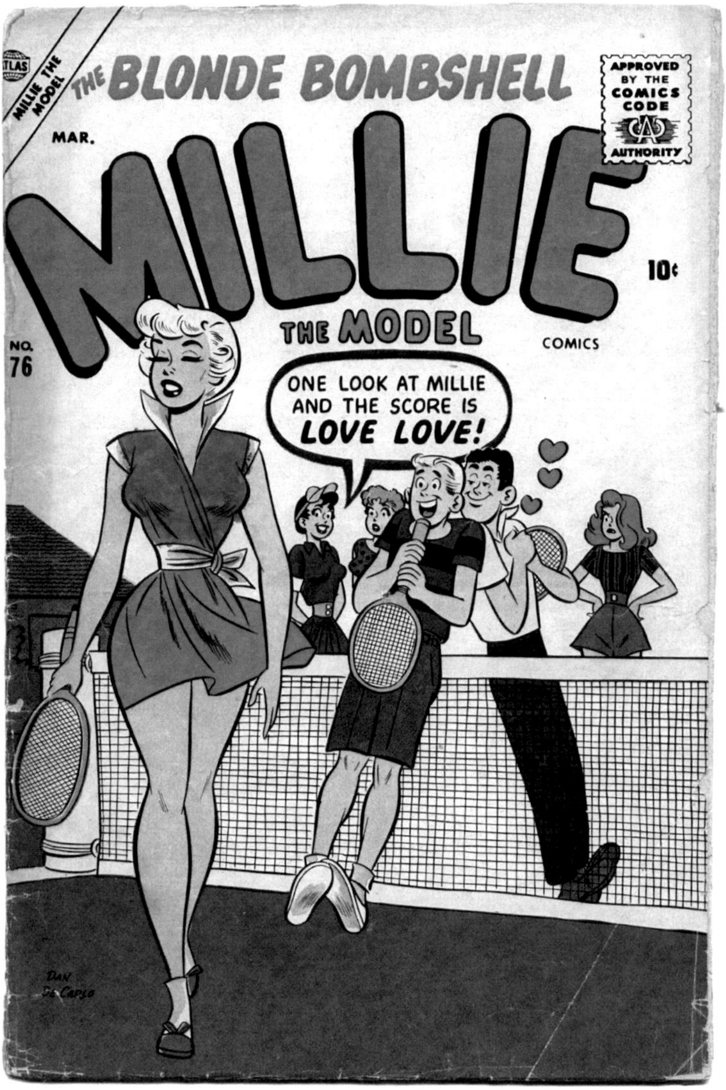

***Millie the Model* #76, March 1957, copyright Sphere Publications, Inc. With the word "love" being part of a score, that joke was used on many tennis covers. Cover by Dan De Carlo.**

Now, as anyone who attends any of several huge annual comic conventions will tell you, females are just as big a part of the crowds as males. It's one of the joyous developments in the hobby's history, which now extends more than half a century back.

Not all of the working girls comics were successful, even with amazingly talented humor artists such as Dan De Carlo at work. De Carlo's Sherry the Showgirl, who appeared in nine issues across two titles in 1956 and '57, is a fine example.

Then there were comics like *Dizzy Dames* from the American Comics Group with six issues in 1952 and '53. Considered by today's standards, this is among the most politically incorrect publications of all time, what with characters like Moronica, Miss Nitwit of (fill in the year).

For that matter, Millie the Model would also be considered politically incorrect. Though the flagship title ran for 207 issues from 1945 to 1973, plus a full dozen giant-size annuals—not to mention dozens of appearances in spin-off titles—this is definitely not a comic book you would see on today's displays of current titles.

Katy Keene from the Archie Series, always portrayed as more mature than the average working girl, did something Millie could not. After Katie disappeared from comics in 1961, at least in her flagship title with #62, she magically reappeared in her own series from 1983 to 1990, in both regular and digest size, totaling 43 issues in all.

Katy first appeared in *Wilbur* #5 in 1945 and was a backup strip in dozens of issues of titles like *Wilbur, Suzie, Laugh Comics* and *Pep Comics*. Katy ran 62 issues in her primary title from 1949 to 1962 and in giant-size issues 23 times in *Katy Keene Pin-Up Parade, Katy Keene Annual* and two issues of *Archie Giant Series*. She also starred in three mid–1950s one-shots and in 13 issues of *Katy Keene Fashion Parade*. All told, she appeared in 102 issues of titles with her name, plus the later 43.

Archie also featured another successful working girl title in *Suzie*, an often ditzy blonde who was the source of many jokes, in 52 issues of her own title from #49–100 after beginning as a support strip in an anthology title. Like Millie and Katy, Suzie joined them as a girl who never lacked for dates.

Marvel also had plenty of luck with 46 issues of *My Friend Irma*, 36 of the original *Nellie the Nurse*, 29 of actress *Hedy DeVine* and 23 of *Tessie the Typist*. In the 1940s and 1950s, especially, there was no lack of a market for comics featuring glamour girls.

Appendix

Teen Humor Comics Outside the Archie Universe, 1940s to 1970s

(Original titles only)

A

Aggie Mack (Four Star/Superior), #1, January 1948–#8, August 1949
Aggie Mack (Dell), Four Color #1335, April–June 1962
Algie (Timor Publications), #1, December 1953–#3, April 1954
All Teen Comics (Marvel), #20/*Teen Comics* #21-on; #20, January 1947; #21, April 1947–#35, May 1950
Andy (Ace), #20, June 1948–#21, August 1948
Andy Hardy (Dell), *Four Color* #389, April 1952; *Four Color* #447, #480, #517, #5, #6, September–November 1954. The first four *Andy Hardy* comic books were erratically published Four Color issues (which were numbered consecutively regardless of the contents over more than 1,300 issues from the 1940s to the 1960s). Dell Comics began what was intended to be a regularly published series with the correct appearance number, so in this case the fifth issue of Andy Hardy was #5 and the sixth issue was #6.

B

Binky (DC, second series); *Leave It to Binky* #61, June–July 1968–#71, February–March 1970; *Binky* #72, April–May 1970–#81, October–November 1971; #82, Summer 1977
Binky's Buddies (DC), #1, January–February 1969–#12, November–December 1970
Blythe (Dell), *Four Color* #1072, January–March 1960

Bunny (Harvey), #1, December 1966–#20, December 1971; #21, November 1976

Buzzy (DC), #1, Winter 1944–1945–#75, February 1957; #76, October 1957; #77, October 1958

C

Candy (Quality), #1, Autumn 1947–#64, July 1956

Cindy (Marvel), #27, Fall 1947–#40, July 1950

Club 16 (Famous Funnies), #1, June 1948–#4, December 1948

Cookie (ACG), #1, April 1946–#55, August–September 1955

Cool Cat (Prize), Volume 8 #6, March–April 1962, no number, May–June 1962, Volume 9 #2, July–August 1962

D

Date with Debbi (DC), #1, January–February 1969–#18, October–November 1972

A Date with Judy (DC), #1, October–November 1947–#79, October–November 1960

A Date with Patsy (Marvel), #1, September 1957

DC Special (DC), #2, January–March 1972

Debbi's Dates (DC), #1, April–May 1969–#11, December 1970–January 1971

Dexter (Dearfield Publications), #1, Summer 1948–#5, July 1949

Dilly (Lev Gleason), #1, May 1953–#3, September 1953

Dollface and Her Gang (Dell), *Four Color* #309, January 1951

Dotty (Ace), #35, June 1948–#39, March 1949 (formerly *Four Teeners*, becomes *Glamorous Romances*)

Dudley (Prize), #1, November–December 1949–#3, March–April 1950

Dunc and Loo (Dell), #1, October–December 1961–#8, October–December 1963

E

Ernie (Ace), #22, September 1948–#25, March 1949 (formerly *Andy*)

Etta Kett (Standard), #11, December 1948–#14, September 1949

Everything Happens to Harvey (DC), #1, September–October 1953–#7, September–October 1954

F

The Farmer's Daughter (Stanhall), #1, February–March 1954–#4, October 1954
Fast Willie Jackson (Fitzgerald), #1, October 1976–#7, 1977
Flat-Top (Nationwide/Harvey), #1, November 1953–#7, September 1955
Four Favorites (Ace), #30, August 1947–#32, December 1947
Four Teeners (Ace), #34, April 1948
Frankie (Marvel), #4, Winter 1946–1947–#17, November 1949
Freckles (Standard), #5, November 1947–#12, August 1949
Freckles (Argo), #1, November 1955–#4, June 1956
Freddy (Charlton), #12, June 1958–#47, February 1965

G

Gabby (Quality), #11, July 1953; #2, September 1953–#9, September 1954
Georgie (Marvel), #1, Spring 1945–#39, October 1952
Gidget (Dell), #1, April 1966–#2, December 1966
Ginger (Archie Series), #1, 1951 (no date)–#10, Summer 1954
Girls' Life (Marvel), #1, January 1954–#6, November 1954
Go-Go (Charlton), #1, June 1966–#9, October 1967
Going Steady with Betty (Avon), #1, November–December 1949–*Betty and Her Steady* #2, March–April 1950

H

Hap Hazard (Ace), #1, Summer 1944–#24, February 1949
Happy Days (Gold Key), #1, March 1979–#6, February 1980
Harold Teen (Dell), *Four Color* #2, 1942
Harold Teen (Dell), *Four Color* #209, January 1949
Harvey (Marvel), #1, October 1970–#2, December 1970; #3, June 1972–#6, December 1972
Harvey Hits (Stevie), #5, January 1958
Hector (Key Publications), #1, November 1953–#3, March 1954
Hedy Wolfe (Marvel), #1, August 1957
Henry Aldrich (Dell), #1, August–September 1950–#22, September–November 1954
Henry Brewster (MF Enterprises), #1, February 1966–#7, September 1967
Here's Howie (DC), #1, January–February 1952–#18, November–December 1954

Hi-Jinx (ACG), #1, July–August 1947–#7, July–August 1948
Homer Hooper (Marvel), #1, July 1953–#4, December 1953

J

Jeanie (Marvel), #13, April 1947–#27, October 1949
Jetta (Standard), #5, December 1952–#7, April 1953
Jim Dandy (Dandy Comics), #1, May 1956–#3, September 1956
Joe College (Hillman), #1, Fall 1949; #2, Winter 1949–1950
Jonesy (Quality), #85, August 1953–#8, October 1954
Josie (Archie Series), #1, February 1963–#106, October 1982 (*She's Josie* #1–16; *Josie and the Pussycats* #45-on)
Junie Prom (Dearfield), #1, Winter 1947–1948–#7, August 1949
Junior Comics (Fox), #9, September 1947–#16, July 1948
Junior Hopp (Stanmoor), #1, February 1952–#3, July 1952
Junior Miss (Marvel), #1, Winter 1944–1945
Junior Miss (Marvel) #24, April 1947–#39 (August 1950) (#37 is all romance)

K

Kathy (Standard), #1, September 1949–#16, September 1953; #17, September 1955
Kathy (Marvel), #1, October 1959–#27, February 1964
The Kellys (Marvel), #23, January 1950–#25, June 1950
The Kilroys (ACG), #1, June–July 1947–#54, June–July 1955
Kitty (St. John), #1, October 1948

L

Leave It to Binky (DC), #1, February–March 1948–#58, February 1957; #59, October 1957; #60, October 1958 (see Binky for second series)
Leroy (Standard), #1, October 1949–#6, November 1950
Linda (Ajax), #1, April–May 1954–#4, October–November 1954
Lucy the Real Gone Gal (St. John), #1, June 1953–#4, December 1953

M

The Many Loves of Dobie Gillis (DC), #1, May–June 1960–#26, October 1964
Margie (Marvel), #35, Winter 1946–1947–#49, December 1949

Mazie (Nationwide), #1, 1950 (no date)–#7, 1951 (no date) (five-cent smaller size)
Mazie (Nationwide/Harvey) #8, October 1952–#13, March 1954; #14, February 1955–#28, August 1958
Meet Corliss Archer (Fox), #1, March 1948–#3, July 1948
Meet Merton (Toby Press), #1, December 1953–#4, June 1954
Meet Miss Bliss (Marvel), #1, May 1955–#4, November 1955
Meet Miss Pepper (St. John), #5, April 1954–#6, June 1954
Miss America (Marvel), #2 (November 1944)–#93, November 1958 (odd numbering system, explained in text; 125 issues after #1, which was superhero only)
Mitzi (Marvel), #1, Spring 1948–#10, December 1949 (#2–7 titled *Mitzi's Boy Friend*; #8–10 titled *Mitzi's Romances*; content same)
Modniks (Gold Key), First issue, August 1967–#2, August 1970
Mortie (Nationwide), #1, December 1952–#3, June 1953
My Date (Hillman), #1, July 1947–#4, January 1948
My Girl Pearl (Marvel), #1, April 1955–#4, October 1955; #5, July 1957-#6, September 1957; #7, August 1960–#11, July 1961

O

Oh, Brother! (Stanhall), #1, January 1953–#5, October 1953
Oscar (Marvel), #24–25, #3–10, #13, Spring 1947–October 1949
Ozzie & Babs (Fawcett), #1, December 1947–#13, Fall 1949

P

Patches (Orbit), #1, March–April 1945–#11, November 1947
Patsy and Hedy (Marvel), #1, February 1952–#110, January 1967
Patsy and Hedy Annual (Marvel), #1, 1963 (no date)
Patsy and Her Pals (Marvel), #1, May 1953–#29, August 1957
Patsy Walker (Marvel), #1, 1945 (no date)–#124, December 1965
Patsy Walker Fashion Parade (Marvel), #1, 1966 (no date)
Penny (Avon), #1, 1947–#6, September–October 1949
Ponytail (Dell/Charlton); #1, July–September 1962–#12, October–December 1965; #13, November 1969–#20, January 1971
Popular Teen-Agers (Star) #5, September 1950 to #8, July 1951 (a continuation of *School-Day Romances* #1-4. More romance comic than teen comic)

R

Ricky (Standard), #5, September 1953
Rodger Dodger (Standard), #5 August 1952
Romeo Tubbs (Fox), #26, May 1950; #28, July 1950
Romeo Tubbs (Green Publications), #27 (December 1952)
Rusty (Marvel), #12, April 1947–#22, September 1949

S

School-Day Romances (Star), #1, November–December 1949–#4, May–June 1950
Scream Comics (Ace), #16, October 1947–#19, April 1948
Scribbly (DC), #1, August–September 1948–#13, August–September 1950; #14, October–November 1951–#15, December 1951–January 1952
Seymour My Son (Archie Series), #1, September 1963; More Seymour, #2, October 1963
Showcase (DC), #70, Binky, September–October 1967; #81, Windy and Willy, March 1969
Slick-Chick Comics (Leader Enterprises), #1, 1947 (no date)–#3, 1947 (no date)
Stevie (Nationwide), #1, November 1952; #6, April 1954
Sugar Bowl (Famous Funnies), #1, May 1948–#5, January 1949
Sunny (Fox), #11, December 1947–#14, June 1948
Susie Q Smith (Dell), *Four Color* #323, March 1951, #377, 453, 553, April 1954
Sweet Sixteen (*Parents Magazine*), #1, August–September 1946–#13, January 1948
Swing with Scooter (DC), #1, June–July 1966–#36, October–November 1972

T

Taffy (Orbit), #5 (November 1946)–#12, February 1948 (first four issues are funny animal)
Teena (ME), #A-1 series 11, 12, 15, 1948 (no dates)
Teena (Standard), #20, August 1949–#22, October 1950
Teen-In (Tower) #1, Summer 1968–#4, Fall 1969
That Wilkin Boy (Archie Series), #1, January 1969–#52, October 1982
Thirteen … Going On Eighteen (Dell), #1, November 1961–January

1962–#25, December 1967; #26, July 1969–#29, January 1971 (last four issues reprint #1–4)

Tippy Teen (Tower), #1, November 1965–#25, October 1969

Tippy Teen Special (Tower), #1, 1969 (no date)

Tippy's Friends Go-Go and Animal (Tower), #1, July 1968–#15, October 1969

Topsy Turvy (Leffingwell), #1, April 1945

TV Teens (Charlton), #14–15, #3–5, February 1954–October–November 1954

V

Vicki (Atlas), #1, February 1975–#4, August 1975 (*Tippy Teen* reprints)

Vicky (Ace), October 1948, no number, first issue; #4, December 1948 (error); no number, January 1949; #4, April 1949, #5, June 1949

W

Wally (Gold Key), #1, December 1962–#4, September 1963

Wendy Parker (Marvel), #1, July 1953–#8, July 1954

Wilbur (Archie Series), #1, Summer 1944–#87, November 1987; #88, September 1963; #89, October 1964; #90, October 1965

Willie (Marvel), #5, Fall 1946–#19, April 1949; #22, January 1950–#23, May 1950

Windy and Willie (DC), #1, May–June 1969–#4, November–December 1969

Y

Young Life (Magazine Enterprises), #1, Summer 1945–#2, Fall 1945; *Teen Life* #3, Winter 1945;–#5, Fall 1946

Z

Zoot Comics (Fox), #5, February 1947–#6, April 1947 (first four issues are funny animal)

Bibliography

Books

Arnold, Mark. *The Harvey Comics Companion*. Albany, GA: BearManor Media, 2017.

Benson, John. *Confessions, Romances, Secrets and Temptations: Archer St. John and the St. John Romance Comics*. Seattle: Fantagraphics Books, 2007.

Daniels, Les. *DC Comics: Sixty Years of the World's Favorite Comic Book Heroes*. Boston and New York: Little, Brown, 1995.

_____. *Marvel: Five Fabulous Decades of the World's Greatest Comics*. New York: Harry N. Abrams, 1991.

Duin, Steve, and Mike Richardson. *Comics: Between the Panels*. Milwaukie, OR: Dark Horse Comics, 1998.

Dunning, John. *Tune in Yesterday: The Ultimate Encyclopedia of Old-Time Radio, 1925–1976*. Englewood Cliffs, N.J.: Prentice Hall, 1976.

Geissman, Grant. *The Complete Junior and Sunny by Al Feldstein*. San Diego: IDW, 2014.

Gerber, Ernst, and Mary Gerber. *The Photo-Journal Guide to Comic Books*. Two Volumes. Minden, NV: Gerber, 1989–1990.

Goulart, Ron. *The Great Comic Book Artists*. Two Volumes. New York: St. Martin's Press, 1986.

_____. The Funnies: *100 Years of American Comic Strips*. Holbrook, MA: Adams Publishing, 1995.

_____, editor. *The Encyclopedia of American Comics from 1997 to the Present*. New York: Facts on File, 1990.

Hadju, David. *The Ten-Cent Plague: The Great Comic-Book Scare and How It Changed America*. New York: Farrar, Straus and Giroux, 2008.

Hamerlinck, P.C., editor. *The Fawcett Companion*. Raleigh, N.C.: TwoMorrows, 2001.

Isabella, Tony. *1,000 Comic Books You Must Read*. Iowa, WI: KP Publications, 2009.

Kooiman, Mike, and Jim Amash. *The Quality Companion*. Raleigh, N.C.: TwoMorrows, 2011.

Levitz, Paul. *75 Years of DC Comics: The Art of Modern Mythmaking*. Italy: Taschen, 2010.

Miller, John Jackson, Maggie Thompson, Peter Bickford, and Brent Frankenhoff. *Comic Buyer's Guide Standard Catalog of Comic Books*, 4th edition. Iowa, WI: KP Books, 2005.

Nolan, Michelle. *Love on the Racks*. Jefferson, NC: McFarland, 2008.

Nyberg, Amy Kiste. *Seal of Approval: The History of the Comics Code*. Jackson: University of Mississippi Press, 1998.

Overstreet, Robert. *The Official Overstreet Comic Book Price Guide*, 49th edition. New York: House of Collectibles and Timonium, MD: Gemstone, 2019.

Phillips, Charles. *Archie: His First 50 Years*. New York: Abbeville Press, 1990.

Plowright, Frank, editor. *The Slings and Arrows Comic Guide*, 2nd edition. Great Britain: Slings and Arrows, 2003.

Robbins, Trina. *A Century of Women Cartoonists*. Northampton, MA: Kitchen Sink Press, 1993.

_____. *From Girls to Grrrlzz: A History of Women's Comics from Teens to Zines*. San Francisco: Chronicle Books, 1999.

_____, and Catherine Yronwode. *Women and the Comics*. Forestville, CA: Eclipse Books, 1985.

Robinson, Jerry. *The Comics: An Illustrated History of Comic Strip Art*. New York: Putnam's, 1974.

Rosen, Rebecca. *Thirteen: "Going on Eigh-*

teen." The John Stanley Library. Montreal: Drawn and Quarterly, 2009.
Schelly, Bill. *John Stanley: Giving Life to Little Lulu*. Seattle: Fantagraphics Books, 2017.
Sheridan, Martin. *Comics and Their Creators: Life Stories of American Cartoonists*. Boston: Hale, Cushman & Flint, 1942.
Simon, Joe, with Jim Simon. *The Comic Book Makers*. New York: Crestwood II Publications, 1990.
Waugh, Colton. *The Comics*. New York: Macmillan, 1947.
Weist, Jerry. *100 Greatest Comics*. Atlanta, GA: Whitman, 2004.
Wertham, Fredric. M.D. *Seduction of the Innocent*. New York: Rhinehart, 1954.
Wright, Bradford W. *Comic Book Nation: The Transformation of Youth Culture in America*. Baltimore and London: The Johns Hopkins University Press, 2001.
Yoe, Craig. *Archie: A Celebration of America's Favorite Teenagers*. San Diego: IDW, Yoe Books, 2011.
_____, editor. *Dan De Carlo's* Jetta. San Diego: IDW, Yoe Books, 2010.

Magazines

Nolan, Michelle. "All Those Marvel-ous Girls," *Comic Book Marketplace* # 99, February 2003.
_____. "There She Goes, Miss America," *Comic Book Marketplace* #115, September 2004.
_____ "They Weren't All Archies!" *Comic Book Marketplace* #34, April 1996.
Vance, Michael. "Forbidden Adventures," *Alter-Ego* #61, August 2006.

Index

Ace Publishing 8, 54–59
Adventures into the Unknown 66
Aggie Mack 93, 100
Algie 187
All American Comics 46
All Funny Comics 40, 42
All Love 57
All Teen 20, 25, 30–31
All Winners Comics 30
Altson, Louise 22
American Comics Group 65–69, 222
America's Best Comics 170
Andy 57–58
Andy Hardy 144–145, 187
Archie 8, 16, 19–20, 37, 60
Archie and Me 162
Archie's Girls Betty and Veronica 20
Archie's Pal Jughead 20
Archie's Rival Reggie 20
Arnold, Mark 156, 227
Around the Block with Dunc and Loo 199–203
Atkinson, Ruth 216
Avon Publishing 96–100

Babe Amazon of the Ozarks 73
Bald, Ken 28, 32
Ben Sangor Shop 67–69, 106–109
Benson, Sally 30
Berg, Dave 191–193
Betty and Me 162
Betz, Betty 145
Bewitched (TV program) 228
Big Shot Comics 73
Binky's Buddies 219
Biro, Charles 193–196
Black Diamond 194
Black Magic 214
Blackhawk 149, 189
Blosser, Merrill 104–105
Blythe 145
Boltinoff, Henry 37
Boy Comics 194
Boy Loves/Meets Girl 194

Brenner, George E. 59
Broadway Hollywood Blackouts 179
Buell, Marjorie Henderson 145
Bunny 198, 226–227
Buzzy 8, 16, 40–47, 65, 111, 121–126, 149

Calling All Girls 10, 15, 76–78
Candy 48–50, 65, 149–152, 189
Captain Atom 153
Charlton Comics 82–83, 219–221
Cindy 18–20, 25–31
Club 16 51–53
Comics Code Authority 111, 165
Como, Perry 78
Confessions of the Lovelorn 67
Conlon, Dolores 11
Cookie 65–69
Cool Cat 214
Cosmo Cat 86
Country-Wide Publications 215
Crack Western 189
Crime and Punishment 194
Crime Does Not Pay 194
Crime Must Pay the Penalty 56

Daredevil (Gleason) 194
Date with Debbi 219
A Date with Judy 8, 37–39, 65, 111, 121–126, 149, 197
A Date with Patsy 117–119
Dearfield Publishing 89–93
Debbi's Dates 219
De Carlo, Dan 111, 134–138, 146–148, 228–231, 235–236
Dell Comics 143–145, 199–203, 222, 231–232
Dennis the Menace 165
Dexter 89–93
Dilly Duncan 187, 194–196
Dizzy Dames 236
Dodo 153
Dollface and Her Gang 145
Dollman 189
Dotty 56–58
Drucker, Mort 218

Dudley 73–75
Dunning, John 37, 143

Eastern Color Publishing 50–53
Eisman, Hy 227
Ellsworth, Whitney 140, 145
Ernie 57–58
Etta Kett 105
Everything Happens to Harvey 111, 121–126, 187

Fagaly, Al 61
Fantastic Four 212
The Farmer's Daughter 175, 178–179
Fass, Myron 215
Fast Willie Jackson 215–216
Fawcett Comics Publishing 80–84
Feldstein, Al 85–89
Fitzgerald, Bertram 216
Flat-Top 153–159, 187
Forbidden Worlds 66
Ford, Glenn 78
Four Favorites 54–56
Four Teeners 56
Fox, Victor 85–88, 180–181
Frankie 25
Freckles and His Friends 105, 187
Freddy 219–221
Frese, George 160–164

Gabby 150–153, 187–189
Gangbusters 37
Geissman, Grant 85–88
Georgie 8 18, 23–27, 33
GI Combat 189
Ginger 112, 160–164
Girls' Life 79
Girls on Probation (film) 8
Glamourous Romances 57
Gleason, Lev 193–196
Go-Go 79, 221
Going Steady with Betty (*Betty and Her Steady*) 96–100
Gold Key Comics 213, 233
Goldberg, Stan 136–138, 210–213
Goldsmith, Clifford 144
Goodman, Jean 11
Goodman, Martin 8, 11, 23, 136
Gordon, Dan 65
Goulart, Ron 105
Green Publishing 180–181
Gross, Milt 69, 106
Gunsmoke Western 136

Haas, Clark 165–168
Haenigson, Harry 96–98
Hap Hazard 8, 16, 54–59
Hartley, Al 15, 57, 114, 139–142
Harvey 213–214
Harvey, Warren 227
Harvey Comics 153–159, 226–227
Heart Throb s 149
Hector 186–187
Hedy DeVine 236
Hedy Wolfe 117–119
Henry 215
Henry Aldrich 143–144
Herbert, F. Hugh 85, 89
Here's Howie 111, 121–126
Hi-Jinx Teen-Age Animal Funnies 106–109
Hickman, Dwayne 218
Hillman Comics 70–75
Holley, Lee 231–232
Homer Hooper 131–133, 187
Hughes, Richard E. 65, 69, 106

I Was a Teen-Age Frankenstein (film) 208
I Was a Teen-Age Werewolf (film) 208
Iger, S.M. "Jerry" 85, 89
Independent News 15

Jack Armstrong 76–77
Jackpot Comics 8, 19–20, 49
Jaffe, Al 116
Jeanie 18–19, 26, 33, 36
Jetta 112, 146–148
Jim Dandy 187, 193–195
Joe College 72–73
Johnson, Van 78
Jonesy 149–153, 187–189
Josie 198, 228–231
Journey Into Mystery 136
Juke Box 51
Junie Prom 89–93
Junior Comics 85–88
Junior Hopp 183–187
Junior Miss 8, 22, 26–29

Kathy (Standard Comics) 165–169
Kathy the Teen-Age Tornado 112, 117, 165, 197, 210–214
Katy Keene 15, 62, 236
Kaye, Danny 83
Kaye, Stan 38
The Kellys 26
Ken Shannon 189
Kid Colt Outlaw 136
Kirby, Jack 70–72
Kitty 100–101
Krank, Ray 102
Kubert, Joe 173–174

Lancaster, Burt 92
Laugh Comics 9, 20, 236
Leader Enterprises 89
Leave It to Binky 8, 40–47, 65, 111, 121–126, 149, 219
Lee, Stan 8, 23, 32; and Kathy, the Teen-Age Tornado 210–214; and *Meet Miss Bliss* 139–142; and *My Girl Pearl* 134–138; and Patsy Walker in the 1940s 10–22, 112–120;

and Wendy Parker 127–133; and working girl comics 234–236
Lemoine, G. 216
Leroy 168–171, 187
Lightning Comics 54
Li'l Jinx 161
Li'l Pan 86
Linda 100
Little Angel 165
Little Archie 161
Loth, Pauline 16
Lovers' Lane 194
Lucky Star 153
Lucy the Real Gone Gal 171–173
Lydon, Jimmy 144
Lynn, Bambi 78

Mad 85
Madison, Guy 78
Magazine Enterprises 78–79, 102–103
Many Loves of Dobie Gillis 198, 218–219
Margie 16, 18–19, 26, 35–36
Marvel Comics *see* Lee, Stan
Marvel Mystery Comics 10
Mary Marvel 23
Master Comics 81–84
Maurer, Norman 173–174
Mayer, Sheldon 43–47, 122
Maynard, Bob 218
Mazie 112, 153–159
Meet Corliss Archer 85, 88
Meet Merton 187, 191–193
Meet Miss Bliss 112, 117, 137, 139–142
Meet Miss Pepper 173–174
Millie the Model 8, 18–19, 23, 111, 204–205, 234–236
Miss America 8, 10–22, 112–120, 150
Mister Anthony's Love Clinic 73
Mister District Attorney 37
Mitzi (*Boyfriends, Romances*) 18–19, 26, 30–33
Morse, Stanley P. 186
Mortie 153–159, 187
My Friend Irma 19, 236
My Girl Pearl 112, 117, 134–138
My Little Margie's Boyfriends 221
My Romantic Adventures 66
My Secret Life 180

Nation-Wide Publishing 153–159
National Comics (DC Comics) 15, 20, 37–47, 65, 111, 121–126, 149, 217–219
Nellie the Nurse 19, 23, 236
New Age Publishing 78–79

Oh, Brother! 175–179, 187
Oksner, Bob 43, 121, 217–219
Orbit Comics 51
Orlando, Joe 219
Oscar 26, 33, 35
Ozzie and Babs 80–84

Parents' Magazine 76–79
Patches 51–53
Patsy & Hedy 111–120, 197, 204–209
Patsy Walker 10–22, 112–120, 197, 204–209
Penny 96–98
Pep Comics 8, 9, 20, 49, 60, 236
Plastic Man 189
Police Comics 23, 48, 189
Polly Pigtails 76
Ponytail 198, 231–232
Powell, Bob 215

Quality Comics 48–50, 149–152, 187–191

Rawhide Kid 136
Real Western Hero 80
Red Rabbit 89
Reggie and Me 162
Renee, Lilly 99–101, 171
Ricky 170, 187
Robbins, Trina 17, 234
Robin Hood Tales 149
Robinson, Jerry 96–98
Robinson, Paul 105
Rodger Dodger 170, 187
Rogers, Gordon "Booty" 73–75
Romantic Confessions 73
Romeo Tubbs 85, 180–181, 187
Rosen, Hy 227
Rule, Chris 116
Rural Home Comics 51
Rusty 18, 26, 35

Sahle, Harry 48–49
St. John Comics 100–101
Schelly, Bill 143, 199–203
Scott, Lizabeth 92
Scream Comics 56–57
Scribbly 40–47, 111
The Secret Life of Walter Mitty (film) 83
Seeger, Hal 175–179
Sensation Comics 39
Seymour 230–231
Sheridan, Martin 105
Sherry the Showgirl 111
Showcase 219
Showgirls 111
Shulman, Max 218
Simon, Joe 70–72; *see also* Kirby, Jack
Sinatra, Frank 78
Slick Chick Comics 89, 93–95
Sparling, Jack 78
Standard Comics 101–104, 165–170
Stanhall Publishing 175–179
Stanley, John 143–145, 199–203
Startling Comics 170
Startling Stories (pulp) 146
Stevenson, Dan 20, 136, 223
Stevie 153–159, 187
Stone, Chic 84

Storm, George 37–38, 40 43
Strange Tales 136
Strange Worlds 210
Sugar Bowl 51
Sullivan, Vincent 78, 102–103
Sunny 85–88
Super Duck 164
Super Mouse 165
Super Mystery Comics 56
Superior Comics 93, 100
Superman's Pal Jimmy Olsen 113
Sure Fire Comics 54
Susie Q Smith 145
Suzie 160, 236
Sweet Sixteen 76–78
Swing with Scooter 198, 219

Taffy 51–53
Tales of Suspense 136
Tales to Astonish 136
Teen Comics 20, 25
Teen-In 223
Teena 102–104
Terry, Hilda 101–104
Tessie the Typist 23, 236
That Wilkin Boy 60, 231
Thirteen 197, 199–203
Thomas, Roy 208
Thrilling Comics 165
Thrilling Wonder Stories (pulp) 146
Tilsam Publications 40
Tippy Teen 198, 222–225
Tippy's Friends Go Go and Animal 222–225
Topsy-Turvy 65–66
Toth, Alex 51
Tower Comics 222–225
True Comics 76
TV Teens 82–83
Two-Gun Kid 136

Vicki 225–226
Vicky 59
Vigoda, Bill 61

Wally 233
Walter, Linda 203
Weld, Tuesday 218
Wendy Parker 14, 19, 112–120, 127–131
Whitney, Ogden 102–103
Wilbur 16, 60–64, 160–164, 236
Williams, Bill 143–145, 175–179, 203
Willie 18, 26, 33, 36
Windy and Willy 219
Woggon, Bill 62
World of Fantasy 210
Wow Comics 80
Wyn, A.A. 54–59

Yoe, Craig 85–89, 146–148
Young Love 214
Young Romance 70, 86 214

Zip Comics 49, 60, 160
Zoot Comics 85, 181–182